RUSSIAN LITERARY CRITICISM

SYRACUSE UNIVERSITY PRESS 1974

RUSSIAN LITERARY CRITICISM

A Short History

R. H. STACY

First Edition

Acknowledgment is made to the following for permission to include material which originally appeared in their publications:

To E. P. Dutton & Co., Inc., for two stanzas from *Eugene Onegin* by Alexander Pushkin, translated by Walter Arndt, © 1963 by Walter Arndt; to Farrar, Straus & Giroux for passages from Vyacheslav Ivanov's *Freedom and the Tragic Life: A Study in Dostoevsky,* translated by Norman Cameron, © 1957 by Farrar, Straus & Giroux, Inc.; to The University of Chicago Press for passages from Mirra Ginsburg's translation of Zamyatin's essays in *A Soviet Heretic: Essays by Yevgeny Zamyatin,* © 1970 by The University of Chicago; and to The University of Wisconsin Press for passages from J. Thomas Shaw's translation of Pushkin's letters in *The Letters of Alexander Pushkin,* © 1967 by the Regents of the University of Wisconsin.

Library of Congress Cataloging in Publication Data
Stacy, Robert H., 1919–
Russian literary criticism, a short history.
Includes bibliographical references.
1. Criticism—Russia—History. I. Title.
PN99.R9S8 801'.95'0947 74-10434
ISBN 0-8156-0107-7 (cloth)
ISBN 0-8156-0108-5 (paperback)

Manufactured in the United States of America

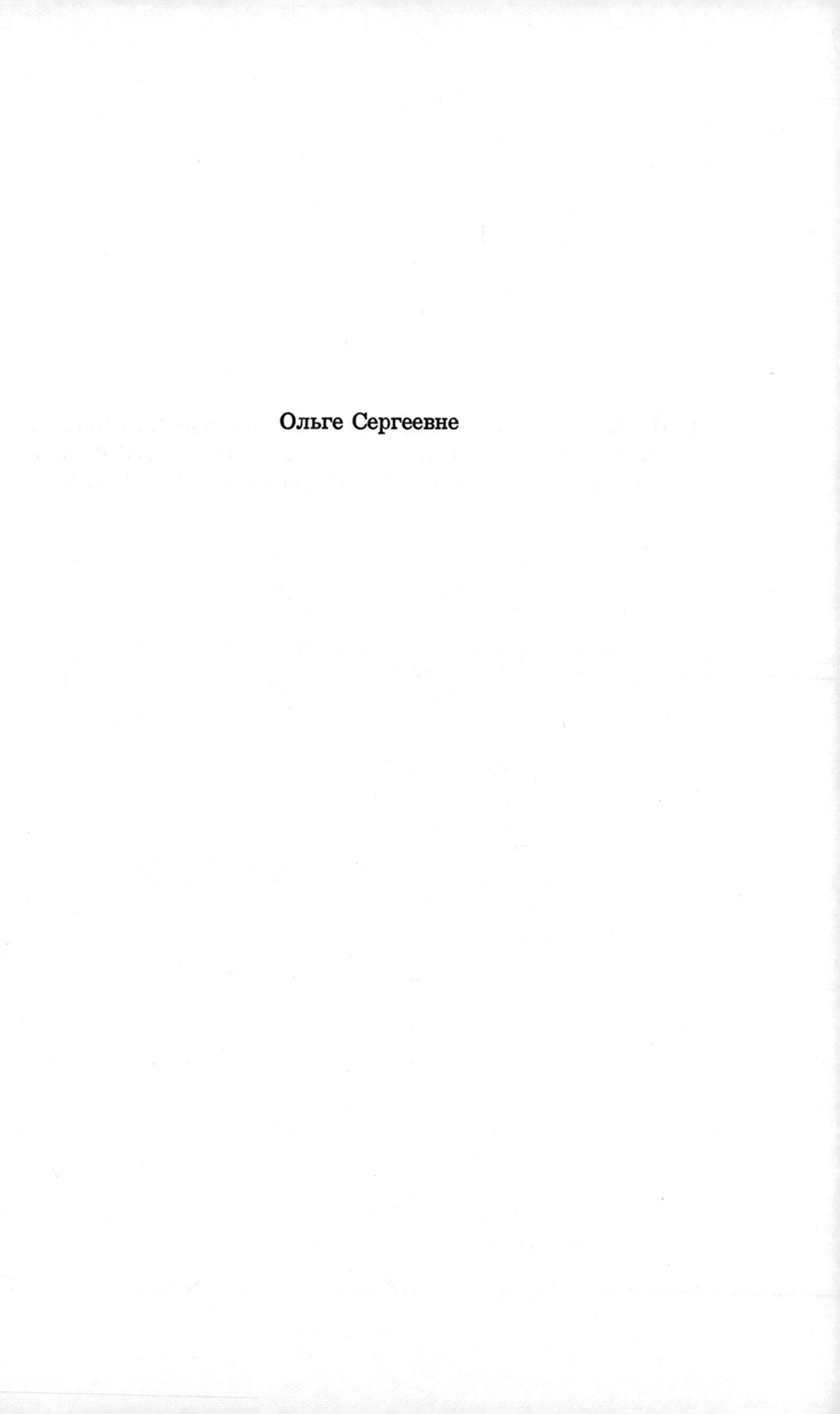

Ольге Сергеевне

R. H. Stacy, Associate Professor of Russian Literature, is chairman of the Slavic Department of Syracuse University. He received the B.A. and M.A. from the University of Michigan and the Ph.D. from Syracuse University.

CONTENTS

PREFACE

This book is primarily intended for readers who do not know Russian but who would like to learn something of the nature and course of Russian literary criticism. From time to time I use Russian words, phrases, and technical terms in transliteration, but these are all accompanied by English translations or equivalents and all passages from the Russian critics are given in English. Where these translations are not my own, I acknowledge the fact and cite my sources. Instead of a single terminal bibliography, at the end of each chapter the reader will find suggested related reading (all available in English and very often in paperback editions) which parallels the discussion in the text.

The book may also be used, of course, to accompany the reading of the Russian texts of the critics under discussion, many of which are now conveniently available in two Oxford Russian Readers: *Russian Critical Essays (XIXth Century)* and *Russian Critical Essays (XXth Century)*.

I have assumed that the reader knows something of the course of European and American literary criticism and have felt free to refer to many names, from Longinus to Eliot, without excessive comment.

R. H. STACY

Syracuse, New York
Spring 1974

RUSSIAN LITERARY CRITICISM

INTRODUCTION

1

This book is a short history of Russian literary criticism and is not by any means a new or original critique of Russian literature. It is, quite simply, a survey of the various ways in which representative Russian critics (often creative writers of renown as well), from the eighteenth century to the present, have viewed not only the literary works of other Russian and non-Russian writers but the problems of literature in general. It would thus be a barren endeavor merely to survey such views without examining the substance behind them; therefore a good deal of attention will also be paid, necessarily, to literary theory. Further, the book does not pretend to offer any startlingly new interpretations of either Russian literature or Russian critical thought, although from time to time value judgments will be made—something that is particularly unavoidable, for instance, in discussing such matters as Russian pseudoclassicism, Russian Formalism, or Russian Marxist criticism.

Russian literary criticism is an integral part of European criticism, and all of the major as well as many of the minor critical trends that we find in the West are reflected in one way or another in the history of Russian criticism. But just as the courses of French, English, and German criticism show certain peculiar or special features and emphases (these often being related to historical factors), so the history of Russian criticism frequently shows unique and interesting developments. Thus the concept of utilitarianism, of English provenance, was taken up by Russian literary critics and carried to what certainly must be an extreme, while other ideas drawn from German idealistic and romantic thought were further elaborated in very distinctive ways. Quite often Russian writers and critics, either after surveying a large bulk of Western European as well as Russian critical theory or as the result of developing variations on some favorite concept, produced remarkable syntheses or interesting new approaches.

A book which claims to be a "Short History of Russian Literary Criticism" must necessarily be selective in two ways: it cannot encompass each and every Russian critic and it cannot even refer to, much less discuss, each and every critical work of those critics who are mentioned. Specialists may object that this or that critic is not considered or that a certain book or article is not referred to. But this book is an introductory survey intended mainly for readers who do not know Russian, and an attempt has been made to limit the survey to what are generally considered the most important critics and critical theories; an effort has also been made to refer whenever possible to books and articles that are readily available in English translation.

Primary attention in this book will be devoted to the major Russian critics and critical movements. But a number of the more significant minor critics will also be mentioned and discussed, and occasionally considerable attention will be paid, for one reason or another, to a critic of otherwise minor importance. It should be noted here, too, that many of the figures discussed in this book were—or are—primarily creative writers, their critical works usually being considered in histories of Russian literature of less significance than their poems, novels, or plays.[1] Though there are some outstanding Russian "professional" critics, it is often very difficult (and, I suppose, futile) to attempt to draw a fine line of distinction between who is and who is not a literary critic in a professional sense. In any case, throughout this book the term "critic" will be used of those selected Russian writers, major and minor, who have in whatever connection written more or less extensively and significantly *about* literature and who very often have, in so doing, made critical judgments and evaluations.

As for the scope of the material in this book, most of the attention will be devoted to criticism of the nineteenth and twentieth centuries. Eighteenth-century criticism will be, for our purposes, represented chiefly by Lomonosov (Chapter I), while pre-eighteenth-century criticism, such as it is and despite the importance it might have for specialists, will only be very briefly mentioned toward the end of this Introduction. Following a chapter on Pushkin and the critics of his age (II), the criticism of Vissarion Belinsky and of his "successors," the so-called Civic Critics, will receive considerable attention (III,

1. Creative writers who from time to time write criticism are often referred to as "occasional critics."

IV). In Chapter V the Aesthetic (or Conservative) Critics, represented chiefly by Apollon Grigoriev, will be discussed. This will be followed by a chapter devoted to the critical writings and observations of Tolstoy and Dostoevsky as well as to a number of other important figures of the late nineteenth century (VI). Chapter VII, the longest in the book, will deal with a large number of critics, loosely (and perhaps in some cases inappropriately) called Modernists. The following chapter (VIII) will consider the very important movement known as Russian Formalism, its leading representatives, and its affiliations and influences. Another rather long chapter (IX) will attempt to cover some of the more important aspects of Soviet Marxist criticism as well as the subject of Socialist Realism. In the final chapter we shall look at some of the critical observations of several modern Russian writers and critics, all of whom are in various ways opposed to Soviet literary canons and especially to the doctrine of Socialist Realism.

Russian literature, perhaps more than any other European literature, has always been markedly oriented toward civic and social values. With a few notable exceptions, this is particularly true of Russian literary criticism; and students of Russian literature, including criticism, are often sorely tempted, like the critics themselves, to digress from the subject of literature and literary values into philosophy, sociology, and politics. But because of this very apparent aspect of Russian literature, frequently commented on in literary histories, some historical and political background is of great importance in understanding both the literary situation and the problems facing Russian critics at any given time. In this book a minimum but, I believe, adequate amount of such background material is provided, especially in connection with the influx at various times of German and other ideologies. Occasionally, in lieu of detailed explanations, a more or less authoritative book on a particular topic is cited in a note.

2

Throughout this book I shall have occasion to refer to many kinds of literary criticism; but there are three major or basic types of criticism and it is best that these be defined and explained at the outset. The first type is normative (prescriptive, legislative) criticism. Such criticism, as the names indicate, prescribes norms or canons for the writer and the critic; it professes, on the basis of some authoritative precedent, to lay down the law for the writer concerning the proper creation of a work of literature and also presumes to legislate on such particular matters as form, language, and style. Its "statutes" also provide the critic with criteria for judging—i.e., approving or condemning—a work of literature. This legalistic aspect of normative criticism is made clear when we note how relevant in its context is such a precept of the law as *stare decisis et non quieta movere*. Like the law, normative criticism relies heavily on tradition. And as the law prefers over-all order and adherence to precedent even at the risk of an occasional miscarriage of justice, so normative criticism is apt to prefer a safe and regular *firma mediocritas* to any irregularity or violation, even by a genius, of its canons. Like the law, too, normative criticism sets a premium on common sense and decorum.

Like the law, finally, normative criticism goes back, so far as European neoclassical movements are concerned (and it is with these that we usually associate normative criticism), directly to Roman and Renaissance rather than to Greek doctrine, to which it is related only indirectly. It should be remembered that both the word *classical* and the concept of classicism itself are of Roman and Renaissance origin. Thus Aulus Gellius in the second century of our era first used the term *scriptor classicus* (as opposed to *scriptor proletarius*), while in the sixteenth century Lodovico Castelvetro formulated the so-called classical unities. Whereas the post-Renaissance development of classical theory and normative criticism produced in France some major works of lasting importance (so that we are quite justified, however derivative the movement might originally have been, in referring to French Classicism), we find in Germany of the late seventeenth and early eighteenth centuries such a cut-and-dried and artificial form of "classicism" that we must somehow modify our terms and use an expression like "pseudoclassicism." It was largely from this degenerate form of classical theory that the Russians borrowed many of the elements of their own pseudoclassicism. The results, especially in criticism, may readily be imagined. Something similar happened a century or so later when, from the detritus of German idealistic philosophy, the Russians borrowed the triadic structure of the dialectic.

The "authoritative precedent" used as the basis of a normative criticism was referred to above. So far as most normative criticism in Europe is concerned, this precedent is contained in a much modified classical theory of, as was mentioned, Roman, Renaissance, and post-Renaissance origin—a theory which eventually had as little in common with Greek classical literature as Pöppelmann's *Zwinger* in Dresden had in common with Greek architecture. But in Soviet Russia another authoritative basis, Marxism-Leninism, has been posited for a new normative criticism. And it is extremely interesting that, although Marxist criticism has given us some valuable insights and at least one major critic (Georg Lukács), the literature produced in conformity with the canons of Russian Socialist Realism (this phrase, by the way, was given currency by that supreme *kritēs,* Joseph Stalin) turns out to be what we might have expected it to be: another quite second-rate body of pseudoclassical writing. The Russian critic Andrey Sinyavsky ("Abram Tertz") has made this point very well, and the whole subject will be discussed below in Chapter IX.

Normative criticism written by a man of superior abilities and taste may constitute a lasting and significant contribution to literary criticism. Perhaps the most familiar normative critic in Europe is Boileau (*Art poétique*[2]), although the Elizabethans also produced one or two names of note. In the hands of a drudge, however, and written on the lowest level, normative criticism frequently has the stench of death about it; the result is, at best, what the Russian critic Dobrolyubov called "proofreader" criticism.

"The great question," Henry James once wrote, "as to a poet or novelist is, How does he feel about life? What, in the last analysis, is his philosophy?" These are the things that interest theoretical critics. Whereas for the normative critic a work of literature is primarily something to be judged, for the theoretical critic a work of literature is the starting point for one or more philosophical disquisitions; and in this context we must usually be prepared to encounter not the jargon of the law but the terminology of philosophy and metayphysics. Often it is aesthetic theory (a branch of philosophy) which preoccupies such a critic and therefore theoretical criticism is sometimes called aesthetic criticism. But just about every conceivable philosophical and metaphysical concept has been, at one time or another, brought to bear on literature—often, it must be said, without specific relevance. One thinks immediately of Plato, of Coleridge, of Lessing, and—in more recent times—of Kenneth Burke.

Russian literature, and especially the novels of Tolstoy and Dostoevsky, has produced a number of works which have provoked lengthy, elaborate, and sometimes incisive theoretical and aesthetic criticism. Though we shall be concerned hereafter only with the Russian theo-

2. Called by Pushkin the "French Koran."

retical critics, amongst whom there are some important figures, the Russian literature of the past still provides rich material for theoretical criticism outside of Russia—witness Sir Isaiah Berlin's *The Hedgehog and the Fox.*

The third major type of criticism is descriptive or analytic criticism. A good descriptive critic—and there have been surprisingly few of them—can reveal facets and levels of meaning in a literary work which the common reader is apt to overlook or never suspect. Such a critic can make the rereading of a poem or a novel into a new and rewarding experience. But this is on the highest level. There are special hazards lying in wait for the descriptive critic who loses sight of his true function or allows his sentiments to become muddled. On the one hand, he may turn out to be merely a vulgar cicerone, a pompous and comical "come-savor-these-delights-with-me" kind of guide through the foothills of Parnassus; or, on the other hand, the result may be the impressionistic critic, more interested in verbalizing his own ecstatic reactions than in describing the work in question or analyzing that "labyrinth of interconnections" (to use Tolstoy's phrase) which is at the heart of all great literature. We are all, of course, carried away at times by the things we read; but the sight and sound of an impressionistic critic being constantly ravished quickly pall. It is something Aristotle might have called *miaros.*

We need descriptive critics—there is no substitute for them. We need especially that particular variety of the descriptive critic, the analytic critic, who brings to his task a wide experience of life, great learning, and a Lyncean vision. But again there is a perverted type of analytic criticism, the type we might call "Pilpul" criticism.[3] The Pilpulist analyzes everything fiercely, endlessly, minutely, and—needlessly; that is to say, he is more concerned with analysis for its own sake than for the purpose of elucidation.

If we agree that the human mind is an instrument designed primarily for analyzing reality, then analytic criticism might appear to be the easiest of the lot. But we must also remember that the objects of literary analysis are synthetic products of this same mind, the most complex structure we know of. In any case, analytic criticism should not be confused with literary scholarship, pure and simple. But where does criticism end and where does literary scholarship begin? The

3. The Pilpulists were the rabbis (especially in Poland) of an earlier age who devoted themselves to an over-refined and hair-splitting study and interpretation of the Torah and the commentaries.

answer here is simple: criticism proper, of whatever variety, always involves evaluation. A work of literary scholarship may be unimpeachably rigorous in its analysis and exposition, tracing with unfailing logic and overwhelming documentation the influence, for example, of one author upon another; but unless it includes or ends in evaluation, it is not, whatever else we may choose to call it, criticism. The critic must, in a sense, go beyond science; he must "stick his neck out" and deal somehow with such matters as Kant's aesthetic paradox. He must try again either to untie this famous knot or, after he has prepared himself long and hard, to cut through it. Bertrand Russell once said that science is what we know and philosophy is what we do not know. In this respect, criticism is akin to philosophy and it follows that the most philosophic criticism is theoretical criticism.

These, then, are the major types of literary criticism, and I should like to add here that in very general terms when we think of normative criticism, we think especially of the French; when we think of theoretical criticism, we think especially of the Germans; and when we think of descriptive criticism, we think especially of the English. Further associations in this connection come readily to mind, e.g., French classicism and rationalism, German metaphysics, and English empiricism. Additional references to these national affiliations, insofar as literary traditions are concerned, will be made in the chapters that follow.

I have mentioned some of the degenerate forms of normative, theoretical, and descriptive criticism. There is also another potential danger which threatens all of these, although theoretical and descriptive critics are most liable to suffer. I refer to the so-called autotelic criticism or criticism which has itself as an end. To paraphrase the pungent language of Marx, autotelic criticism is to proper criticism what autoerotism is to love. The autotelic critic not only tends to forget or ignore the true purpose of criticism, which is to elucidate and evaluate, but he also forgets that criticism has an ancillary function. Whereas criticism in its authentic form is properly a metalanguage ("a comment on a comment, a secondary language . . . applied to a primary language"[4]), the autotelic critic in effect perverts, often with the most laudable of intentions, this metalinguistic and ancillary function of criticism and he himself becomes a "creative writer" of sorts—in English criticism the name of Walter Pater immediately suggests itself.

4. Roland Barthes, "Criticism as Language," in *The Critical Moment: Literary Criticism in the 1960's* (New York: McGraw-Hill, 1964), p. 126.

On the lowest level the autotelic critic is almost bound to produce mere irrelevancies. On the highest level, however, when the critic writes a fine piece of authentic judicial criticism couched in a language which, though stylistically brilliant itself, does not obfuscate, then we are willing (as in the case of Sainte-Beuve) to apply the term "autotelic" without the usual pejorative connotations. There is, of course, no reason why criticism should not be well or even beautifully written. But the fact remains that critics like Sainte-Beuve are exceptions and that, from the time of Aristotle (whose notoriously crabbed style is perhaps less the Master's fault than his students'), the language of literary criticism has varied between what is now called "technical writing" and that rambling autoschediastic style that we usually associate with the name of George Saintsbury.

So far as Russian criticism is concerned, in the chapters that follow we shall see numerous examples of the three major types of criticism mentioned above as well as instances of impressionistic and autotelic criticism. Russian eighteenth-century criticism, as noted earlier, is overwhelmingly normative, and the same applies to Soviet Marxist criticism. During the nineteenth and early twentieth centuries (down to the Revolution) most significant criticism is of the theoretical variety, this being due to the very marked tendency of the Russian critics to use a literary text as a springboard for largely non-literary discussion, a phenomenon that will be referred to on several occasions in the following chapters. The best examples of Russian impressionistic and autotelic criticism will be found amongst the critics discussed in Chapter VII, while analytic criticism occurs rarely and somewhat indiscriminately. The Formalists (Chapter VIII) are to a great extent analytic critics, but many of their comments on literary texts are apt to be highly theoretical as well. In a more general sense, there is a range of Russian criticism from a very informal, journalistic style (especially in the cases of Belinsky and the Civic Critics) to the learned and classical style of a critic such as Shestov (Chapter VII, section 5) or from the severely moralistic and religiose criticism of Tolstoy to the mordant and intricate wit of Nabokov.

3

From the earliest period of Russian literature down to the beginning of the eighteenth century there is very little that is important, much less interesting, in the way of literary criticism. The only things of any possible interest to us—and even these are purely marginal—are the manuals of poetics and rhetoric. The *Izbornik* of 1073, a sort of anthology or miscellany copied from a Bulgarian original, contains, for instance, what is frequently referred to as a "treatise on poetics." Actually this is a Slavic version of the *peri tropōn poiētikōn* ("On Figures of Speech in Poetry") of Georgios Choiroboskos ("George the Shepherd"), a Byzantine Church-affiliated scholar of the sixth century. By no stretch of the imagination can it be called criticism, being essentially a frigid list of polysyllabic names of figures or tropes—some twenty-seven in all. Among the works on rhetoric, I may mention two Slavic versions of Skouphos' trite Greek *Rhetoric,* one made in the late seventeenth century and the other revised in 1705 by Kozma Grek ("Cosmas the Greek"), a Greek teacher who had, like a number of his compatriots, come to Muscovy. Kozma Grek's version, though valuable for its lexical contents and as a monument of Russian Baroque, is again hardly of interest as criticism. There were many such manuals in Russia by the time of Lomonosov (1711–65), although their use was limited to ecclesiastical (i.e., homiletic) purposes. Rhetoric in post-classical times is usually associated not with the Greeks but with the Romans (hence many technical terms of rhetoric in general use—exordium, peroration, etc.—are of Latin origin). And it was especially Latin school rhetoric, emanating chiefly from the Kiev Academy[5] that, along with German and French pseudoclassical doctrine, reached Lomonosov in the eighteenth century.

But, someone may ask, What about the Greeks and the Byzantine legacy? Despite the quaint comparisons that are made from time to time between ancient Greek poetry and Russian poetry or even between the ancient Greeks and the Russians, I suggest that Weidlé is quite correct in asserting that the Russians are of all peoples, with the

5. This famous institution was founded in 1631 to counter Jesuit influence after the Union of Lublin, but its own teaching methods were based largely on Jesuit pedagogical practice.

possible exception of the Germans, the least Greek in temperament.[6] We can, I think, state categorically that there is simply no Greek influence on Russian literary criticism. It must be remembered that there was no renascence in Russia, no rediscovery of the classics, and certainly nothing comparable to Dryden's *An Essay of Dramatic Poesy.* As for the Byzantine inheritance, we are forever reading about such matters as the reappearance of "Byzantine cruelty" either in Imperial or Soviet Russia or about the vestiges of "Byzantine ritualism" and Byzantine caesaropapism in Russia. With these, however, I have no concern; nor have I any concern, beyond a few remarks to be made shortly, with the actual Byzantine heritage: the religion of the Eastern Church, the law (both civil and ecclesiastical), and those poor remnants of an already desiccated literature which eventually reached Russia after undergoing monkish censorship. There is, by the way, no literature or body of criticism in the Western world in which censorship, in all its forms and involving all aspects of literary and artistic activity, appears with such persistence as it does in Russia.[7] Thus V. S. Pritchett, in an introduction to some tales by Leskov, may quite justifiably write that "the sound of the lash has always been heard in Russian literary criticism." Though this "sound of the lash" grew noticeably stronger during the Soviet era, censorship by either Church or State authorities has been a regular phenomenon throughout Russian history. In early Russia, for example, the Church not only emasculated such secular literature as was allowed entry by expurgating almost all references to romantic love (thus depriving Russian literature of the various motifs of courtly love, so familiar in the West); but it also did irreparable damage to native traditions by condemning folk poetry and songs (because of their pagan and too unabashedly secular content) and thus preventing to a large extent their preservation in writing.

It is especially interesting that, despite Russia's proximity to the capital of the Eastern Roman Empire (which fell to the Turks in 1453), despite its affiliations with the Eastern Church, and despite the "Byzantine inheritance," it is West European influence which we encounter at the beginnings not only of Russian literary theory but of many other areas of Russian culture as well. It was to open a window

6. See Wladimir Weidlé, *Russia: Absent and Present* (New York: Random House Vintage Books, 1961), p. 163.

7. Should anyone doubt this, let him read Mirsky's *History of Russian Literature* or Marc Slonim's *Russian Theater* and tick off the references to censorship.

to the West that Peter the Great founded St. Petersburg; it was from the West that the sources of Russia's baroque age (in the seventeenth century) came; it was from the West that pseudoclassical doctrine came; it was from the West that a belated romanticism, including romantic nationalism or "Slavophilism," came (this time the Church could not stem the tide); and, finally, it was from the West that the teachings of Schelling, Hegel, and Marx came. It has constantly been the "decadent West" (and those familiar with Russian history and literature can recall innumerable examples of such a description of Western Europe or America by Russian writers, from the earliest times to the present) that, despite all the barriers that have been thrown up, has largely moulded Russian political and literary thought, to name only two areas. Thus it comes as no surprise that again, in spite of all the walls, iron curtains, and other restrictive devices which the Soviet Union has erected to protect Orthodox Russia, we see today everywhere in that land the growing influence of Western ideas: in economics, psychology, psychiatry, cybernetics, semantics, etc. And for the mainland Chinese, who are relatively recent converts to communism, the Soviet Union, precisely because of these very obvious Western leanings, is no longer the land of orthodoxy but of heterodoxy and rank heresy.

Although the subject will concern us no further in this book, I should like, before turning to Lomonosov, to say one or two more things about the Eastern—more particularly, the Russian—Orthodox Church. To anyone who stems from the Christian tradition of the West, whether he be Roman Catholic, Protestant, or Christian apostate, a study of Eastern Orthodoxy may be very enlightening; and a reading of, for example, Ernst Benz's *The Eastern Orthodox Church* will provide some revealing insights not only into the history of Christianity but also into a branch of Christianity that differs in many respects from that of the West. Persons of the Jewish faith might also be interested in reading such a book, since there are in Eastern Orthodoxy some special connections with Judaism—e.g., in the doctrine of Heavenly Wisdom. For serious students of Russian literature something more than a cursory knowledge of the Eastern Church is of course necessary. But the importance of Orthodoxy may be exaggerated. When we think of the Russian Orthodox Church and Russian literature, we usually think of Tolstoy and Dostoevsky: the former for his excommunication and the latter for his compliance. Dostoevsky, amongst his numerous hariolations, said such things as "the Russian people is entire in its Orthodoxy. He who does not understand Orthodoxy will never have the slightest understanding of the people." Now this may or may not be true—I shall not argue the point here. But I have heard essentially the same thing said of Dostoevsky himself and his novels and this, I think, is quite wrong. Belinsky once remarked that it is very easy to speak of Russian literature in extremes. George Steiner, although there is a modicum of truth in what he says, still exaggerates when he writes that "it is possible to read a major portion of Dostoevskyan fiction as a gloss on the New Testament." I suggest that what is really needed to understand Dostoevsky is (in addition to a rudimentary knowledge of Christian theodicy) a knowledge of European literature. It is interesting and significant, for instance, that the so-called core of *The Brothers Karamazov*, the controversial "Legend of the Grand Inquisitor," does not involve any esoteric eastern or Byzantine doctrines; it was probably inspired by a scene in a play by Schiller and clearly displays one of Dostoevsky's many aversions—his animus, in this case, against the Roman Catholic Church.

SUGGESTED READING

Watson, George, *The Literary Critics* (Baltimore: Penguin Books, 1962).

Hall, Vernon, *A Short History of Literary Criticism* (New York: New York University Press, 1963).

Wimsatt, William K., and Brooks, Cleanth, *Literary Criticism: A Short History* (New York: Alfred A. Knopf, 1962).

Wellek, René, *A History of Modern Criticism: 1750–1950* (New Haven: Yale University Press, 1955–65).

Mirsky, D. S., *A History of Russian Literature* (New York: Alfred A. Knopf, 1949), Book One, chapters 1 and 2.

I MIKHAIL LOMONOSOV

1

Seen from our Western vantage point in the seventies of the twentieth century, Russian literary criticism both begins and ends badly. This is true whether we begin with Lomonosov and pseudoclassical doctrine or with the later sociopolitical and journalistic criticism of Vissarion Belinsky; and it is certainly true of the present state of Soviet Russian Marxist-Leninist criticism. To a certain extent, these unimpressive beginnings and present state of Russian criticism are due to the effects of German influences—influences which we encounter very early (notably in the cases of both Lomonosov and Belinsky) as well as at the roots of Russian Marxist criticism. On the other hand, the same influence can be seen in the origins of Russian Formalism which, while still representing an essentially erroneous and distorted view to official Soviet critics, is often considered by Western observers as a high point in Russian criticism. One can also see this German influence (Hegelianism) even in the case of such an outstanding critic as Zamyatin (Chapter VII, section 10), although it is here by no means pervasive or dominant.

Mikhail Vasilievich Lomonosov was born in 1711, the son of a prosperous fisherman on the island of Kurostrov in the mouth of the Northern Dvina, some fifty miles from the port of Archangel. Technically, Lomonosov was a "peasant" (*krest'janin*). Thus, for whatever the observation is worth, modern Russian literature, which is now (officially at least) in proletarian hands, also had a proletarian beginning, a fact which Soviet authorities make the most of. The young Lomonosov, although he served at sea with his father for a brief period, early showed unusual scholastic aptitudes and evidently had no vocation for a life of fishing. He set off for Moscow in 1730 with slight financial help from his father; but, in order to enter the so-called Slavonic-Greek-Latin Academy at the Zaikonospassky Monastery, he had to falsify his credentials by calling himself "the son of a nobleman," since the Academy did not admit the children of serfs or peasants. Later this falsification was discovered, but in view of the young scholar's exceptional promise it was overlooked.

He completed the course of studies very successfully and was selected, together with eleven other students, to be sent to St. Petersburg (a city then only a little over thirty years old) to study at the Academy of Sciences which functioned both as a scientific society and an institution of learning, providing instruction on the secondary and college levels. Within the same year Lomonosov was again selected to be sent first to the University of Marburg in Germany and then to Freiburg to study mining. The University of Marburg is a familiar name in the annals of Russian literature, Pasternak being one of the more recent figures of note to have attended this university. In Lomonosov's day the great name at Marburg was Christian Wolf (later Freiherr von Wolf), a mathematician and natural philosopher of considerable learning though not of exceptional brilliance. Lomonosov attended his lectures, concentrated on scientific studies, and then, three years later, moved on to Freiburg. Here personal differences between Lomonosov and Johann Henckel, the professor of metallurgy, erupted into mutual recriminations and open animosity, a foretaste of the difficulties with the German academic hierarchy that were later to plague Lomonosov back in Russia.

In 1740 Lomonosov, after less than a year at his mining studies, left Freiburg without official permission from Russian authorities. Short of funds and often in dire straits, he traveled here and there seeking assistance. Finally, fearful of re-entering Russia without authorization, he returned to Marburg. Here he married a German girl and was able to return to Russia the following year. A year later he was appointed what we would call an assistant professor or lecturer in chemistry at the Academy. This was the beginning of his professional academic career and I shall dwell no further on the facts of his life, since all the material is readily available elsewhere.[1] I shall only add that, shortly after his appointment, he became embroiled with the Germans who were in virtual control of the Academy (at one time this institution was called the *dreifüssige Akademie,* a pun on the name of Nicholas Fuss and his two sons) and, after the situation had

1. See, for example, B. Menshutkin, *Russia's Lomonosov* (Princeton, N.J.: Princeton University Press, 1952).

actually come to blows, Lomonosov was arrested and placed under detention for several months.

Lomonosov died in 1765, broken, worn out, and addicted to drink. Pushkin once said that Lomonosov was himself a university; his achievements were many in many fields: he was an original thinker, experimental scientist, poet, and graphic artist of no mean ability. Despite his many activities, however, I shall be concerned here with only one work by Lomonosov—his *Rhetoric.*

The *Rhetoric,* completed in 1744 and published in 1748, is the major monument of Russian pseudoclassical literary theory. A neatly arranged "codex" of the law literary, it contains 326 sections, while the Russian text runs to some 280 pages. It is a work of criticism, i.e., a work dealing with evaluation, only in the sense that its rather frigid precepts *imply* the proper criteria for literary judgment.

It cannot be said that the work is, in any but minor respects, original. Such handbooks of rhetoric were legion in Europe of the time and in the preceding century (Martin Opitz's *Buch von deutschen Poeterei,* 1624, is a good example) and it was from some of these that Lomonosov borrowed heavily. But it should be remembered that, in the "classical" context, no stigma was attached to literary borrowing (or, to be franker, the extensive "lifting" of attractive or useful passages without acknowledgment[2]) and that it was part of the pseudoclassical program to perpetuate traditions and not to innovate or, in modern parlance, to "rock the boat."

A good deal is known about Lomonosov's sources. In addition to drawing upon the standard works of such French neoclassicists as Caussin and Pomay, he also made use of the *Ausführliche Redekunst* (1736) of Johann Christoph Gottsched, a professor at Leipzig (professors are usually very prominent, as might be expected, in any "neo-," "pseudo-," or "Alexandrian" period) and one of the leading figures in the German pseudoclassical movement proper (c.1680–1750). It was Pushkin himself who once wrote that "German is the only language in which the critics appeared before the authors." But Lomonosov's work, however derivative it may be, was still a pioneering venture: the *Rhetoric* played no small part in bridging the gap between Russian letters and the mainland of secular Western thought. One thinks immediately of Peter the Great and indeed it was Belinsky, having in

2. Though plagiarism is not new, having been perpetrated quite elegantly by some of the greatest writers, the concept of literary theft as cause for court action is a comparatively modern development.

mind the entire corpus of Lomonosov's writings, who called him the Peter of Russian literature.

Professor B. Kudryavtsev, in a small book published in the Soviet Union in 1954, after pointing out in the approved fashion the ideological content in the *Rhetoric* (he is referring to illustrative material quoted by Lomonosov), makes the following profound comment: "Speech, the great scientist wrote, can take the form of prose or verse." And in point of fact there is much of the most elementary propaedeutic in the *Rhetoric;* for example, Lomonosov provides (in discussing evidence or proof) the following guide for the thinking author: "Here we have a father and a mother; consequently there are children, since otherwise they could not be father and mother" (§86). This of course is Roman school *probatio* and indicates, as does much of the matter in the *Rhetoric,* the origins in Kievan and Latin school rhetoric. For instance, the three main divisions in the work are: *izobretenie* (the Latin *inventio*), *ukrashenie* (*ornatio*), and *raspolozhenie* (*dispositio*). It is interesting, too, that Lomonosov's famous hierarchy of styles (discussed in an essay he published in 1757, "On the Use of Church Books in the Russian Language"[3]) is also of Roman origin (e.g., Quintilian), although the *ultimate* sources are Greek. Lomonosov posits three styles (high, middle, and low), the differences being primarily lexical, depending on the ratio of Church Slavonic words. Thus odes and tragedy should employ the high style; satires, elegy, and drama (something less than high tragedy) should employ the middle style; and comedies, epigrams, and songs should use the low style. Such stylistic legislation is characteristically classicist but the greatest writers have consistently violated—and well they did—such constrictive and artificial rules, Shakespeare being in this respect an archcriminal in the eyes of classicists. This explains why the Bard has always been *persona haud grata* in France, while the Germans and the Russians, who are romantic often to a distressing degree, adore him. In fact, there has been at least one attempt by Teutonic scholar-

3. By "Church Books" Lomonosov means works written in Church Slavonic. Church Slavonic is a modified form of Old Church Slavonic, the language—also known as Old Bulgarian—into which Saints Cyril and Methodius translated certain ecclesiastical works in the ninth century. Church Slavonic words are (roughly) to Russian words what Greek and Latin roots are to English, and they are readily drawn upon for forming "learned" or technical terms. Thus the Russian word for *milk* is *moloko,* while the Church Slavonic is *mleko.* But as we draw upon Latin to form *mammal,* so Russian draws upon Church Slavonic to form the equivalent—*mlekopitajushchee.*

ship to claim him as a German; the Russians have not as yet gone quite this far.

The *Rhetoric* exhibits the full panoply of ancient (mainly protreptic[4]) rhetoric, most of the examples being drawn from ancient authors but with occasional and refreshing—though not always enlightening—allusions to things Russian. Thus, in the chapter on *izobretenie,* as an example of how etymologies (and ancient etymologies were notorious for their sheer fantasy) may be used to bolster an argument, Lomonosov writes the following: "If the Greek noun *theos* comes from the verb *thein* (to run), the Russian *bog* from the noun *beg* (running), and the German *Gott* from the verb *geht,* one may very well conclude that the ancient Greeks, the Slavs, and the Germans considered as divine those things that are in constant motion—the Sun, the Moon, the stars, or mighty rivers" (§83).[5] Lomonosov discusses in typical textbook style, section by section, such matters as grammatical and rhetorical figures including antonomasia (replacing the phrase "rich man," for instance, by the name Croesus), enthymemes (rhetorical syllogisms), periodic sentence structure, as well as the ancient chria. This was an aphorism, quotation, or historic saying developed along strictly prescribed lines into a short essay. It is noteworthy that Lomonosov here preserves, handed down through the centuries, the entire eight steps of the traditional Roman formula. The examples he quotes are all ancient (§§254–65).

Most of the material I have so far referred to is of purely academic interest, but there is one aspect of the *Rhetoric* that is more significant from the point of view of criticism. This is what has been called Lomonosov's "baroque poetics." The term "baroque" has been one of the most debated terms in literary history ever since Wölfflin first applied it to literature in his *Renaissance und Barock* (1888).[6] In 1929 Helmut Hatzfeld voiced the opinion that French neoclassicism was baroque and many scholars have since come to share this view, while Ortega y Gasset not only included such movements as Gon-

4. The first sentence in the first paragraph reads: "Rhetoric is the art of speaking elegantly on any given subject and thereby of winning over others to one's own way of thinking."

5. Trediakovsky, a contemporary of Lomonosov's, derived the Russian word for *Celts, Kelty,* from *zhëltyj* (*yellow*), since he believed that the Celts were blond. I have met at least one American newspaperman who really believed that the word *news* is derived from N, E, W, S (i.e., the points of the compass).

6. The term had been used since the eighteenth century in art to mean "extravagant" or "bizarre."

gorism, Marinism, and Euphuism in the baroque but also expressed the view that what is often called ancient classicism is actually baroque (e.g., the poems of Pindar). In his studies of Ovid, the Cambridge scholar L. P. Wilkinson has also referred to "Hellenistic baroque" and "Greco-Roman baroque," and he finds strong baroque elements in Ovid.

In the literary history of Russia, some scholars (notably Dmitry Chizhevsky in his *History of Russian Literature from the Eleventh Century to the End of the Baroque*) now designate the period c. 1640–1740 as the age of the baroque. This is somewhat later (as one might expect) and of somewhat longer duration than the period of German baroque literature (c. 1600–80). This is not the place to enter upon a detailed discussion of something that is more the concern of literary history and comparative literature than criticism; suffice it to say that the recognition of the baroque in Russian literature as a sort of "pre-classicism," related to the following age of classicism (or pseudoclassicism) in much the same way that preromanticism (or sentimentalism) is related to the following romantic age, is of considerable value.[7] For instance, it helps us to distinguish meaningfully some important differences between the first and second halves of the eighteenth century in Russian literature and, more particularly, it helps us explain the presence in the Rhetoric of elements "far removed," as Chizhevsky writes, "from the 'rationalist' poetics of classicism."

Thus it is at first surprising to read in the *Rhetoric* that "profound reasoning and arguments are not so moving [as to arouse the passions] and they cannot inflame the passions; for this, reason must be brought down from its high seat to the senses and must be united with them so that it may be set aflame with passion" (§100). To this typically baroque emphasis on the passions and on "inflammation" is added Lomonosov's predilection for lush ornamentation, for magnificence (*velikolepie*) and richness of expression (*izobilie*)—predilections which are at the very opposite from classical litotes or meiosis ("*le classicisme tend tout entier vers la litote*"—Gide). But the most baroque feature of the *Rhetoric* is the preference for 'involved turns of phrase" (*vitievatye rechi*) with words arranged in "strange, unusual, and unnatural" ways (§129ff.). It is revealing, too, that Lomonosov should quote (to show the efficacy of opposing passions in conflict)

7. René Wellek recognizes the relevance and usefulness of the term "baroque." See his *Concepts of Criticism* (New Haven: Yale University Press, 1963), pp. 69 ff.

lines from the *Medea* of Seneca. This writer of the Silver Age of Latin literature, whose influence on the Elizabethan stage is notorious, has also—and quite rightly—been called baroque, excessively fond as he is of bloody scenes, startling effects, novel turns of speech, and learned conceits.[8]

Yet we must not exaggerate Lomonosov's baroque leanings; he is, after all (as he tells us), advocating devices or "stratagems" by which the writer can, in effect, deceive and enchant his readers (§150). What he is actually outlining is a crude theory of what the Russian Formalist critics were later to call the "device of making strange" (see Chapter VIII). And the tendency amongst post-classical students of the Latin language and literature in various parts of Europe to produce stylistic monstrosities, to prefer the odd construction to the normal or the rare usage to the common, has always been strong, although the *reductio ad absurdum* was reached long before the seventeenth and eighteenth centuries in the Middle Ages in what W. P. Ker calls the "ineffable *Hisperica Famina*."[9] Lomonosov does prefer, for instance, a word order in literary Russian based upon the highly artificial word order in literary Latin, especially poetry. But in this respect Antioch Kantemir (died 1744) outdid Lomonosov, and some of his poetical hyperbata are nothing less than grotesque.

Baroque, too, is Lomonosov's "psychophonetic" theory (§170ff.): that is, the analysis of the vowels and consonants as vehicles for specific emotional color. There are adumbrations of such a theory in ancient rhetoric, while various baroque poetics elaborated on this, and it was taken up again in more recent times by the French Symbolists (in their constant search for overtones) and by the Russian Futurists and Formalist critics. The close reading and exhaustive analysis of some of the New Critics also occasionally involve such interpretation. The obvious shortcoming in Lomonosov's theory, however, is that he is too mechanically specific: the consonants S, F, and R, for example, suggest the mighty and the impressive, Z, V, L, and M suggest "delicate and tender" matters, and so on.

Though we may well agree with Mirsky when he writes (and he has in mind, of course, the entire body of Lomonosov's writings, both prose and poetry) that Lomonosov's "importance as the legislator and actual *founder* of the literary language of modern Russia cannot be

8. Macaulay once wrote that "to read Seneca through is like dining exclusively on anchovy sauce and *pâté de foie gras*."

9. See his *The Dark Ages* (New York: Mentor Books, 1958), p. 31.

exaggerated," Lomonosov's critical legacy, as enshrined in the *Rhetoric,* is as antiquated now as is the language of his formal odes. The romantic movement that began in Russia early in the nineteenth century was to make radically different demands on the writer and we see in Russia, as throughout most of Europe, the beginnings of a breakdown in that formal decorum, that nice sense of propriety which are hallmarks of classicism. But though Lomonosov the critic has little to say to us in the West today (we can read "Longinus On the Sublime" with immeasurably greater enjoyment and sympathy), his rhetorical precepts are, unfortunately, relevant to many aspects of Soviet writing. One cannot, in fact, read very much Soviet verse or very many Soviet novels without being struck quite soon by the disturbing presence of literary affectations and mannerisms: the conventional epithet, pretentious decorum and propriety, pompous nationalism and stilted encomia, the affected and unnatural language (Tolstoy was one of the first to notice the latter defect in the writings of Gorky, the author of —among other things—*The Mother,* the classic prototype of the Socialist Realist novel), and especially the incongruous and infuriatingly frequent euphuistic substitution of "literary" periphrases and genteel expressions for simple nouns, adjectives, and verbs. This strange similarity (strange, that is, to find in what was originally supposed to be a revolutionary new proletarian literature) between eighteenth-century Russian classicism and twentieth-century Soviet literature is the burden of a famous essay by Sinyavsky (see below, Chapter IX, section 7).

2

Two other figures of the eighteenth century deserve at least passing mention before we turn to the contributions of Karamzin, Pushkin, and other writers and critics of the early nineteenth century. Vasily Trediakovsky (1703–69), the son of a priest, also attended the Slavonic-Greek-Latin Academy and subsequently studied at The Hague and in Paris at the Sorbonne. Upon his return to Russia in 1730 he was first appointed a translator at the Academy and eventually became "Professor of Eloquence" there. Frequently humiliated by court nobles because of his humble origin, Trediakovsky had a rather unhappy life and was often engaged in polemics with other Russian writers, notably Lomonosov and Sumarokov. He retired in 1759 and died ten years later, unknown and impecunious.

Though an indefatigable worker (Peter the Great called him an "eternal toiler") and though rightfully disparaged as a creative writer of quite undistinguished abilities, Trediakovsky must be given credit for what was, in fact, his yeoman service in promulgating pseudoclassical theory and practice (he translated Boileau's *Art poétique* into Russian). It was Trediakovsky who introduced classical hexameters into Russian poetry and he is usually acknowledged, along with Lomonosov and Sumarokov, as one of the founders of modern Russian literature. Perhaps Trediakovsky is best known, in the history of Russian poetry, as a pioneer in advocating (in 1735) syllabotonic prosody as a replacement for the then current but unsuitable syllabic system, here anticipating Lomonosov, who advocated a similar change. But Trediakovsky was too much of a classicist to suggest violent reform, and he still wanted the syllabic system retained for short lines. Like many classicists of his time and later, he used the terms "long" and "short" (derived from classical quantitative metrics) to mean "accented" and "unaccented" and he was strongly opposed to enjambement (*perenos*).

On the basis of several of his essays, including "Three Dissertations on the Three Most Important Russian Antiquities (1773), there is good reason, too, for seeing in Trediakovsky a pioneer in the study of Russian antiquities as well as of literary history and philology, despite the fact that his etymologies were, as noted in the preceding section, rather absurd. Aside from his own literary productions, he also provided Russian readers with translations of popular French works, e.g., Fénelon's *Télémaque* and Tallemant's *Voyage de l'îsle d'Amour*. This latter translation was a particular success, introducing the Russian reading public as it did to the novelistic treatment of romantic love. Equally important, however, was the fact that Trediakovsky used (as he explains in his Preface) ordinary Russian rather than a language heavily larded with Church Slavonic.

Alexander Sumarokov (1718–77), of noble descent, was the foremost dramatist of the eighteenth century and, according to Mirsky, the "first *gentleman* in Russia to choose the profession of letters." Educated in St. Petersburg at a cadet school, he later served as an adjutant to two influential counts and in 1756 was appointed director of the "Russian Theater," a newly founded enterprise in St. Petersburg.

Sumarokov, too, was an arch-classicist, and he refers in one of his Epistles to Boileau as "secretary of the muses." His earliest tragedy, *Khorev* (1747), based upon early Russian legendary history but written in accordance with French neoclassical canons, is seldom read today but often cited as the first regular Russian classical tragedy. In his adaptation of Shakespeare's *Hamlet* (the first in a long series of Russian versions), Sumarokov attempts, quite unsuccessfully, to "tame and order" Voltaire's "drunken savage."

Sumarokov made use of just about all the classically approved literary genres. Though in many of these he expresses no more than the commonplaces of neoclassical taste or satirizes government clerks in a kind of pseudo-Juvenalian manner, his literary products are frigid, uninspired, and pedestrian. Indeed, in both his works and authoritarian canons of judgment he reminds us, curiously, of Soviet literature and literary criticism. In two Horatian Epistles (first published in 1748 but later revised and consolidated) Sumarokov attempts to provide Russian writers, readers, and critics with the neoclassical norms and standards which he felt were necessary guidelines during the initial stages of a new and more sophisticated literature.[10] The subject of the first Epistle is primarily language. Following some preliminary and traditional remarks on language ("With our voice we divide our thoughts into small parts") and the function of image-making or representation (*izobrazhenie*) which allows us to "penetrate the hearts of others," Sumarokov recites a number of practical suggestions for the writer and the translator. In a tradition going back to Horace and, earlier, to the Stoics, Nature is held up as a guide, while the quaintly versified language is often (as so frequently is the case in Russian literature) on the rustic side: thus the serious writer is likened to the "industrious bee" that takes into its honeycomb both the fragrance of roses and particles of manure.

The second Epistle is addressed to those "who strive to reach Parnassus," i.e., to poets. Here more direct influence of Boileau's *Art poétique* is clearly apparent and we find, of course, most of the paraphernalia of classical allusion, antonomasia, and metaphor. Some of the genres mentioned and discussed by Boileau, however, are ignored or only cursorily referred to by Sumarokov. The novel in verse, for instance, is not treated, whereas the fable and mock-epic, which were

10. There is an English prose translation of these *Epistles* in H. B. Segel, *The Literature of Eighteenth-Century Russia* (New York: Dutton, 1967), I, 221–38.

popular in Russia, are given considerable attention. The Epistle ends with an oft-quoted line, one of a long series of such comments by later Russian writers on the Russian language: "Our beautiful language is capable of everything."

Although Lomonosov (as well as Trediakovsky) criticized Sumarokov for his faulty knowledge of Church Slavonic, Pushkin later noted that Sumarokov knew Russian better than Lomonosov. In his own poetic practice, Sumarokov made extensive use of the written and spoken language of educated Moscow society; he advocated simplicity and naturalness of expression as opposed to both the artificial Slavonic rhetoric of the clergy and what he called the pomposity and verbosity of Lomonosov's "high style." He also spoke out against the then popular linguistic Gallomania and the practice (noted above at the end of the section on Lomonosov) of substituting involved periphrases for simple words and phrases, a practice usually explained as stemming from the classicist's avoidance of particulars. And in asking, "Why should we not write as we speak?" Sumarokov anticipated Karamzin who, as we shall see, prepared the way for Pushkin.

Thus the literary and critical labors of Lomonosov, Trediakovsky, and Sumarokov, as well as of other writers of the eighteenth century in Russia, represent to a great extent linguistic and stylistic pioneering, an attempt to establish and stabilize a suitable literary language. They are of course important names in Russian literary history and criticism for their advocacy and promulgation of neoclassical poetics as well as for their own creative endeavors, weak and uninspired though these appear to us now. But it was out of their work and their polemics that eventually, with the subsequent contributions of a number of early nineteenth-century writers and critics, there emerged a strong, flexible, and sensitive literary language. About a century had to intervene between Trediakovsky's essay on accentual prosody and Pushkin's *Eugene Onegin*, whereas only about forty years separate this latter work and Tolstoy's monumental *War and Peace*. One can, in fact, see a direct line of affiliation running from a figure such as Sumarokov through Pushkin to Tolstoy (and thereafter through Gorky to many Soviet Russian authors) in contrast to another tradition beginning roughly with Gogol and running through Dostoevsky to quite a different breed of modern and contemporary Russian writers. These two traditions, though largely a matter of literary history, will nevertheless be referred to from time to time in connection with literary theory in the chapters that follow.

SUGGESTED READING

Mirsky, D. S., *A History of Russian Literature* (New York: Alfred A. Knopf, 1949), Book One, Chapter 3.

Chizhevsky, Dmitry, *A History of Russian Literature from the Eleventh Century to the End of the Baroque* (The Hague: Mouton, 1960), p. 401 ff.

Menshutkin, B., *Russia's Lomonosov* (Princeton: Princeton University Press, 1952).

Wellek, René, *A History of Modern Criticism: 1750–1950* (New Haven: Yale University Press, 1955–65), Vol. III, Chapter 7.

II THE AGE OF PUSHKIN

1

In 1766, the year following the death of Lomonosov, Nikolay Karamzin was born near Simbirsk (now Ulyanovsk, the city having been renamed in honor of Lenin). In a way, then, Karamzin—who died in 1826—bridges the gap between Lomonosov and Pushkin (1799–1837). Neither Karamzin nor Pushkin was a critic in the professional sense; yet both figures loom so large in the making of Russian literature—the former as the harbinger of romanticism as well as writer and historian in his own right, and the latter as the greatest of the Russian poets—that neither the literary theory of the one nor the critical observations of the other can possibly be omitted in any survey of Russian criticism.

Karamzin was educated privately in Moscow and, having been introduced to N. I. Novikov, the prominent journalist, he began to write for the latter's publications. At first a publisher of satirical journals, Novikov turned, after 1744 (when Catherine the Great shut down all such periodicals), to editing and publishing. "From 1775 to 1789," writes Mirsky, "his press turned out a greater number of books than had been printed in Russia since the beginning of printing. He may be said to have formed the Russian reading public." This is no mean achievement even when we realize that, toward the close of the eighteenth and during the early nineteenth centuries, there were tremendous (in their implications) technical improvements in mass printing methods and a consequent proliferation of cheap printed material—especially of the novel. But of Karamzin Mirsky also writes that "the ultimate justification of Karamzin's language is that it became the language of Pushkin." What does he mean by this?

What Karamzin did, essentially, was to reduce Lomonosov's tripartite system of styles (which was based mainly on lexical criteria) to a single style: the middle style. He sought to—and did—establish a canon more suitable to the time, a time in which the "cult of sensibility" was making its way into Russia and when a preromantic movement (sometimes referred to as sentimentalism) was about to flourish, this to be followed by a full-blown romantic movement (c. 1820–40). Karamzin wanted a cultivated but not archaic style suitable for the expression of the "elegant and noble" feelings associated with preromanticism so that authors could "write as they speak and speak as they write" (actually the Karamzinian style strikes us today as affected and artificial in its own way). He advocated, in opposition to such eminent figures as Admiral Shishkov (the leader of the literary conservatives and champion of the Greco-Slavonic tradition), the exclusion of archaic Slavonicisms (which Pushkin called *bibleizmy*—"biblisms") and the introduction and adoption of new words and expressions, especially abstract nouns, often drawn from or based upon words or phrases in Western European languages.

Karamzin, who was by no means a great creative writer (although his sentimental tale, *Poor Liza,* was immensely popular in its day), carried out his innovations under the strong influence of such romantic writers as Rousseau, Sterne, Thomson, and Ewald von Kleist. He was the first Russian to translate Sterne—who was to have a significant influence on subsequent Russian writers—directly from the English, and he produced the first Russian version of Shakespeare's *Julius Caesar.* In his Preface to this version, Karamzin also provides us with the first Russian defense of Shakespeare, the violator of all received canons, lauding the playwright for the emotional range of his characters and the almost limitless inventiveness of his imagination. The entire Russian romantic movement was highly derivative; even in the case of Pushkin (who utilized romantic themes but preserved an eminently austere and classical style) we see this "derived" quality. Incidentally, the adoption of foreign—especially French—phrases into Russian (these are called loan translations or calques), a practice strongly advocated by Karamzin, was continued by Pushkin. Perhaps the most readable introduction in English to this aspect of Pushkin is an essay by Vladimir Nabokov, entitled "The Servile Path."[1] This is a brief account of Nabokov's research in re-establishing the French original, often including the specific source, of various Pushkinian words and phrases.

1. In *On Translation,* ed. by Reuben A. Brower (Cambridge: Harvard University Press, 1959), pp. 97 ff.

2

In 1815 some of the followers of Karamzin (Zhukovsky, Batyushkov, and Vyazemsky among them) founded the Arzamas society. This was a convivial gathering of gentlemen-poets who, in addition to supporting the reforms advocated by Karamzin, indulged in the writing of light verse and in parodying the stilted style and manner of the Shishkovians (who included some major figures—e.g., Griboedov, the playwright—and who had their own society, called Beseda). Before Pushkin left the Lyceum of Tsarskoe Selo, which he attended from 1811 until 1817 (i.e., between the ages of twelve and eighteen), he had not only joined Arzamas but had already published some of his verse. This is not, however, the place either to outline his tragic life thereafter or even to enumerate, much less discuss, his many writings; these have been and will continue to be analyzed and re-analyzed in multitudes of volumes and articles—even Pushkin's "Leporello list" (*Don Zhuanskij spisok*) has been studied and commented upon. We must confine ourselves here to examples of his critical remarks, of which there are many and various and, rather than attempt to establish any consistent critical theory (there is none in Pushkin), examine some at least of his literary *obiter dicta.*

The letters of Pushkin, which are now available in an excellent English translation,[2] contain a great variety of opinion on the nature of poetry, on the Russian literary scene, and on censorship and the Russian government, as well as many judgements on works by contemporaries. One of the most striking things in the letters (aside from the imprecations and the frequent indulgence in *matershchina,* or the ultimate in vituperation, involving the word *mother*) is Pushkin's repeated assertion that he writes only for money. Indeed, the point is made so often and so aggressively, one suspects (and genteel lovers of Pushkin hope) that it is not true at all. He is at times blasphemous ("The Holy Spirit is sometimes to my liking but I prefer Goethe and

2. *The Letters of Alexander Pushkin,* ed. by J. Thomas Shaw (Madison: University of Wisconsin Press, 1967). All my quotations are drawn from this edition. The figure in parentheses after each relevant quotation is the letter number in Professor Shaw's translation.

Shakespeare"), exultant ("My tragedy is finished; I reread it aloud, alone, and I clapped my hands and shouted, 'at a boy, Pushkn,' at a boy, you son of a bitch!"), violently angry, usually about the state ("When you live in a privy, you get used to the smell of s—") or the censorship ("that bitch, the censorship"), generally cynical about love ("Lawful sex is like a warm cap with ears. One's whole head disappears into it," "I will point out to you only that the less one loves a woman, the surer one is of possessing her"), pugnaciously proud of his partly Negro ancestry ("my brothers the Negroes"[3]), occasionally meditative ("Holy Russia is becoming unbearable to me"), and he frequently misquotes Latin (*Heu fugant, Posthume, Posthume, labuntur anni*).

One of the best things in the collection is a short passage in a letter to Pletnev concerning Pushkin's uncle, Vasily, who had just died. It shows Pushkin's fine sense of humor and is, in miniature, a perfect picture: it might well be a passage, *mutatis mutandis*, from an English letter of the same age concerning some notable country eccentric:

> Poor Uncle Vasily! Do you know what his last words were? I came to see him, found him unconscious; he came to, recognized me, was mournful and silent a little while, and then: "How boring Katenin's articles are!" And not another word. What do you think of that? That's what it means to die an honorable warrior on one's shield, *le cri de guerre à la bouche!* (313)

The most striking aspect of Pushkin's critical statements is their neat elegance of phrasing, their incisiveness, and their cogency. He himself set the tone when, in another letter to Pletnev, he advised: "Do not write *kind* criticism! Be sharp-tongued and beware of excessive sweetness!" "I have read Kyukhelbeker's verses and prose. What a strange fellow! Only into his head could come the Jewish thought of lauding Greece—magnificent, classical, poetic Greece; Greece, where everything breathes of mythology and heroism—in Slavonic-Russian verses taken completely from Jeremiah. What would Homer and

3. Pushkin's maternal great-grandfather was Hannibal, an Ethiopian Negro obtained for Peter the Great by the Russian envoy in Turkey. It later became almost a commonplace for social critics to refer to the Russians as "white Negroes" (Belinsky) or the "Negroes of the North" (Herzen), and the poet Tsvetaeva once asked, "What poet is not a Negro?"

Pindar have said?" (31). "He [i.e., Thomas Moore] is excessively Eastern. He imitates childishly and in an ugly manner the childishness and ugliness of Saadi, Hafiz, and Mohammed. A European, even in the rapture of Oriental splendor, must preserve the taste and eye of a European. That is why Byron is so charming in *The Giaour,* in *The Bride of Abydos,* etc." (114). "That strange man [i.e., Derzhavin] knew neither the Russian ABC's nor the spirit of the Russian language . . . his genius thought in Tatar" (126). You [i.e., Bestuzhev] —and, I think, Vyazemsky—are the only ones of our men of letters who are learning; all the rest are unlearning" (164).

He touches on almost all genres. "Years," he writes, "incline one towards prose" (30). "A novel requires chatter: say everything out plainly" (125). "For goodness sake, honor poetry—as a good, intelligent old woman whom one may drop in on sometimes so as to forget for a moment the gossip, the newspapers, and the cares and bothers of life, to be diverted by her pleasant chattering and her stories; but to fall in love with her is unwise" (11). "The classicists and the romanticists have all based their laws on verisimilitude and that is precisely what the nature of drama excludes. Not to speak of time, etc., what the devil verisimilitude is there in a hall cut in two halves, of which one is occupied by two thousand people who are supposed to be unseen by those who are on the boards?" (139).

In addition to Professor Shaw's edition of Pushkin's letters in English translation, two other excellent collections of Pushkin's critical writings, also in English translation, have recently appeared. One is *The Critical Prose of Alexander Pushkin,* translated and edited by Carl Proffer. This book contains a brief introduction to the beginnings of Russian literary criticism as well as to Pushkin's own literary views; in an appendix there are short critical articles by three of the critics to be mentioned below—Vyazemsky, Ryleev, and Kyukhelbeker. The other collection, *Pushkin on Literature,* contains a wealth of selections translated and edited by Tatiana Wolff. Of special interest here is an appendix containing a short-title list of the non-Russian books in Pushkin's libary.

Scattered throughout much of Pushkin's verse and prose fiction is a kind of paracriticism. Occasionally this is in the form of parody (e.g., *History of the Manor of Goryukhino*), which the late English critic Hugh Kingsmill has called the most perfect form of criticism, involving an exercise of the imagination rather than an assertion of the will. In *Eugene Onegin* there are numerous references to literary movements and fashions. Here, for example, are two stanzas, the first

(III, 12) commenting on the gothic novel, and the second (III, 28) revealing some personal tastes:

But minds are all unhinged at present,
True worth is boring to this age;
Outside of novels, vice seems pleasant,
And in them it is all the rage.
The British Muse's eerie ravings
Haunt Missie in her sleep; her cravings
Are all for brooding vampires now,
Or wandering Melmoth, dark of brow,
Or doomed Ahasverus who drifted
From land to land, or bold Corsair,
Or Sbogar with his secret air.
Lord Byron's apt conceits have lifted
Bleak egoism up to shine
In the Romantic's gloomy shrine.

Send me, Almighty, I petition,
In porticoes or at a ball
No bonneted academician,
No seminarist in a yellow shawl!
No more than in red lips unsmiling
Can I find anything beguiling
In grammar-perfect Russian speech.
What purist magazines beseech,
A novel breed of belles may heed it
And bend us (for my life of sin)
To strict grammatic discipline,
Prescribing meter, too, where needed;
But I—what is all this to me?
I like things as they used to be.[4]

Though we would be hard put to find any consistent theory of either literature or of literary criticism in Pushkin, we can pretty well conclude what his tastes were. He shows a clear sympathy with and predilection for the classical qualities of decorum and propriety, of

4. These two stanzas are quoted from Walter Arndt's translation (New York: Dutton, 1963).

understatement and restraint, and his preferences are generally conservative ("I like things as they used to be"), and he has an almost congenital aversion for the vulgar, the muddled, and the erratic. While his own works give an impression—at first—of simplicity and plainness (*Il est plat, votre poète,* said Flaubert), there is beneath the surface a rich complexity of thought, the product of a well-stocked, sound, and vulpine mind. The illusion of simplicity comes from a superb and felicitous command of language, a masterful feeling for *le mot juste* in situations where a less talented writer would squander adjectives and adverbs. This sensitive, connoisseur-like discrimination in the precise meaning and use of individual words and in the synergical effect of exactly the right combinations of words (the real secret of the *Mehrwert* or "epiphenomenal" quality of great poets) is seen not only in Pushkin's own works but also in the technical advice he gives other Russian poets in his letters.

3

Of the poets and critics who were friends of Pushkin in a "literary aristocracy" (some of them members of the so-called Pushkin Pleiad), Vasily Zhukovsky (1783–1852) has—after the poet Baratynsky—the greatest renown. He produced, in addition to some original verse of high rank, superb translations from the English (e.g., Gray's *Elegy*) and especially from the German poets (notably Schiller). Zhukovsky was a Germanophile, married a young German girl after his retirement from court service, and died in Baden-Baden. He befriended Pushkin in the latter's time of troubles and was instrumental in the emancipation from serfdom of the Ukrainian poet, Shevchenko, whom the Russian government treated despicably. Carrying on the Karamzinian tradition, by virtue of his innovations in metrics and diction and his controlled handling of emotions, he has rightly been called the "father of modern Russian poetry." In the field of criticism (peripheral to his accomplishments in poetry and translation) he was one of the first Russian poets to attempt an appraisal of his predecessors and he wrote studies of the unique fabulist, Krylov, and of the satires of Kantemir.

Prince Peter Vyazemsky (1792–1878), whom Belinsky once referred to derogatively as "that prince in the aristocracy and helot in literature," was a close friend of Pushkin—whom he called the successor to Zhukovsky—and he wrote the foreword to Pushkin's *Prisoner of the Caucasus*. Their correspondence is, according to Mirsky, "a treasure house of wit, fine criticism, and good Russian." Vyazemsky, however (unlike Pushkin), was a dedicated exponent of romanticism as freedom from all rules, and, although an aristocrat, he argued for a literature that would be both popular and national. (It is interesting that the advocacy of a popular literature with "mass appeal" comes so often from noblemen—witness Count Lev Tolstoy.) Prince Vyazemsky, who was also a poet, advocated the continued introduction of Gallicisms into Russian; and Pushkin, commenting on this in one of his letters, complained that the Russian metaphysical language of his day was in a savage condition. But Vyazemsky's judgment is frequently erratic—when, for instance, he calls Dmitriev a better fabulist than Krylov.

Kondraty Ryleev (1795–1826), another member of the gentry, was hanged for his part in the Decembrist uprising of 1825. Ryleev was a revolutionary poet in both word and deed, but he has left us some brief critical comments on such matters as the quarrel between the classical and the romantic (i.e., the French and the German influence), a quarrel which he felt was artificial and needless. Alexander Bestuzhev (1797–1837), best known in Russian literature as a novelist, was exiled to the Caucasus for his part in the Decembrist affair. Writing of the new German influence, he remarked that "there was a time when at every turn we sighed in the manner of Sterne and paid courtly compliments in the French fashion: now, following the Germans, we have flown off into the blue ethereal." Bestuzhev's taste is questionable and his language shallow and vague; e.g., "Glinka [a minor religious poet and a cousin of the composer] is a master of the language of feelings." As for his judgment, it is almost sophomoric. In an article entitled "A Glance at Russian Literature During 1824 and at the Beginning of 1825," Bestuzhev claimed that it is in the early age of a literature that the geniuses appear—an idle contention easily countered by Pushkin. Bestuzhev goes on to say that "we have criticism but we do not have a literature," to which Pushkin replies that exactly the opposite is true; and Bestuzhev's claim that encouragement or patronage inspires only mediocre talent is brilliantly refuted again by Pushkin through a mere citation of great names from Horace to Voltaire.

Vilgelm Kyukhelbeker (1797–1846) was another young Russian, this time of German origin, who took part in the Decembrist revolt, for which he spent ten years in prison and the last decade of his life as an exile in Siberia. His wife has been set forth by the twentieth-century writer and critic, Yury Tynyanov, in *Kyukhlya* (1925), an excellent historical novel. At first a romantic and a follower of Karamzin and Zhukovsky, Kyukhelbeker edited briefly (prior to his arrest and exile) *Mnemosyne,* a literary journal voicing the aspirations of the young pro-German idealists; but later he became a literary conservative, called himself "a romantic in classicism," and joined the party of Shishkov. "Let us be thankful to Zhukovsky," he wrote, "that he freed us from the yoke of French literature and from control by the laws of the schools of La Harpe and Batteux; but we shall allow neither him nor any other, even though he have a ten-fold greater genius, to impose on us the shackles of German or English domination." Kyukhelbeker is often, because of his unrestrained behavior and the rather odd language of his poetry, called "quixotic" (Pushkin sometimes referred to him as "Anacharsis Cloots"). And although Mirsky places Kyukhelbeker, along with Kireevsky (see below), in first place amongst the critics of the Golden Age, Pushkin was closer to the truth when he wrote that "Kyukhlya" was a madcap, clever with his pen. The essential smallness of Kyukhelbeker may be seen in most of his critical judgments—for example, in his admiration for the quite minor poet, Shirinsky-Shikhmatov.

Of all the friends, associates, and defenders of Pushkin, it is perhaps Orest Somov (1793–1833) who, before Belinsky, comes closest to being a professional critic. We cannot, of course, call him a "professional" in the strictly technical sense, since he worked as a private citizen for the Russian-American Company (the main function of which was, prior to 1867, to exploit the fur riches of Alaska); nor can we call him a major critic. But in his articles (many of which appeared in the journal *Northern Flowers*[5]) we find something approaching consistent romantic literary and critical theory. Somov is best known for his essay "On Romantic Poetry" (1823), a sort of romanticist manifesto, and it was Somov, alone of all critics, who saw hope and promise for a young writer following the miserable fiasco of *Hans Küchelgarten,* the pitiful narrative poem that marked Gogol's debut in Russian literature. Further evidence of Somov's good taste and judgment is seen in his comments (still eminently relevant) on the poetry of Baratynsky.

5. See J. Mersereau, *Baron Delvig's* Northern Flowers, *1825–1832. A Literary Almanac of the Pushkin Pleiad* (Carbondale: Southern Illinois University Press, 1967). There is an interesting chapter (IV) on literary criticism, most of it being Somov's.

Somov was primarily interested in the problem of Russian prose. He felt that, whereas Russian poetry had already acquired (largely through the efforts of the Karamzinian reformers) an adequately conventional language, Russian prose was still inchoate. "Prose," he wrote with sound insight, "demands of us a most extensive and solid knowledge of the language. It requires greater exactness and more precision in those locutions which a writer, almost constantly, must create for himself, since we are still poor in models." Somov, however, was lamenting the absence of an effective narrative and epistolary prose style (*slog*) precisely at the time Pushkin, in his letters and his *Tales of Belkin,* was forging these very qualities. Somov was an ardent defender of Pushkin, although he saw fit to criticize the torture scene in *Poltava* on the basis of plausibility and verisimilitude.

Somov was remarkably objective and moderate in his critical reviews and he complained of the personal, vituperative, and recriminatory nature of Russian journalistic criticism: "Our tedious polemics include anti-criticism, re-criticism, and re-anti-criticism. And these are often protracted into a continous series of new re- and re-anti-critiques." But the situation remained essentially unchanged, and Russian literary criticism as written by Belinsky and his successors and—with few exceptions—right down to the present day in the Soviet Union has always contained a very strong admixture of quite non-objective personal invective and abuse. More will be said of this in the chapter on Belinsky.

4

Three other names deserve passing mention. Ivan Kireevsky (1806–56) is best known as a philosopher and a leader of the Slavophiles. But his so-called philosophy is rather a congeries of obscure and meaningless comments on a moribund religion than a critical analysis of reality.[6] As a Slavophile, he steered clear of the two extremes, vaunting neither the purely Western nor the purely Russian, and thus displeased both

6. Mirsky calls Kireevsky "the fountainhead of all modern Orthodox culture." What he means by this, I do not know; but some idea of what Russians mean by *philosophy* may be had by reading N. Lossky, *History of Russian Philosophy* (New York: International Universities Press, 1969).

friend and foe. Belinsky, commenting maliciously but accurately on the name "Ivan Vasilievich" (the name of a silly hero in a popular novel but also Kireevsky's given name and patronymic), wrote: "Now we shall know what to call all fantasizers of this kind." Kireevsky edited briefly—and Pushkin placed great but futile hopes in this—a literary review entitled *The European;* but because Nicholas I discovered some political allusions in one article and because Kireevsky admitted under questioning that he thought the serfs should be liberated, the journal was suppressed and Kireevsky placed under police surveillance. Kireevsky was a better critic, however, than philosopher. Even though his criticism is very often a medium for philosophical discussion, Pushkin thought highly of his judgement—despite the fact that it was Kireevsky who first pointed out what is perhaps the principal flaw in *Poltava*: the somewhat awkard juxtaposition of romance and epic.

Prince Vladimir Odoevsky (1803–69) was a rather amazing gentleman, famous for his encyclopedic knowledge and with a popularity that was once just below that of Pushkin and Gogol. He was the first to decipher the notational system of the old Russian liturgical music; he wrote children's stories of lasting appeal; he once published a collection of his own stories with a six-color title page printed by a process he invented; and he tried—unsucessfully—to introduce a new system of punctuation. In his *Russian Nights* (1844),[7] a strange "philosophical" novel, he outlines the first systematic criticism of the culture of Western Europe (i.e., from the Russian point of view); and in another, this time unfinished, utopian novel, *The Year 4338*, he gives us what he considered to be an inspiring picture of the world unified under tsarist absolutism. Odoevsky believed that Russia would bring to Europe a new spiritual force; this is, of course, what eventually happened, but not quite as he had predicted. He also—being a religious gentleman—attributed Beethoven's irascibility and his constant, dissatisfied search for new harmonies to his lack of faith. Unfortunately, most of Odoevsky's literary criticism concerns writers now long forgotton, although his review, entitled "How Novels Are Written Amongst Us," of a novel by Alexander Stepanov is an early, albeit minor, contribution to criticism of the novel. Incidentally, this article appeared in the illustrious *Contemporary,* the literary review founded by Pushkin.

Stepan Shevyrev (1806–64) was a Slavophile professor of literature at Moscow University who wrote some professorial articles on

7. This work is now available in English in a paperback edition. The footnotes (by Odoevsky) are frequently more interesting than the text.

Pushkin; but he is best known as the object of Belinsky's ire in "On the Literary Criticism and Views of the *Moscow Observer*" (of which Shevyrev was chief critic): Shevyrev had unfortunately stressed the "genteel" and the "feminine genteel" in literature as "elevating" qualities. Pushkin, however, lauded Shevyrev, but primarily because he had written a devastating criticism of Faddey Bulgarin (see next chapter) whom Pushkin despised. In a scholarly work, *A Theory of Poetry* (1836), Shevyrev notes correctly that Longinus "searches in pagan writers for those very ideas which are closer to the spirit of our age"—that Longinus is, in short, a romantic critic. When Dostoevsky's early works first appeared in print, Shevyrev discerned (but this did not demand great perspicacity) the very apparent Gogolian coloring of his prose.

The critics noted in this chapter are thus a rather heterogeneous group. They made no important formal contributions to critical theory and it would be difficult to find amongst them any common feature in the criteria they employed for judging literature, except possibly a kind of upper-class sensibility and taste. The old classical proprieties were rapidly passing away, becoming objects of ridicule and mockery, but these critics, though necessarily affected by the charms of romanticism, managed to preserve something of the earlier respect for the past as well as a comparatively relaxed and levelheaded attitude toward literature as primarily a gentleman's avocation. I strongly suspect that much of the offhand and cavalier nature of the criticism, such as it was, written by the persons mentioned in this chapter, including Pushkin himself, is the result not only of the journalistic demands of the time but also of a certain aristocratic disdain for what the Greeks called *banausia*: a professional or technical and therefore demeaning preoccupation with something resembling a trade—in this case, a narrow and professional (as opposed to a dilettante and avocational) concern with literature. If this is so, then the appearance of Belinsky as both *raznochinets*[8] and professional critic is readily understandable against the background of changing social conditions in Russia. But I would also venture to state that anyone with a modicum of taste who reads through the delightful and touching body of Pushkin's letters, despite the protestations, cynicism, and obscenity, will agree that many a single letter or single phrase by Pushkin, with his sureness of judgment and his knack of hitting the nail on the head, is worth more than volumes of speculation by either prince or professor.

8. See following chapter, section 3.

SUGGESTED READING

Hingley, Ronald, *Russian Writers and Society, 1825–1904* (New York: McGraw-Hill, 1967).

Nebel, H. M., trans., *Selected Prose of N. M. Karamzin* (Evanston: Northwestern University Press, 1969).

Segel, Harold, ed., *The Literature of Eighteenth-Century Russia* in two volumes (New York: Dutton, 1967). Volume I contains several short essays by Karamzin.

Proffer, Carl, ed., *The Critical Prose of Alexander Pushkin* (Bloomington: Indiana University Press, 1969). This volume also contains articles by Kyukhelbeker, Vyazemsky, and Ryleev.

Wolff, Tatiana, ed., *Pushkin on Literature* (London: Methuen, 1971).

Pushkin, Alexander, *Eugene Onegin,* trans. by Walter Arndt (New York: Dutton, 1963).

Mirsky, D. S., *Pushkin* (New York: Dutton, 1963).

Shaw, J. Thomas, ed., *The Letters of Alexander Pushkin* (Madison: University of Wisconsin Press, 1967).

Mersereau, John, *Baron Delvig's* Northern Flowers, *1825–1832. A Literary Almanac of the Pushkin Pleiad* (Carbondale: Southern Illinois University Press, 1967).

Odoevsky, V. F., *Russian Nights,* trans. by O. Koshansky-Olienikov and R. Matlaw (New York: Dutton, 1965).

Wellek, René, *A History of Modern Criticism: 1750–1950* (New Haven: Yale University Press, 1955–65), Vol. III, Chapter 7.

Mirsky, D. S., *A History of Russian Literature* (New York: Alfred A. Knopf, 1949), Book One, Chapter 4.

III BELINSKY

1

In 1836 a Moscow periodical published one of Peter Chaadaev's "Philosophical Letters" on the meaning of history and thereby caused a furor. Chaadaev, a former Hussar of the Guards and a friend of Pushkin, had originally written these documents in French, and they had been circulated, as was often (and still is) the practice, for private reading. But when the first *Letter* appeared publicly in Russian (incredibly it had been passed by a censor[1]), it was, as Alexander Herzen later put it, "like a shot that rang out in the dark night—it forced all to awaken." The published *Philosophical Letter* severely criticized the course and status of Russian history:

> The history of other nations is that of their emancipation. Russian history is one of serfdom and autocracy. . . . Of all the peoples of the world, we alone have given nothing to the world and we have learned nothing from it. . . . There is something in our blood that rejects all true progress.

In effect, Chaadaev condemned Russia as inferior to the West and said that she could only move forward by learning from the West (which in fact was and has been the case). Chaadaev himself was declared insane, while the periodical that had published his *Letter* was closed down by the police.

But the principal result of this rather notorious incident was the crystalization and hardening of lines between two opposed but loosely organized factions in Russian thought, the Westernists and the Slavophiles. The latter group (led by such eminent figures as Alexey

1. His explanation that he had approved the article while playing whist with some lady friends was not accepted, and he was dismissed from the service.

Khomyakov[2] and the brothers Kireevsky) supported "Orthodoxy, Autocracy, and Nationalism"; they believed that Russia's strength as well as her future lay in cherishing native traditions, both cultural and political, and in rejecting the West as a source of corruption. On the other hand, the Westernists, following Chaadaev, held that Russia was an integral part of Europe and European civilization, that her cultural progress had been seriously retarded by the Tatar Yoke, and that she must waste no time in catching up with the West by assimilating, as rapidly as possible, everything progressive and technologically advanced. It is, however, of particular interest that both parties drew upon German philosophical thought to bolster their separate positions. The Slavophiles were strongly influenced by German "romantic nationalism" and, insofar as they were generally also pan-slavists, by Herder in particular,[3] while the writings of such leaders of the Westernists as Belinsky and Herzen are literally replete with German romantic and idealistic ideology. Even more interesting is the fact that both factions were persecuted by the tsarist regime with almost equal ferocity (instead, for example, of sympathizing with Balken liberation movements, supported by the Slavophiles as pan-slavists, the regime sided with the Austro-Hungarian Empire in putting these down).

The distinction between the Westernists and the Slavophiles is an important and significant one, since these two factions, albeit under different names and in varying guises, can be traced right down to the present day in Soviet Russia. The tradition of the Slavophiles, going back to Shishkov and his followers and, even earlier, to the opponents of Peter the Great's reforms, continues in such figures as Leontiev (Chapter V) and Dostoevsky (Chapter VI), as well as in the "Scythians" (Chapter VII), in Stalinism, and in present-day "hard-line" Communists, with their intransigent suspicion and hatred of the West. The tradition of the Westernists, going back to the supporters of Peter the Great's reforms, is apparent in the views of the Modernist critics (Chapter VII), the Formalists (Chapter VIII), in Leninism and

2. Concerning Khomyakov (who was also a theologian) and Chaadaev, Berdyaev writes: "It is characteristic of Russian thought and of its irregularity that the first Russian philosopher of history, Chaadaev, was an officer of the Life-guard Hussars, and the first original theologian, Khomyakov, was an officer of the Horse-guards. Pushkin wrote of Chaadaev, 'in Rome he would have been a Brutus, in Athens a Pericles, among us he is an officer of the Hussars'" (*The Russian Idea*).

3. See Hans Kohn, *Pan-Slavism: Its History and Ideology.* It was a Slovak, Jan Herkel, who, writing in Latin, first used the term *panslawismus* in 1826.

Trotskyism (as opposed to Stalinism), and in the "dissonant voices" amongst the writers, thinkers, artists, and scientists—Marxist or not—of contemporary Soviet Russia.

2

One of the most remarkable aspects of the early nineteenth century in Russia and, indeed, of the century as a whole is the powerful influx of German ideology and the preponderant influence of German philosophical, aesthetic, and literary theory. The Russian Formalist critic Tynyanov went so far as to say that, insofar as Russian literature is concerned, the nineteenth century *means* German influence just as the eighteenth century meant French influence. A good deal of study has been devoted to this phenomenon, and there are many and learned monographs and volumes devoted to the influence in Russia of Schiller, of Goethe, of Hegel. But what exactly was the nature of this German thought which the Russian intellectuals imbibed in such heady draughts?

The eighteenth century had been an age of enlightenment, rationalism, and empiricism. But toward the end of the century there developed in Germany, following the long and barren period that succeeded the crippling Thirty Years War, a very manifest reaction: a profoundly metaphysical view of reality. In opposition to the rationalism of the French and the empiricism of the English, the Germans offered the aesthetic idealism of Schiller, the "organic" *Naturphilosophie* of Schelling, the metaphysical historicism of Herder, and the dialectic of Hegel. If we view the fervor with which these new concepts were received in Russia as religious in nature (and the language of the recipients strongly suggests this), then Schiller was

> the John the Baptist of the new faith. The "men of the thirties and of the forties" invariably began their German education with him, to be followed only later by Schelling and Hegel, the other great representatives of German influence in Russia. Rival Germans there no doubt were: Goethe, Jean-Paul Richter, Hoffmann, Herder, Fichte, and later Heine. . . . But it was Schiller, Schelling, and Hegel who were the structural ribbing of the edifice of

German influence in Russia, and Schiller was the very head of the corner.[4]

But appealing alike to poets, *lyubomudry*[5], and radicals was the seeming universality of, as they received it, this farrago of German idealism in which reason and sentiment appeared to fuse. It had at once religious appeal, the self, all mankind, and even the universe being merged into one harmonious whole; it was, with its pseudo-logic of analogy, in a sense "scientific" and "progressive," since it offered an organic view of growth and development, not only of nations but of literatures as well; it was both highly individualistic (Schiller's concept of *Schönseeligkeit* made a tremendous impact[6]) and collective (exalting history and the *Volk*); and it provided a device and a program for those who were anxious to remake the world—Alexander Herzen once called the philosophy of Hegel the "algebra of revolution."

3

Vissarion Belinsky (1811–48) was, as mentioned earlier, the first professional Russian literary critic, and his position as the "father" of Russian criticism is upheld in the Soviet Union largely because of his emphasis on the ideological and sociological content of works of art (as opposed to merely aesthetic or formalist analysis) but also because of his generally radical outlook (the Soviet Union now tolerates only dead radicals) and his atheism. But Belinsky was a great critic, and, though he unwittingly founded a "school" of lesser epigones (the Civic critics, to be discussed in the next chapter), his work deserves careful consideration. To dismiss him because the Soviets pay homage to him would be tantamount to dismissing Pushkin because his poetry is read—and presumably even loved—by Communists.

Fallible, however, he certainly was, especially in his judgments of

4. Martin Malia, *Alexander Herzen and the Birth of Russian Socialism* (New York: Grosset & Dunlap, 1965), p. 39.

5. The Slavonic translation of *philosophoi*. The *lyubomudry* were a Moscow circle of young idealists, adherents of the cult of Goethe and Schelling.

6. A Russian word—*prekrasnodushie*—was coined on the German model.

foreign writers. Thus his favorite foreign novelist was George Sand, he felt that Eugène Sue had more talent than Balzac, and he once expressed the opinion that E. T. A. Hoffmann was to be ranked with Shakespeare and Goethe. And his harsh criticism of Shevchenko, the great Ukrainian poet, though due in large part to a congenital Great Russian prejudice, must be viewed as a serious blot upon his reputation as a critic. In what follows, however, I shall deal only with Belinsky the critic of Russian letters; and here it is a commonplace in histories of Russian literature to mention the soundness of his judgment. Turgenev spoke of his "fine, sure taste," and Mirsky, although he disparages Belinsky's dreadful style (Belinsky was certainly no autotelic critic) and regrets his baleful influence on later "high journalese" in Russia, writes the following: "His judgments on writers who began their work between 1830 and 1848 may be accepted almost without qualification. This is high praise for a critic, and one that few deserve."[7]

In addition to his fame as a critic, Belinsky's name is also associated with two important aspects of Russian thought emergent in the thirties of the nineteenth century. He was, first of all, a spokesman of the Russian intelligentsia. This latter word, a transliteration of the Russian form of the Latin abstract noun *intelligentia,* was probably introduced into Russian toward the end of the eighteenth century by a German Mason teaching at the University of Moscow, Johann Georg Schwarz, and later (toward the end of the nineteenth century) given currency in the novels of Boborykin.[8] In Russian the word took on a special meaning (less neutral than our *intellectual* or Coleridge's *clerisy,* although the difference these days is less clear-cut), and it referred properly to that part of an educated society—the literati—which holds radical views (in Russian an *intelligent* is a member of the intelligentsia). Second, Belinsky was one of the *raznochintsy.* This word, which means simply "persons of various classes," was applied to men of other than gentry or noble origin who, after receiving an education, entered upon a career other than the traditional one for their class.[9] This was,

7. *History of Russian Literature,* p. 167. This is indeed high praise. See Henri Peyre's *The Failures of Criticism* for some of the amazing *gaffes* of the great critics.

8. For a history of the Russian intelligentsia, see M. Raeff, *The Origins of the Russian Intelligentsia* (New York: Harcourt, Brace & World, 1966).

9. More accurately, even the son of a nobleman, if he did not follow in the family tradition (entering the army or the diplomatic service), might become a *raznochinets.*

in itself, a radical break with tradition, and the process was often difficult and accompanied by considerable hardship. Not unnaturally, then, many of the *raznochintsy* were also *intelligenty,* radical literati, critics of the status quo, and advocates of reform. Prior to the thirties the great majority of the figures in Russian literary and intellectual life had been members of the gentry; after 1830, however, more and more of the eminent names are those of *raznochintsy*. Belinsky is thus (to use a term beloved of the Russian critics) the coryphaeus of both movements: the ever-widening role of "men of various classes" in Russian literary and intellectual life and the rise of a radical clerisy. Belinsky may well be called (as Lenin called Tolstoy) a "mirror of the Revolution." "He supplied the solvent which began the process of eating away the foundations of the old order" (Sir John Maynard). It is interesting, too, that the *Communist Manifesto* was written in the year Belinsky died.

The son of a poor doctor, Belinsky attended Moscow University for three years, during which time (it is reported) he neither took nor passed a single examination. He pursued the study of literature, the field that was to remain his lifelong love; but he wrote a play that was critical of serfdom and was expelled before taking his degree. This happened in the early thirties during the reign of Nicholas I, whose realm, as noted in the previous chapter, Pushkin likened to an outhouse.[10] In 1833 Belinsky began to write for Nadezhdin's *Telescope*. But this periodical was suppressed in 1836 (for publishing Chaadaev's *Philosophical Letter*), and three years later Belinsky moved to St. Petersburg where he became the chief critic for *Fatherland Notes*. In 1846 Nekrasov invited him to join the prestigious *Contemporary* (founded by Pushkin) as literary critic. In 1847 Belinsky, who was suffering from the ravages of tuberculosis, went abroad and died shortly after his return to Russia in 1848.

Belinsky thus lived a short but intense life, almost constantly preoccupied with literary criticism and polemics. Although he compensated for his expulsion from the university by educating himself through wide and intensive reading, he had a poor working knowledge of German and he learned what he did of intoxicating German philosophical thought mostly through reading excerpts of the philosophers in translation. But the most striking feature of Belinsky was the

10. In his book on Gogol, Vladimir Nabokov writes of Nicholas I: "a bland, philandering Tsar, an ignoramus and a cad, whose whole reign was not worth a foot of Pushkin's verse." In *Hadji Murad* Tolstoy gives us another chilling picture of Nicholas I.

intensity of his engagement in the study of literature as a guide for the good life, an intensity which earned him the epithet of "Furious" (*neistovyj*).[11] Here is what Alexander Herzen writes of him:

> But that shy man, that frail body, contained a mighty spirit, the spirit of a gladiator! Yes, he was a powerful fighter! He could not preach or lecture; what he needed was argument. If he was not contradicted, if he was not stirred by irritation, he did not speak well. But when he was touched to the quick, when his cherished convictions were challenged, when the muscles of his cheeks began to quiver and his voice trembled, then he was worth seeing. He pounced on his opponent like a panther; he tore him to pieces, made him look ridiculous and pitiful, and incidentally developed his own thought with extraordinary force, with extraordinary poetry. The discussion would often end with blood coming from the sick man's throat; pale, gasping, his eyes fixed upon the man with whom he was speaking, he would lift his handkerchief to his mouth with shaking hand and stop, deeply mortified by his physical weakness. How I loved and pitied him at these moments![12]

The Nadezhdin mentioned above, the editor of the *Telescope,* was Nikolay Nadezhdin. Critic, journalist, and professor of literature at Moscow University, he is particularly relevant here both as a teacher and predecessor of Belinsky in urging that literature be "natural, original, and national." Nadezhdin was conversant with German romantic idealism (especially Schelling), knew the Schlegels, and passed on his enthusiasm to Belinsky. The influence of German idealism on Belinsky is profound, and he began his career as a critic under the aegis of Schelling's *Naturphilosophie.* Passage after passage in Belinsky, though the subject under discussion is almost always Russian literature, shows the German background: art is an organic whole; literature is the expression of the national spirit; the poet "thinks in

11. Belinsky's passionate approach reminds one of Victor Hugo's *"La haute critique a son point de départ dans l'enthousiasme"* or Anatole France's *"J'ai toujours préféré la folie des passions à la sagesse de l'indifférence."*

12. Perhaps the best example of the "Furious Vissarion" may be found in the fiercely vehement "Letter to N. V. Gogol," one of the great documents of epistolary Russian. This may be read in *Belinsky, Chernyshevsky, and Dobrolyubov: Selected Criticism,* ed. by Ralph Matlaw (New York: Dutton, 1962), pp. 83 ff. The passage by Herzen is quoted from Professor Matlaw's Introduction.

images"; etc. But he is not completely subservient to German ideology: he dislikes, in general, Slavic folklore and speaks derogatively of oral literature, shows no nostalgic affection for *die alten Griechen,* and even in his Hegelian period does not share the German philosopher's view of the coming demise of art. One of the remarkable aspects of Belinsky's criticism, in fact, is, despite all the German influence, its surprising homogeneity over the years so far as categories and procedures go. This point is well made by René Wellek, who compares Belinsky's development as a critic to that of Ruge, De Sanctis, Carlyle, and Taine.

Another point must be made here, a necessary reminder for anyone who intends to read Belinsky. We have already referred to Mirsky's judgment of Belinsky's execrable style: it is often ponderous and diffuse, frequently involved in elementary explanation, with numerous and abrupt digressions and repetitions and long-forgotten quarrels with long-forgotten personalities. In short, except for a *caput mortuum* well worth extracting, it has all the defects of ephemeral journalism. But the reader of Russian literary criticism, once he is beyond the banal normative statutes of Lomonosov, the candid paralegomena of Pushkin, and the elegant banter of Prince Vyazemsky, must realize (and Chernyshevsky pointed this out long ago) that the Russian review article—in which a goodly amount of Russian criticism is embodied—has always, under censor-ridden regimes, served as a more or less safe vehicle for the expression of non-literary ideas. Since the censorship appeared to be less severe on apparently long-winded and tedious reviews of equally boring treatises, the Russian critic, eager for a means of expression and more often than not at odds with the regime, has always been strongly tempted to stray from the text at hand (and, I suspect, to "pad" his article with matter that would surely cause the censor to nod). For one who has read the great English and French critics, with their generally very close attention to the text (they had manifold other outlets for political polemics), it is sometimes an exasperating and discouraging experience to begin an article by Belinsky, his successors, or many of the other critics we shall have occasion to mention (with the notable exception of the Formalists). But, with these stipulations in mind, there is ample compensation in reading Belinsky. He may not be a Sainte-Beuve, "but he has a kind of impressive massiveness, a pathos of devotion to his country's literature and to the progress of its society, that cannot be easily matched in the West. Considering the conditions under which he labored, the temptation to which he was exposed as a public figure, and the violence of his volatile temperament, one must admire his generally firm hold on the nature of art, the high standards he applied and upheld, the vigor and penetration of many of his criticisms, and the power of characterization he displayed."[13]

Amongst specific literary concepts which have become associated with or colored by Belinsky's activities, we may note here the term "belletristics" (*belletristika*) to which he gave new currency in the Russian critical language. But in the Russian usage this term does not signify merely "belles lettres" or artistic literature; it refers rather (as Vinogradov and others have pointed out) to a mixed genre, half-publicistic and half-artistic, involving not only a concern for aesthetic and cultural values but also a preoccupation with ideological, political, and moral didacticism. In addition, Belinsky was particularly instrumental in introducing into Russian criticism a good deal of abstract philosophical and metaphysical terminology coined on the basis of German models, a fact noted—and parodied—by his contemporaries. The late Soviet Russian scholar, Viktor Vinogradov, goes so far as to say that Belinsky "refashioned the Russian literary language" and participated in a "restructuring" of the very concept of "literature."[14] Some idea of what Vinogradov meant may be gotten from the paragraphs that follow.

There are three distinct periods in Belinsky's career as a critic. During the first period (1834–38) his criticism, in addition to showing a marked German influence, is brash, radical, and bellicose with, as he himself once remarked of Herzen, *cet air de matador* about it. During the short *détente* period (1838–41) Belinsky became a "right" Hegelian, adopting the famous formula, "All that is real is rational and all that is rational is real." To the astonishment and chagrin of his friends, he now accepted (as the formula demanded) the social order which he had earlier so bitterly attacked, and he concerned himself briefly with more universal and less polemical themes. But he soon saw his error (it was characteristic of Belinsky to admit error), and from 1841 until his premature death he considered art as a criticism of life (in the sense of social reality). In his "Discourse on Criticism" (1842) he writes, for example: "What is the art of our time? It is

13. René Wellek, *A History of Modern Criticism: 1750–1950* (New Haven: Yale University Press, 1955–65), III, 264.

14. V. Vinogradov, *The History of the Russian Literary Language from the Seventeenth Century to the Nineteenth,* condensed and trans. by L. Thomas (Madison: University of Wisconsin Press, 1969), pp. 199–201.

judgment and analysis and therefore criticism of society. . . . For our time a work of art is dead if it depicts life only for the sake of depicting it, without the powerful subjective motivation that stems from the prevailing thought of the age, if it is not a cry of suffering or a rapturous dithyramb, if it is not either a question or an answer to a question."

This periodization of Belinsky's criticism has a significant counterpart in his views of Schiller. Until about 1838 Belinsky was generally rapturous in his praise of Schiller—"Schiller has given us the mysteries of heaven, has revealed to us the wondrous beauty of life!" During the subsequent Hegelian period of "reconciliation with reality" he frequently, in stronger and stronger terms, expressed his disillusionment with Schiller—"I have broken completely with Schiller. . . . Why this hatred? For his subjective ethical point of view, for his terrible concept of duty, for his abstract heroism, for his aesthetic war on realism—for everything I suffered in his name!" And then, after the short-lived Hegelian phase, he returns to his earlier ardor—"I curse my shameful proclivity to reconciliation with foul reality! Long live the great Schiller, the noble spokesman of humanity . . . !" There is later an almost identical sequence of acceptance-rejection-acceptance in Dostoevsky's attitude toward Schiller.[15]

Perhaps the best-known example of Belinsky's critical reaction is seen in his response to two early works by Dostoevsky, *Poor Folk* and *The Double*, both published in 1846. The first novel was enthusiastically hailed by Belinsky as a work of social protest and in the Gogolian "naturalist" tradition (see below). Now in many ways this novelette was significant: it is, first of all, an extremely promising endeavor for a twenty-five-year-old tyro; it foreshadows much to come in Dostoevsky ("the banal is made to reveal love as the essence of life"—F. D. Reeve); and, by rejecting the purely sentimental and romantic, it presages the later great age of Russian realism with its marked humanistic and philanthropic tendency. But it is not a "proletarian" novel, and Belinsky, in effect, misread the work, exaggerating the sympathy shown the poor and quite neglecting the essentially—although still embryonic—Dostoevskian psychological analysis. As for *The Double*, which still strikes the modern reader as inchoate and unsuccessful, this work Belinsky dismissed and castigated—not as mere *ébauche*, however, but as lunatic fantasy. For Belinsky, who demanded in so

15. See E. Kostka, *Schiller in Russian Literature* (Philadelphia: University of Pennsylvania Press, 1965), Chapters III and VII.

many words that there be the closest possible resemblance between literary characters and their "models" in real life, the fantastic and the grotesque had no place in Russian literature. And although we can see how, in emphasizing social content and didacticism and in rejecting the fantastic (which provides numerous occasions for ambiguity and irony,[16] Belinsky anticipates modern Soviet canons of judgment, still it is surprising that he felt the way he did in view of his particular conception of literary realism. This deserves special attention.

In the 1840s Faddey Bulgarin, a writer and journalist (and possibly police spy and informer) of Polish origin, began to disparage those writers who imitated Gogol's description of lowly characters as members of the "natural school." Certainly Bulgarin, who was something of a hack, had no idea of what Gogol was doing (which is not too surprising, since it appears that Gogol himself did not know). In any case, Belinsky, who recognized the greatness of Gogol but who ranked him high because of the "realistic" exposure and satire of the seamy side of Russian life, seized upon the term "natural" and used it in a laudatory sense and as a synonym for "realistic." But the interesting thing is that, when it comes to defining realism, Belinsky writes: "A man drinks, eats, and dresses—this is a world of phantoms . . . but a man feels, thinks, and recognizes himself as an organ, a vessel of the spirit, a finite particle of the general and infinite—this is the world of reality [*dejstvitel'nost'*]." This definition has obvious affinities with the "romantic realism" of, for instance, Novalis: *Nach innen geht der geheimnisreiche Weg. In uns oder nirgends ist die Ewigkeit mit ihren Welten, die Vergangenheit und Zukunft. Die Aussenwelt ist die Schattenwelt.*" But Belinsky's definition, although of course it may be quoted in support of literature as a vehicle for supposedly "universal" ideas (and in this sense it fits very well into the Hegelian Marxist-Leninist tradition), may also be read as a defense of the very technique which Dostoevsky essayed in *The Double* and which Kafka perfected in *The Metamorphosis.*

Definitions of literary or artistic realism are many and they make fascinating reading. Some would hold that any such definition depends, in the final analysis, on what exactly one means by the "real" world: Is it the "outer" world of easily verifiable phenomena or the "inner" world of thought, dream, and fantasy? Others feel rather that the term "realism" is simply the name of a "product" which appears

16. One of the leading advocates in modern Russian literature of the fantastic and the grotesque has been Andrey Sinyavsky. See below, Chapter X, section 2.

under various "brand names"; such a view allows for the easy and convenient proliferation of dozens of species: radical realism, critical realism, romantic realism, lyrical realism, manor realism, and so on. But what Belinsky was getting at in his definition of, and other statements about, realism was this: that, whereas what we call naturalism represents an indiscriminate inclusion of events simply because they occur,[17] realism represents a discriminate view of reality, i.e., reality ordered in the mind of the artist on the basis of a particular *Weltanschauung* (*mirosozertsanie*) or philosophy. This is the soundest way of looking at realism, and it is the view of Lukács, the Marxist critic.[18] But one does not have to be a Marxist to agree with him. Thus John Bayley writes (discussing Tolstoy): "realism to a Russian is a method of getting at what should be as well as what is." This particular doctrine of literary realism reminds one of the Aristotelian doctrine of *mimesis.* Just as some writers and critics have insisted that realism portray with meticulous verisimilitude the real world around us, so for generations Aristotle's term *mimesis* was misinterpreted to mean a faithful representation or imitation of this same "real" world. But Aristotle makes it clear, first, that art imitates (*mimeitai*) not only characters and actions but emotions as well and, second, that it, like *paideia* (education in the widest sense), supplies the deficiencies of nature; that, in short, *mimesis* is a *creative revelation of the ideal.*

Closely related to Belinsky's views on realism is his distinction (made first in an article written in 1836) between "real" and "ideal" poetry (or art in a more general sense). This again represents the adoption of German aesthetic theory, since the above distinction was Friedrich Schlegel's, while Schiller's earlier and better known distinction between "naive" and "sentimental" poetry makes essentially the same point. On the basis, then, of the formula, "Realism deals with life, idealism with ideas," Belinsky distinguishes between works like *Don Quixote* (always popular in Russia) and *Eugene Onegin* as "real" poetry and Goethe's *Faust* as "ideal" poetry. He especially exalts Shakespeare and Scott.[19] Art for Belinsky is necessarily related, in the

17. *Indiscriminate* is perhaps the wrong word to use here, since naturalists are attracted, as we know, to *certain* aspects of reality.

18. It is sad, however, to hear Lukács say: "Those who have arrived at such [Marxist] knowledge know, in spite of all temporary darkness, both whence we have come and where we are going."

19. Tolstoy will later, but in a much more severe and ruthless fashion, make further distinctions between two types of literature. According to his formula, not only will Shakespeare be dismissed but Tolstoy's own great novels as well.

ways we have mentioned, to real life rather than being based upon abstract concepts of beauty, theory, or (as we might say today) myth; and Shakespeare's works, mirroring reality as they do, represent the acme of non-idealistic creation. But Belinsky's thought in this area as well shows two tendencies. On the one hand he increasingly emphasizes works of literature as organic wholes exhibiting the Hegelian "sensuous expression of the Idea"; he praises Gogol in "Old World Landowners" for *not* copying from reality and for creating types which, while remaining individuals, assume universal significance.[20] "Art," Belinsky goes so far as to say, "purifies reality." On the other hand, while still holding that the function of criticism is to distinguish between the temporal and the eternal, he elaborates (in articles on Lermontov and Pushkin) what René Wellek has called a "mystique of time": he sees literature as the result of a historical process, progressing through a series of genres from the lyric to the drama and the novel.[21] History itself determined that Pushkin would eventually turn, as in fact he did, to the novel and that Lermontov would write drama. Though Belinsky's "official" Hegelian period was brief, these notions show the lasting influence on his thought of Hegelian meliorism and historical determinism.

Quite frequently in his articles Belinsky will merely exclaim enthusiastically over the beauty or—more often—the veracity of a passage (this is what F. Schlegel called *"Potztausend!"* criticism); occasionally he will dissect and analyze, but very often this is apt, in a manner which has been called "typically Russian," to be rather a labored treatment of a literary character as if he or she were a real person with a past and a future than a stylistic or aesthetic analysis. The critic Pavel Annenkov (see Chapter V), who has left us a splendid account of the "age of Belinsky,"[22] calls Belinsky's analysis (1840) of Lermontov's *A Hero of Our Time* "superb." Yet here Belinsky, who rationalized the erratic behavior of Pechorin (a famous "superfluous man" in Russian literature) as a developmental defect, goes on to theorize about Pechorin's *future:* that he will eventually, in some better world, find peace within himself and reconciliation with his en-

20. See W. Wimsatt's essay, "The Concrete Universal," in *The Verbal Icon.* Goethe also developed an ontologically oriented theory of types and symbolism.

21. Although the concept of organic growth in the arts is also German, we usually think of the French critic Brunetière in this connection (*L'Évolution des genres dans l'histoire de la littérature,* 1890).

22. See P. V. Annenkov, *The Extraordinary Decade,* ed. by A. P. Mendel (Ann Arbor: University of Michigan Press, 1968). The translation is by Irwin Titunik.

vironment! In Lermontov's poem *The Demon* Belinsky sees a defense of man's right to unlimited freedom. "The drama of the poem," writes Annenkov, "though it involved mythical beings, had a completely real content for Belinsky, like a biography or a theme taken from the life of an actual person."

In his analysis of Gogol's *The Inspector General,* Belinsky compares it with Griboedov's classical *Wit Works Woe.* Annenkov refers to this as "aesthetic criticism," although it is hardly such in the French, English, or German sense of the term. The principal point Belinsky makes is that Gogol's inimitable comedy is an organic whole (as if *Wit Works Woe* were not) with one dominating central figure—Khlestakov (whom Nabokov calls the "government specter"). The play, Belinsky writes, "is more than a mirror of reality—it is more like reality than reality itself; it is artistic reality."[23] On the other hand, Belinsky sees in Griboedov's comedy (the source, it has been computed, of some sixty-one phrases that have become proverbial in Russian) only a series of vignettes; furthermore he criticizes it, oddly enough, because it is satire. Here again Belinsky, in his furious search for relevance in literature (despite the German metaphysics), seems to be reading Gogol's play—itself one of the greatest satires, if not *the* greatest satire, in Russian literature—as a "documentary" picture of reality.

Belinsky's use of certain terms (e.g., "pathos" in the Hegelian sense of "moral passion") is peculiar. For example, in speaking of Pushkin's development, he says that prose "killed romanticism." One might think he means by "prose" either "not poetry" or realism. But he calls Pushkin's *Mozart and Salieri, The Stone Guest,* and other works in verse "pure prose." For Belinsky "prose" means "richness of inner poetic content, virile maturity, and strength of mind"; it is "the real fact seen through the poet's imagination and brightened by the light of universal meaning—as a portrait in which the man represented may be more like himself than in a daguerrotype."[24] Here once more Belinsky restates what is essentially his romantic view of reality—*a realibus ad realiora* (to use the Latin tag later given currency by the Russian Symbolist poet, Vyacheslav Ivanov). Of special interest, too, is his comparison of art and nascent photography; but critics who continue to make such inane comparisons, always to the detriment of photography, seem never to recall that we have had our Steichens.

23. Thus, again, art supplements reality. Compare Gorky's definition of what was later called Socialist Realism in Chapter IX, section 1.

24. Lev Tolstoy also praised poetry he liked by calling it "prose."

It is a commonplace—and the point has been made by many critics—that much so-called poetry contains large doses of prose, while much prose contains real poetry. But some light, I think, is thrown on Belinsky's *ad hoc* meaning of the term "prose" by a statement Macaulay once made in his *Essay on Milton:* "In proportion as men know more and think more, they look less at individuals and more at classes. They therefore make better theories and worse poems." Relevant also is T. S. Eliot's observation that, whereas his poetry reflected the *reality* around him, his prose reflected his *ideals.* And René Ghil was thinking along similar lines when he remarked that Zola was the "poet" and Mallarmé the "realist."

Belinsky distinguishes, as have many critics, between the artist and the belletrist: the former is the rare creator who supplements reality (whose works are "more real than reality itself") and the latter is the imitator. In a later age the critic Ivanov-Razumnik elaborated this distinction by saying that the artist (poet) shows or discloses (*pokazyvaet*) reality, while the belletrist talks about or relates (*rasskazyvaet*) reality. Yet the belletrist is not summarily dismissed. "Great and exemplary works of art and science," Belinsky writes, "have been and will continue to be the only elucidators of all problems of life, knowledge, and morality. But until such works appear, works which often keep us waiting long, the activity of belles lettres is essential. During the long intervals their function is to occupy, nourish, and inspire minds which would be doomed to idleness." In contemporary Russian letters this is an appropriate comment on Solzhenitsyn.

Needless to say, Belinsky stresses content. "Only content—not language or style—can save a writer from oblivion, given the changes in the language, customs, and ideas of a society." Though he recognizes the stature of Lomonosov (whom he would call a belletrist of genius), Belinsky refers to his poems as having merely historical interest and nothing more. It is here, perhaps, in his outspoken emphasis on content that Belinsky's views are most clearly opposed by modern criticism in the West and by a series of critics in Russia (to be discussed in subsequent chapters of this book). Thus the late Richard P. Blackmur spoke of the "commonplaceness of great poets." "Most poetry," he wrote, "is on commonplace themes and the freshness, what the poet supplies, is in the language."[25] Belinsky cites the case of Rabelais as a writer who has had lasting significance and appeal by virtue only

25. In Pasternak's novel Doctor Zhivago writes: "Only the familiar transformed by genius is truly great." See below, Chapter VIII, section 2, on "defamiliarization."

of the content of his fiction; but we would disagree and hold that it is rather his style and language that are determining factors.

Finally, from the Russian Marxist-Leninist point of view, Belinsky was the founder of what is called "democratic literary criticism." The words *democracy* and *democratic* are, even in the West, notorious weasel-words, although we do at least have some crude notions of the workings of representative democracy and of the value of its necessary concomitant, liberalism; but for the toadies of a government which has, more than any government in history, insulted the meaning of democracy, of literature, and of literary criticism, making a cruel and despicable mockery of each, to use the term "democratic criticism" in either Russian or English is a gross indecency. And though we may appreciate and sympathize with the moral zealousness and earnestness of Belinsky, though we might hope he would be, were he able to observe the execrable scene in Russia, amongst the first to condemn it, still we must remember that it was Belinsky who wrote the following words: "People are so stupid that they must be led toward happiness by force . . . *fiat justitia, pereat mundus!*"

Let us now turn to the successors of Belinsky, the so-called Civic critics.

SUGGESTED READING

Matlaw, Ralph, ed., *Belinsky, Chernyshevsky, and Dobrolyubov: Selected Criticism* (New York: Dutton, 1962).

Bowman, Herbert, *Vissarion Belinski, 1811–1848: A Study in the Origins of Social Criticism in Russia* (Cambridge: Harvard University Press, 1954).

Terras, Victor, *Belinskij and Russian Literary Criticism: The Heritage of Organic Aesthetics* (Madison: University of Wisconsin Press, 1974).

Proctor, Thelwall, *Dostoevskij and the Belinskij School of Literary Criticism* (The Hague: Mouton, 1969).

Annenkov, P. V., *The Extraordinary Decade*, ed. A. P. Mendel (Ann Arbor: University of Michigan Press, 1968).

Wellek, René, *A History of Modern Criticism: 1750–1950* (New Haven: Yale University Press, 1955–65), Vol. III, Chapter 7.

Mirsky, D. S., *A History of Russian Literature* (New York: Alfred A. Knopf, 1949), Book One, Chapter 5.

Seduro, Vladimir, *Dostoyevski in Russian Literary Criticism, 1846–1956* (New York: Octagon Books, 1969), Part I, Chapter 1.

IV THE CIVIC CRITICS

1

The Civic or radical critics (the "democratic critics" in Soviet usage), however much one may dislike their reading of literature, are an interesting group. There are really only three of them: Nikolay Dobrolyubov (1836–61), Dmitry Pisarev (1840–68), and Nikolay Chernyshevsky (1828–89). The first and the last were sons of priests and former seminary students; Pisarev was a member of the gentry. Dobrolyubov and Pisarev, who were principally critics, died, as we see, quite young, while Chernyshevsky, who lived on almost to the last decade of the nineteenth century, was also a novelist. As a novelist, however, he is for all practical purposes a *homo unius libri:* this work, *What Is to Be Done?* (1863), has occasionally been called the worst novel ever written.[1] Chernyshevsky also has the minor honor of having been the first critic to use the phrase "inner (interior) monologue" (*vnutrennij monolog*). Pisarev was the *enfant terrible* amongst the Civic critics, and the whole radical movement in utilitarian criticism reached its ultimate development (referred to in Russian as *Pisarevshchina*) in his polemical and truculent essays. Pisarev, who served time in prison (as did Chernyshevsky), once said that the intellectual brilliance of the eighteenth century was due to the widespread drinking of tea and coffee (Voltaire is reported to have drunk seventy-five cups of coffee a day) and was one of the few Russian critics who have dared to disparage Pushkin.[2] The Civic critics received a good deal of abuse and

1. The novel is available in paperback. Benjamin Tucker's 1883 translation has been revised and abridged by Ludmila Turkevich, with an Introduction by E. H. Carr (New York: Vintage Books, 1961). In his Preface, Chernyshevsky tells us how his novel will end and he assures us, quite candidly, that the reader will find neither talent nor art in the novel, only the "truth."

2. But Mirsky writes: "His famous uncrowning of Pushkin, for all its naiveté, may still be read with pleasure."

a *Schimpflexikon* could be composed on this score.[3] Herzen called Chernyshevsky and Dobrolyubov the "bilious ones" (*zhelchniki*) and Turgenev once told Chernyshevsky: "You are just a plain snake, but Dobrolyubov is a cobra!" But such language (which reminds one of the vilification heaped today upon activists or dissidents) is quite unfair, especially in the case of Chernyshevsky whose almost saintly purity of character was noted even by his jailers. The Marxist or Soviet point of view regarding Chernyshevsky and Dobrolyubov is stated thus by Lukács: "Chernyshevsky and Dobrolyubov are to this day the last great thinkers of the revolutionary-democratic enlightenment in Europe. Their work, to this day, represents the last major and inwardly continuous offensive thrust of the democratic philosophy of the Enlightenment."

Chernyshevsky is the central figure in a group known as the "men of the sixties." The "men of the forties" (Bakunin, Herzen, Turgenev, and Belinsky, to name only four) were men brought up in a tradition, somewhat distorted and second-hand, of Western liberalism and, as we have noted, strongly under the influence of German philosophical idealism. They were particularly—notoriously, in the eyes of the younger generation—weak in having no concrete or workable program for either reform or revolution; indeed, they often seemed to be more interested, despite their occasional iconoclastic talk, in the beauty of their souls and in self-improvement than in radical social melioration. But the "men of the sixties" were not only devotees of a veritable cult of Reason, Science, and Progress but militant activists as well. The phrase "cult of Reason" reminds us, of course, of France, and in point of fact the sixties in Russia have frequently been referred to as Russia's Age of Reason. As E. H. Carr writes, "Faith in progress and in the ultimate attainment of the goal is common to all the characters in *What Is to Be Done?* Here, too, Chernyshevsky harks back to the Enlightenment and may be regarded as the disciple of Condorcet quite as much as of Darwin."[4] Yet the German influence still lingers on, and the "men of the sixties" (satirized as nihilists in Turgenev's *Fathers and Sons*) loved to read Büchner and to quote Feuerbach ("*Der Mensch ist, was er isst*") while their ethics were based on En-

3. Probably the best-known *Schimpflexikon* is that composed by the American journalist and critic, H. L. Mencken, containing a long list of the names he was called, especially by men of the cloth. But the Russian writer Korney Chukovsky compiled one for Leonid Andreev, a much-reviled prerevolutionary author.

4. In the Introduction to the edition mentioned in note 1. On the *Éclaircissement*, see below, Chapter VI, section 1 (on Tolstoy).

glish utilitarianism. As militants, the "men of the sixties"—and especially Chernyshevsky—are often regarded as forerunners of the Bolsheviks. Lenin, in any case, cherished the works of Chernyshevsky, and Karl Marx was inspired to study Russian by a desire to read the writings of Chernyshevsky on economics.

Chernyshevsky was educated at a theological school and at the University of St. Petersburg and joined the staff of *The Contemporary* (then edited by Nekrasov) as its literary critic in 1855. In his Master's thesis, "The Aesthetic Relations Between Art and Reality," which he defended publicly in the same year, Chernyshevsky sets the utilitarian (and Platonic) tone in Russian criticism by arguing that art, far from having any special ontological status of its own, is but an inferior reproduction of reality and that its sole function is didactic edification: to disseminate knowledge of reality. This, of course, represents a radical break with Belinsky's romantic view of a work of art as something "more real than reality itself." The aesthetic qualities of a work of art are dismissed as mere sensuous adornment (much as modern linguists use the term "enrichment"). In his "documentary" *Studies in the Age of Gogol* (1856) Chernyshevsky continued his exposition of utilitarian literary theory, at the same time reviving an interest in Belinsky (whose name had become taboo during the period of reaction following the "Year of Revolutions," 1848) and correcting—in the sense of giving a more utilitarian interpretation to—the views of his great predecessor. This work, together with his Master's thesis, was instrumental in alienating other critics associated with *The Contemporary;* Druzhinin and Annenkov (to be discussed in the following chapter) began, since they were Aesthetic critics, to publish elsewhere. In 1857 Chernyshevsky relinquished his post of literary critic to his disciple, Dobrolyubov, and turned his attention to more purely political and economic matters. He also became more deeply involved in radical activism and in 1862, following the Edict of Emancipation (with which he was extremely dissatisfied), he was arrested on what appear to have been false charges. After his trial he was subjected to the so-called civil execution in St. Petersburg: he was placed upon a scaffold against a "pillar of shame," a placard reading "State Criminal" was suspended from his neck, a sword was broken over his head, and his sentence read aloud.[5] Concerning the whole affair, Berdyaev writes: "The Chernyshevsky case represented one of the most revolting falsi-

5. During the reading of the sentence it is reported that Chernyshevsky spent the time nonchalantly spitting.

fications perpetrated by the Russian Government. He was condemned to nineteen years in penal servitude; as a man who might have had a deleterious effect on the young, he had to be gotten out of the way. He bore his penal servitude heroically—it might even be said that he suffered his martyrdom with Christian humility. He said 'I fight for freedom but I do not want freedom for myself, lest it should be said that I am not fighting for disinterested ends.'"

René Wellek, though he quite rightly states that Chernyshevsky must be ranked lowest as a literary critic amongst his fellows, recognizes that he had the makings of a good critic.[6] (One wonders what kind of criticism Coleridge might have written had he lived under a Nicholas I or even an Alexander II.) But although Chernyshevsky sacrificed everything to his political militancy and put all his convictions, publicly at least, in reason and science, we can nevertheless see another side of the man in a letter to Nekrasov:

> I of course know from experience that convictions are not everything in life. There are the demands of the heart, and in the life of the heart there is real joy and there is real sorrow for us all. I know this from experience and I know it better than others. . . . I know that the poetry of the heart has equal rights with the poetry of the mind. . . . I have taken the liberty of being this candid not merely to tell you that I read poetry not at all exclusively from the political point of view. On the contrary, only by force does politics make its way into my heart and my heart does not live by this alone or at least would rather not live by it.

Chernyshevsky's prose style is no better than Belinsky's. It is tediously repetitious, meandering, and turgid, heavily larded with the "scientific" jargon of the time. More easily than any other critic mentioned in this survey, he slips from the text into Civic criticism. Thus, in what is perhaps his best-known article, "The Russian at the Rendezvous,"[7] ostensibly a critical review of Turgenev's story *Asya,* he attacks Russian liberalism. As for the typically Turgenevian lyrical treatment

6. *A History of Modern Criticism,* IV, 238 ff. In his novel *The Gift,* Vladimir Nabokov devotes the fourth chapter to a "biography" of Chernyshevsky; see below, Chapter X, section 4.

7. An English version of this essay may be found in *Belinsky, Chernyshevsky, and Dobrolyubov: Selected Criticism,* ed. by Ralph Matlaw (New York: Dutton, 1962).

of frustrated love, he writes (as a contemporary Soviet critic might): "Those erotic questions, forget about them! They are not for the reader of our age, preoccupied as he is with problems of administrative and judiciary reforms." In almost any one of his didactic and homiletic articles we can find an abundance of quotable matter ("It is better not to raise a man at all than to raise him without the influence of ideas concerning civil affairs"), but the relevance is always non-literary. It is in his article on Tolstoy, however, that Chernyshevsky comes closest to something resembling literary criticism. He recognized (and was apparently the first to do so) Tolstoy's particular technique of describing psychic processes, "those half-dream, half-reflective conjunctions of ideas and sensations that grow, move, and change before our very eyes," contrasting this with Lermontov's earlier and pioneering venture in writing a psychological novel.[8] Using the specious but richly suggestive graphic simile, he likens Tolstoy's art of description to that of the painter who catches the shimmer of sunlight on rustling leaves, thus anticipating later critics who compared Tolstoy's style, for example, to the impressionism of the *plein-airistes.*

Chernyshevsky thinks rather highly of Pushkin but only as a sort of revered national poet, a classic figure of the past; yet he sees (but disparages) an essential quality in Pushkin when he writes: "In some talents the power of observation is characterized by something cold and dispassionate, and the most remarkable representative of that special trait in our literature was Pushkin." Without realizing the full implication of his statement, he continues (discussing Pushkin's description of the customs and habits of the old Russian landowner in *Dubrovsky*): "But it is difficult to decide what Pushkin himself thought about the traits he depicted." In other words, Chernyshevsky felt that Pushkin should have been more frankly committed and made his ethical and political position crystal clear. Furthermore, whereas Pushkin seems too derivative (reminding one now of Byron, now of Shakespeare), Gogol is seen as the creator of a Russian literature free of foreign influence and the real founder of the "critical tendency" in this literature. Here Chernyshevsky chooses to ignore the various marked influences on Gogol—notably that of Hoffmann.

8. It is in his article reviewing Tolstoy's *Sevastopol Sketches* that Chernyshevsky uses the phrase "inner monologue." An English version of this article may also be found in the work cited in the previous note.

2

Nikolay Dobrolyubov, like Chernyshevsky the son of an Orthodox priest, received his education in a theological seminary and at a pedagogical institute. Having replaced Chernyshevsky as literary critic on the staff of *The Contemporary,* he repeated *ad nauseam* and with exceeding little grace the tenets of his predecessor. Still, despite the overriding pressure of his rigidly utilitarian convictions, he was exceptionally gifted and he shows a considerably keener critical judgment than Chernyshevsky. He comes close to elaborating a critical theory of types, and his name is inseparably linked with two themes in Russian literature and criticism, "Oblomovism" (*Oblomovshchina*)[9] and the "Superfluous Man" (*lishnij chelovek*). In one essay (on Dostoevsky's *The Insulted and the Injured*) there is even outlined a "holistic" view of the poet's function and an intimation of the catalytic role of the imagination in an almost Coleridgean sense: "The poet creates a whole; he finds the vital link, fuses and transforms the diverse aspects of living reality."

A brief review of three of Dobrolyubov's critical essays will give the gist of his method. In "What Is Oblomovism?"[10] he uses the notorious indolence and acedia of the hero of Goncharov's novel (a "land-locked" novel which contains, amongst much else, a beautiful *locus classicus* on the sea) mainly as a text for an extended social criticism of Russian life, a procedure which he candidly admits will disturb "true" critics. But some of the formal qualities of the novel are touched upon (and disparaged): e.g., the relentless repertory of detail (the description of the ink and paper used in writing a letter) and the attention paid (in a manner Gogol brought to hilarious perfection) to "peripheral" characters. And he notes the "role" played by Oblomov's famous dressing gown—an "Ibsenian symbol" according to a later, non-Russian critic.[11] As a brash young critic of very radical persuasions

9. Occasionally rendered "Oblomovitis."

10. An English version of this essay may be found in the work cited in note 7.

11. The dressing gown (*khalat*) appears frequently in Russian literature of the

(we must remember that he died at the age of twenty-five), Dobrolyubov too frequently uses a somewhat heavy-handed sarcasm: "No doubt *Oblomov* will elicit a good deal of criticism. Some of this will probably be of the proofreader type and will detect certain flaws in the language and style. Some of it will be emotional and will contain numerous exclamations about the charm of scenes and characters. And some of it will be of the apothecary-aesthetic type and carefully examine the novel to see whether all the characters have been given the precisely proper doses of such and such qualities."

Dobrolyubov's name is also associated with the dramatist Ostrovsky and he has two articles on his work, "The Kingdom of Darkness"[12] and "A Ray of Light in the Kingdom of Darkness." In the former, Dobrolyubov expatiates on the type of the domestic merchant-tyrant, the *samodur*, and, as if he were a historian rummaging through source documents, he tries to get at the underlying social factors. Dobrolyubov loses sight of the play as a piece of dramatic art requiring exceptional technical skill on the part of the artist, and he regards it essentially as a corpus of sociological data. The economic dependence of certain characters on others is more important than stagecraft. The other essay, on Ostrovsky's *The Storm*, centers around Katerina (the unfortunate heroine of the play) whom Dobrolyubov sees as a symbol of "a great national idea"—in effect, the symbol of revolution; an interpretation, as René Wellek puts it, "that seems the very height of what could be called 'loss of contact' with the text."[13]

One of Dobrolyubov's most apparent weaknesses as a critic—even in the context of Russian Civic criticism—is seen in his tendency to discuss literary characters as if "they" were real persons, actually existing in a social milieu, with a past history and a contingent future, a procedure which is futile and inane. Of course he is not unique in this respects (for example, the word *Hamlet* in a matrix of other words has received similar treatment in the West); but he represents, as does Chernyshevsky, an extreme development. This marked tendency, by the way, not only amongst the Civic critics but also amongst the great majority of other Russian critics, to refuse to accept the self-sufficiency

nineteenth century. Vyazemsky has a poem in which old age is likened to a threadbare dressing gown.

12. The phrase refers to the Russian merchant class.

13. *A History of Modern Criticism,* IV, 252. In their constant search for revolutionary precedents, Soviet students of the drama have settled on Lope de Vega's *Fuente Ovejuna* as the first "proletarian" drama.

of literary characters has two important parallels. First, there is a definite, traditional, and I would say bitter hostility amongst Russian critics and writers as well as the general reading public toward the aesthetic doctrine of *ars gratia artis.* (I have met very few *émigré* Russians who express any liking for Vladimir Nabokov's novels—with the possible exception of *Pnin.*) Second, the Russian seems extremely reluctant—be he either Orthodox Christian or devout Communist—to believe that the meaning of a man's life may be self-sufficient or pointless in any teleological sense. "He is inclined," as John Berger writes, "to think that his destiny is larger than his interests."[14]

On the credit side, Dobrolyubov's principal contribution is his notion of social types based upon the assumption that the types of characters which a particular author creates in his fiction (or the types created by various authors in a given literature or literary period) reveal, more accurately than any stated or implied intentions, the actual outlook and philosophy of the writer. "What an author intended to say," writes Dobrolyubov "is much less important for us than what he really did say, possibly without realizing it, simply as a result of the correct representation of the facts as he saw them." But this concept has been expressed by other critics and theoreticians, from William Blake (on Milton) to Rozanov and Shestov (on Dostoevsky), while Kant has some similar remarks on this point in his *Critique of Pure Reason.*

3

Dmitry Pisarev, the most radical of the Civic critics, not only condemns Shakespeare and Pushkin (among other names of note) as worthless, but even attacks Belinsky for having been fatuous enough actually to take Pushkin's writings seriously. As a painter may make himself most useful (according to Pisarev) by illustrating a book on insect pests, so the writer best fulfills his calling by expounding positivist and scientific knowledge. Thus the present-day "technical writer" would receive Pisarev's most ardent praise.[15] Pisarev shares the general

14. *Art and Revolution* (New York: Pantheon Books, 1969). This book deals mainly with the sculpture of Ernst Neizvestny.

15. In the satirical novel *We* by Zamyatin (to be discussed as a critic in Chapter

radical background of Belinsky, Chernyshevsky, and Dobrolyubov ("Belinsky begat Chernyshevsky, Chernyshevsky begat Dobrolyubov, Dobrolyubov begat Pisarev"—Ivanov-Razumnik) but he carries the utilitarianism, rationalism, and materialism of the latter two critics to a point where, like the character Bazarov in Turgenev's *Fathers and Sons*, he cuts himself off completely from the entire romantic past. He is an "aesthetic nihilist," representing the *reductio ad absurdum* of Civic criticism. Discussions of Pisarev's writings are usually replete with such adjectives as *vicious*, *crude*, and *notorious*, these reflecting the shock and natural reaction of the romantic mind to hearing its pet velleities set at naught. Though there is an obvious *pour épater le bourgeois* quality about Pisarev's forays, his iconoclastic views furnish a refreshing antidote to a good deal of maudlin adulation of the written word.[16]

Less "notorious" than his article "The Destruction of Aesthetics" and less "vicious" than his "Pushkin and Belinsky" is his article on Turgenev's *Fathers and Sons*. Here, in defining the "new man" of the sixties and beyond, he analyzes Bazarov's character, motivation, and significance in terms that can still be read with enjoyment. On the whole, Pisarev is rather easy on Turgenev: he likes his women and he sees in the author's treatment of Bazarov an "ambivalent" attitude (reminding us of Dobrolyubov's theory of revelatory types). But he regrets the accidental death of Bazarov (whose story the future itself will complete, however) and his replacement in *Smoke* by such a disappointing character as Litvinov. Turgenev, by the way, had sent a copy of his novel *Smoke* to Pisarev and had asked the young man's opinion of it.

Pisarev died (by drowning, possibly suicide) when he was twenty-eight. Although he spent a number of years in prison for having published radical propaganda, he was not actually an extreme revolutionary: he believed that the situation in Russia could be alleviated through a rational reorganization of private enterprise by "men of good will." He was deeply disturbed (and the relevance to our own age is to be noted) by the fact that Russia had conservatories of music

---

VII) the denizens of the dystopian society of the distant future have preserved what they consider the best of "ancient" literature—railroad schedules.

16. In a three-volume anthology, edited by James Edie, *Russian Philosophy* (Chicago: Quadrangle Books, 1969), there are four of Pisarev's philosophical essays (in Vol. II). There is also an excerpt from Pisarev's essay on Dostoevsky's *Crime and Punishment* in *Crime and Punishment and the Critics*, ed. by Edward Wasiolek (San Francisco: Wadsworth, 1961).

while famines were rife and that expeditions were sent to Mesopotamia to study cuneiform inscriptions when masses of Russians could not read Cyrillic. René Wellek, however, while minimizing Pisarev's importance as a literary critic, places him in a notable tradition: "He must be grouped with a long line of thinkers that begins with Plato, goes through the Elizabethan puritans, the 'geometrical' partisans of the Moderns under Louis XIV, to the Benthamite Utilitarians and men like Proudhon, who all wanted to banish the poets from the Republic."[17]

4

Before we turn to another important group of Russian critics, a few words should be said of Valerian Maykov (1823–47). A brother of the poet Apollon Maykov, he was a brilliant young man who gave promise of great things to come. He received his *kandidat* degree—equivalent to our doctorate—when he was nineteen, and he had, by the time of his premature death, authored a rather astounding variety of works, from a long but unfinished essay, "The Social Sciences in Russia," to the first volume of a *Pocket Dictionary of Foreign Words Used in Russian.* In 1846, when Belinsky left the staff of Kraevsky's *Fatherland Notes,* Maykov took his place as literary critic. Although a Comtian positivist and a Civic critic in a technical sense, emphasizing sociological themes in literature and judging art on the basis of its relevance to vital and social issues, he neither became infatuated with German philosophy nor developed extreme or iconoclastic utilitarian views. His early death, however, and the fact that he was something of a polymath prevented him from leaving us any substantial critical legacy. Still, on the basis of his sensitive evaluation of Dostoevsky's earliest works and his articulate appreciation of Tyutchev's poetry, he deserves at least passing mention. Indeed, Mirsky rates him highly, calling him "a *critic,* one of the small number of genuine critics in Russian literature." Maykov, writing in the year of his death, was keen enough to detect and point out, in opposition to many who saw in the early Dostoevsky only another Gogol, at least one real difference between the two. "Both Gogol and Dostoevsky," he wrote, "portray actual so-

17. *A History of Modern Criticism,* IV, 256.

ciety. But Gogol is first of all a social writer, while Dostoevsky is a psychological one. For the former, the individual is meaningful as the representative of a certain society or circle; for the latter, society is interesting only insofar as it influences the personality of the individdual." Incidentally, Maykov's interest in Dostoevsky foreshadows the growing concern, in the last decades of the nineteenth century, with the works of this novelist that we will observe especially in the writings of the critics to be discussed in Chapter VII.

SUGGESTED READING

Matlaw, Ralph, ed., *Belinsky, Chernyshevsky, and Dobrolyubov: Selected Criticism* (New York: Dutton, 1962).

Gifford, Henry, ed., *Leo Tolstoy* (Harmondsworth: Penguin Critical Anthologies, 1971), contains an excerpt from Chernyshevsky's essay on Tolstoy.

Edie, James, and others, *Russian Philosophy*, 3 vols. (Chicago: Quadrangle Books, 1969). Volume II contains essays by Chernyshevsky and Pisarev.

Wasiolek, Edward, *Crime and Punishment and the Critics* (San Francisco: Wadsworth, 1961), contains an excerpt from an essay by Pisarev on Dostoevsky.

Proctor, Thelwall, *Dostoevskij and the Belinskij School of Literary Criticism* (The Hague: Mouton, 1969). Chapters III–V survey the criticism of Chernyshevsky, Dobrolyubov, and Pisarev.

Woehrlin, William, *Chernyshevskij* (Cambridge: Harvard University Press, 1971). Chapter VI deals with Chernyshevsky's aesthetics and literary criticism.

Wellek, René, *A History of Modern Criticism, 1750–1950* (New Haven: Yale University Press, 1955–65), Vol. IV, Chapter 11.

Mirsky, D. S., *A History of Russian Literature* (New York: Alfred A. Knopf, 1949), Book One, Chapter 7.

Seduro, Vladimir, *Dostoyevski in Russian Literary Criticism* (New York: Octagon Books, 1969), Part I, Chapter 1.

V THE AESTHETIC CRITICS

1

We have seen how the considerable emphasis which Belinsky laid on the social significance of literature was taken up and carried to extremes by the majority of his "disciples." It was natural that certain other critics should have reacted negatively to what, in their opinion, was a one-sided and misdirected emphasis and that they should have attempted to correct what they considered distorted interpretations. Those who voiced their dissent from about the middle of the nineteenth century to the eighties are known as the Aesthetic critics.[1] For the most part, they are a comparatively genteel lot, not given to passionate diatribe or frenzied sociological analysis. They take a more Laodicean or Horatian view of the world and the written word and have consequently (because of their "reactionary" views) been quite ignored in Soviet Russia; and, because a good deal of literary scholarship *in partibus infidelium* is curiously Soviet in its orientation and taste, they are (as Wellek notes) "doubly unknown in the West." This is not, however, a great loss, since they added nothing really significant to modern critical thought. In this chapter we shall mention several of these critics, although particular attention will be paid to one, Apollon Grigoriev.

Alexander Druzhinin (1824–64) was a novelist as well as critic, the author of the once popular Sandian "problem" novel, *Polinka Sachs*. He was intimate with both Turgenev and Tolstoy, but thought that Lev Tolstoy's brother, Nikolay, had a superior command of the Russian language. Druzhinin was a serious student of English litera-

1. They are also frequently referred to as the Conservative critics. The term "aesthetics" (*èstetika*) with its "art-for-art's-sake" overtones, when used in any non-Marxist context, is looked upon askance in Soviet Russia. The word *aestheticizers* (*èstetstvujushchie*) has become a regular term of abuse.

ture, wrote some fairly interesting articles on Dr. Johnson, Boswell, and Scott, and translated several of Shakespeare's plays. He noted (as have many others) similarities between Dickens and Dostoevsky, especially in their treatment of children, while his comments on Tolstoy, although to the point, are hardly unique. Thus he cautions Tolstoy regarding his tendency toward excessively subtle analysis and informs him (as some critic might have informed Pushkin or any other major writer) that all his merits bore within themselves the seeds of imperfection. Like so many critics, too, Druzhinin feels that Tolstoy's notorious "psychosomatic parallelism" is often too finely drawn: that the appearance of so-and-so's thigh, for instance, really cannot indicate a wish to travel to India.

Pavel Annenkov (1813–87) is best known for a scholarly Russian classic of *Kulturgeschichte, Pushkin in the Age of Alexander I,* and for some valuable memoirs, a good portion of which is now available in English translation under the title of *The Extraordinary Decade.* He was at one time Gogol's secretary and, like Druzhinin, an intimate friend of Turgenev (the Aesthetic critics naturally gravitated toward Turgenev, a devotee of the "good and the beautiful" and hence mercilessly parodied by Dostoevsky in *The Possessed.*) But he also knew most of the eminent men of the age, not only in Russia but in Western Europe as well. Of gentry origin, Annenkov was a wealthy landowner and had the aristocratic tastes of the age he knew best—the age of Pushkin. He was a connoisseur and a dilettante and showed at times an aggravating lack of conviction. Turgenev himself once remarked that Annenkov was hardly ever heard to state his own views about anything and that he tended to agree with the opinions of anybody of note. Marx regarded him contemptuously as an "Epicurean,"[2] while Lavrov, the Populist leader, called him an "aesthetic tourist." But his non-involvement served him well as a memoirist, and his objectivity differentiates him sharply from his radical colleagues.

But we must not exaggerate Annenkov's lack of involvement. It is only about things that do not interest one, it has been said, that one can give an unbiased—and usually worthless—opinion. Literature, however, interested Annenkov immensely, and he brought to bear on the books he read if not the acumen of genius, at least a cultivated and liberal taste. Despite the fact that the friendship between Annenkov and Turgenev was life long, the critic spoke out concerning the novel-

2. Marx's doctoral dissertation was a study of the contrasts between the philosophies of Democritus and Epicurus.

ist's "poetic lies"; he noted something affected in Turgenev—the desire constantly to produce a literary effect. Although it is a commonplace now to contrast Turgenev's strong women and his weak men, Annenkov saw deeper and perceived a strong feminine streak in the author himself.[3]

2

Apollon Grigoriev (1822–64), although best known as a critic, was also a minor prose writer and poet (he has one poem in Dimitri Obolensky's Penguin anthology), an accomplished pianist, and a composer of romances and adaptations of popular Gypsy songs—notably the familiar *Two Guitars*. He was also something of a textual critic, having supplied some brilliant emendations to Yakushkin's collection of folk songs. Grigoriev was born into a family of the minor nobility (his grandfather had attained the requisite rank in the civil service and had acquired a patent of nobility), but with one drawback, something that presaged the unhappiness that was to dog his life: he was a "natural" or illegitimate son.[4] The infant was sent to a foundling home but "reclaimed" a year later, and he was brought up in the notoriously middle-class Zamoskvarechye district of Moscow, the stronghold of the merchantry. He attended Moscow University and took a degree in law in 1843, acquiring in the meantime an excellent knowledge of French and German. Grigoriev had an unhappy marriage and two profoundly disturbing and unsuccessful love affairs, but these are hardly of immediate concern. In any case, beginning as a librarian at Moscow University and moving from appointment to appointment (he once taught civil law at an institution called "The Alexander Institute for Foundlings"), he came eventually to lead what is usually termed a Bohemian life and was, over a number of years, in and out of debtors' prison. Prior to his death by a stroke in 1864 he felt that his life and

3. In his *Literature and Western Man* the English critic and novelist J. B. Priestley is constantly finding "feminine streaks" in the great European novelists. Turgenev, incidentally, once said that the only time he was blissfully happy was when a woman stamped her heel on his neck and pressed his nose into the dirt.

4. Grigoriev later befriended the poet Fet, also a natural son but legitimized in 1873.

his efforts on behalf of literature had been failures and he signed one of his last articles "An Unnecessary Man."

Grigoriev, in addition to being termed either an "aesthetic" or "conservative" critic, is more accurately an advocate of "organic" criticism (*organicheskaja kritika*). But his organic criticism has its roots in two sources. On the one hand, it draws heavily on the "organic" *Naturphilosophie* of Schelling (whom Grigoriev once called the "Plato of the modern world") and German idealistic philosophy in general. Grigoriev encountered German philosophy at Moscow University and, with Fet's help, studied German and thereafter continued his reading of Schelling and Hegel.[5] All reality, according to Schelling, is one great organism in a dynamic state of purposeful growth, constantly striving toward more refined and highly perfected forms and higher levels of consciousness. The very culmination of this process is man as artist; and art or the creative act (often partly, by its very nature, unconscious and frequently prophetic) is an organic part of the process of growth. Art *is* Life. Moreover, art is national, the repository of a nation's heritage. Also of considerable importance is the influence of Carlyle, the English Germanophile critic and historian (he received Prussia's highest award, *Pour le Mérite*—the "Blue Max"—for his history of Frederick the Great). Grigoriev rates Carlyle almost as the founder of organic criticism and calls him, in Carlylean language, "the great dreamer, poet-philosopher-historian-prophet."

On the other hand there is the native Slavophile background.[6] In 1850 Grigoriev became editor of Pogodin's very conservative and nationalistic journal, *The Muscovite*. Mikhail Pogodin (1800–75) was a writer and publisher as well as a professor of history at the University of Moscow. In his journal, which came to an end in 1856, he defended the official ideological triad of "Orthodoxy, Autocracy, and Nationalism," was a staunch supporter of the Slavophile movement, and suffered the consequent obloquy of the liberals and radicals. Grigoriev was also intimate with the dramatist, Ostrovsky, and was the leader of a group of young men who, while not fanatically anti-Western, were extremely keen on furthering an independent and original Russian cul-

5. The reader will by now have noticed the strange coexistence of so much abstract philosophical thought and discussion and one of the most autocratic regimes in European history. The Marquis de Custine, traveling in Russia in 1839 (while Nicholas I was Tsar), wrote: "Everywhere I hear the language of philosophy and everywhere I see oppression as the order of the day."

6. See above, Chapter III, section 1.

ture. They sought a "renewed faith in the earth, in the soil, and in the people, a restoration in the mind and heart of everything of immediate importance." The Russian word for *soil* is *pochva* and hence these men were called the *pochvenniki* or "men of the soil" (*pochvennichestvo* being the abstract name of the movement). Occasionally Grigoriev's criticism is referred to, rather misleadingly, as "soil-bound criticism" (e.g., in Utechin's *Concise Encyclopedia of Russia*).

The only major work by Grigoriev readily available in English translation is his *My Literary and Moral Wanderings* (1864).[7] Unfortunately, this is largely autobiographical and memoiristic rather than critical, although it is a good introduction to Grigoriev's unique style. Stylistically, though we dub Grigoriev an Aesthetic critic (see below), there is not too great a difference between him and his fellow Civic critics. Mirsky puts this rather harshly but to the point: "Grigoriev's writings are all more or less unkempt and slovenly journalism where flashes of genius and intuition are stifled by the overgrown weeds of verbosity." Grigoriev felt it necessary to introduce new terminology, such as *vejanie* or *drift*—the total or organic tendency of an age or period (something like Herbert Read's usage in *The Drift of Modern Poetry*)—and his references are apt frequently to be synaesthetic: he will speak, for example, of the "aroma and color of an epoch." He makes frequent use of *ad hoc* hyphenated compound nouns and adjectives, and, in order to despecificate and to render the notion of impalpability, he is fond of employing such phrases as "some sort of," "some kind of," or "a certain kind of."

It is interesting that Grigoriev's language is occasionally compared to that of the Russian "metaphysical" poet, Tyutchev. Tyutchev, too, was influenced by Schelling, and he expressed in what is perhaps his most famous poem, *Silentium*, the *topos* that "a spoken thought is a lie." The Russian symbolist poet and critic, Vyacheslav Ivanov, once wrote that "Russian symbolism had its first beginnings in the poetry of Tyutchev"; and there is a striking modernity of idiom in Grigoriev who, as R. E. Matlaw puts it, "was very sensitive to delicate and evanescent sensations that we have learned to take as a matter of course since the impressionist and symbolist eras."[8] As a critic, Grigor-

7. New York, 1962. This paperback edition also contains three other autobiographical pieces. The translation and the Introduction are by Professor R. E. Matlaw.

8. *Ibid.*, p. xxix.

iev, with his attention to and emphasis on nuances and suggestion, his wide literary and linguistic background, and his almost total devotion to literature, reminds one of modern critics such as Richard P. Blackmur or Kenneth Burke. We get an idea of the scope and range of Grigoriev's critical studies from a mere enumeration of some titles; "The Development of the Concept of Nationality Since the Death of Pushkin"; "Contemporary Literature as Related to Its Historical Point of Departure"; "A View of Russian Literature Since the Death of Pushkin"; "The Relationship Between Critical Consciousness and Romanticism"; "Westernism in Russian Literature"; "Realism and Idealism in Our Literature"; and "Belinsky and the Negative View of Literature."

Before we review some of Grigoriev's judgments of literature, a word must be said about the term "aesthetic" frequently applied to him. He is hardly an Aesthetic critic in the ordinary (say, French or English) sense. He is opposed to purely social and Civic criticism, to be sure, or the view that literature is a mere reflection of life; but he is equally opposed to the view that literature, or the critical language dealing with it, can in any way be divorced from life. Such a view would, in any case, be impossible in the context of his overall organic theory. It is worth noting here that neither Belinsky nor Grigoriev nor a Marxist critic could (although their reasoning might be different) accept the statement by Baudelaire that "poetry has no other end but itself. . . . If a poet has pursued a moral goal, he has diminished his poetic force and the result is most likely to be bad." Pushkin would probably agree with this, certainly Nabokov would, and a handful of minor figures in the Russian symbolist movement as well as the Formalists would concur; but on the whole such a view is quite un-Russian.

Grigoriev is not unusual, as a Russian critic, in thinking highly of Pushkin; he wrote that there was nothing in the literature of the time (the 1850s) that had not had its beginnings in Pushkin. Grigoriev was particularly interested in Pushkin's *Tales of Belkin,* as well as Lermontov's *A Hero of Our Time,* and the emergence of "meek types," such as Belkin and Maxim Maximovich, to counter the "predatory types" represented by Onegin and Pechorin. The "meek" hero (the ultimate development appeared after Grigoriev's death in Dostoevsky's Prince Myshkin, the hero of *The Idiot*) was the true rendering of the Russian character, while those "predatory" types represented the corrupt European man at his worst. But Grigoriev saw in Pushkin the beginnings of an entirely new art, the "Homeric, Dantesque, and Shakespearean art of a new world." This new art—which, in the organic context, meant a new life—Grigoriev associates with Russian Orthodoxy, thus foisting upon Pushkin, as Dostoevsky was later to do again, religious and nationalistic views which the great poet quite apparently did not share.

One of the striking inconsistencies—and there are a number of them—in Grigoriev is, in view of his overall and marked romantic proclivities (Schiller, Victor Hugo, Byron, Schelling), his particular attraction toward Pushkin. Mirsky writes in this connection: "In fact nothing that was romantic was alien to him, and for all his love for the classical and balanced geniuses of Pushkin and Ostrovsky, his innermost sympathy went to the most exuberant of the romanticists and to the sublimest of the idealists."[9] The juxtaposition of Pushkin and the second-rate Ostrovsky is slightly incongruous in itself, but Grigoriev, who was an inveterate theatrophile, esteemed the Russian playwright most highly; or, to be quite blunt, he overrated and exaggerated his virtues. Ostrovsky, the author of some forty-two plays, was hardly the "classical and balanced genius" that Pushkin was, and it cannot be said that he observes in his drama the classical principle of making the most of a minimum of resources. His plays are loosely constructed and uneconomical from the technical point of view. But Grigoriev did not see in Ostrovsky technical competence, not to mention literary qualities, so much as validation for his own organic and nationalistic theory. Ostrovsky, after all, was producing a body of Russian national drama depicting in an acceptably realistic manner traditional, *echt russische* modes of behavior. For Grigoriev, Ostrovsky was thus not so much the dramatist as a "poet of folk traditions." Although Grigoriev accused Dobrolyubov of being blinded by theory in claiming Ostrovsky as a satirist of the "Kingdom of Darkness," his own judgment of Ostrovsky is based precisely on theoretical extrapolation rather than on an analysis of intrinsic merits.

Aside from any other terms we may use to describe Grigoriev's criticism (and we have already used three: aesthetic, conservative, and organic), there is one major category into which he falls without the shadow of a doubt: romantic criticism. Dominating all his other qualities as a critic and most patent of them all are his romantic sympathies. Mirsky, quoted above, has commented on this, and René Wellek concludes his discussion of Grigoriev on this note.[10] The key terms

9. *History of Russian Literature,* p. 208.

10. *A History of Modern Criticism,* IV, 266–70.

running throughout Grigoriev's writings—growth, individuality, originality, nationality, spontaneity, feeling, naturalism, even art as prophecy—are all "classical" hallmarks of the romantic outlook. But if he is a romantic critic, he has much in common with a great number of modern critics. For instance, when T. S. Eliot remarks that "the whole of the literature of Europe from Homer . . . has a simultaneous existence and composes a simultaneous order," we see again the pervading impact of romantic thought.[11] Romantic criticism is not limited to Europe—I have always felt that the key term in the *Dhvani* school of Indian literary criticism, namely *dhvani* (which means *reverberation*), is exactly the sort of terminology one might find in Grigoriev.

Grigoriev dismisses Goncharov's Oblomov as a "contrived" character and lauds Turgenev's Lavretsky in *A Nest of Gentlefolk* as a "positive" Russian type, a character that was "born and not invented." A good deal of Grigoriev's treatment of literary characters, it will be noted, is in the Civic vein; thus Wellek writes: "his criticism of individual writers remains within the curious circle of preoccupation with social types." Although Grigoriev saw (it is now a commonplace) the importance of Gogol's Ukrainian background and recognized that he was not, in the accepted sense of the word, a realist, he had the strange notion that Gogol was essentially a humorist. Such a view is even more absurd than calling Gogol a realist, and it is justifiably mocked in Nabokov's essay on Gogol. Grigoriev sees a continuation of Gogolian "naturalism" in Dostoevsky's *Poor Folk* and finds *The Double* repulsive, reacting here in quite the same manner as Belinsky. Of Tolstoy he admires especially the brilliant *Family Happiness* (a bravura achievement in which the author, Tiresias-like, recounts the *cristallisation de l'amour* from the woman's point of view); but he also notes—as have many other critics—the two faces of Tolstoy: particularly, such a contradiction between the Count's real sentiments and the excessive development of the "meek" type that we see in *Resurrection.*

As for realism in literature, Grigoriev had grave doubts about this. He recognized at least one lasting contribution of the realist movement—the importance for a writer of an exact, even a meticulous knowledge of *realia* and manners and customs (*byt*); yet he felt that realism

11. It is interesting, too, that Eliot has written that "the greatness of literature cannot be determined solely by literary standards." This statement, made in connection with Eliot's religious thinking, fits with surprising accuracy into the Russian—including the Marxist—context.

had an innate tendency to become grossly materialistic and nihilistic (and hence not "organic") and to be a mere "servile attendance on life." He believed that the practice of realism as a technical achievement was a necessary stage and that it had to, and eventually would, be exhausted and replaced. But his fears in this particular respect, for Russian literature at least, were unfounded. Though he noted in Tolstoy the persistent inclination to analyze everything to excess and though in fact Tolstoy does go to extremes—in describing, for instance, the symptoms of death with clinical and pathological detail[12]—the direction Russian realism took prevented it from even approaching an "exhaustion" of the technique. It is in France that the method is being carried to what may be its real limits.[13]

There are some especially interesting connections between Grigoriev and Dostoevsky. Of course, the critic died before he could ever know the real, mature Dostoevsky; but, although his reactions to Dostoevsky's early works were something less than favorable, he came to appreciate *The Insulted and the Injured* (1861), Dostoevsky's first long novel. There is also some development, as we shall see, of Grigoriev's ideas in Dostoevsky's thoughts on literature (Wellek goes so far as to call Dostoevsky Grigoriev's disciple). In a letter dated 1857, however, Grigoriev (writing to a friend) outlines certain concepts which we usually associate with Dostoevsky, particularly in *The Possessed* (1872) and in the "Legend of the Grand Inquisitor" in *The Brothers Karamazov* (1880). Grigoriev writes: "The ideas of Socialism and Jesuitism really coincide. . . . To the same degree both Jesuitism and Socialism transform men into swine with their snouts down—on the theory, perhaps, that they will be more contented this way." Finally, it was Dostoevsky who, faced with the vagueness of Grigoriev's theories, asked the critic to give a more precise definition of his *Weltanschauung*. The critic responded with, characteristically, his "Paradoxes of Organic Criticism." The following excerpt points up, better than anything else, the intuitional nature of Grigoriev's thought: "Life is something mysterious and inexhaustible, an abyss that engulfs all

12. In both Shakespeare (e.g., *Henry the Fifth*) and in Tolstoy (e.g., *Anna Karenina*) there is reference, rare in literature, to a sign of imminent death known as tilmus.

13. I refer to such novelists as Robbe-Grillet and Sarraute. See below, Chapter VIII, section 2, for an interesting comment by Shklovsky on Tolstoy and Sarraute.

finite reason, an unspannable ocean, the logical conclusion of the wisest brain—something even ironical, and at the same time full of love, procreating one world after another."

3

Konstantin Leontiev (1831–91) is, though Berdyaev calls him "the first Russian aesthete," more properly an Orthodox critic. A fierce enemy of enlightenment, egalitarianism, and liberalism, a defender of pogroms, and such an ultra-conservative in religion and politics that even Dostoevsky's "humanitarianism" shocked him, he defended the Byzantine heritage, glorified war (he thought that Russia needed more Vronskys and fewer Levins), and predicted that Russia would, following her downward path, ultimately bring forth the anti-Christ. Toward the end of his life, however, he thought that the Russian Tsar should "take over" and organize socialism "as Constantine organized Christianity."[14]

Leontiev is one of the most irritating critics to read, both because of his rebarbative style and the repellingly reactionary views he expresses. Thus, in discussing Tolstoy, he is apt to say such things as "we can allow this passage" or "I knew in advance when an unpleasant stumbling stone was about to appear and, almost without hesitation, I would cast it from the splendid flowering path." He likes to refer to the "laws" of aesthetics and to "noble and profound ideals," occasionally condescends (for the sake of comparing tastes) to mention "them" (i.e., Russian lower classes and servants), and is offended (much as Gorky might have been) when Tolstoy denigrates a mother's heart.

Leontiev was educated at Moscow University, where he studied medicine, and he served during the Crimean War as an army surgeon. He later entered the consular service and spent a number of years in Greece and Turkey. A marriage to a young and illiterate Greek girl was disastrous: he told her, it seems, of his numerous erotic activities and she eventually lost her mind. Leontiev's life was, to a great extent,

14. Some of Leontiev's writings are now available in English translation. See *Essays in Russian Literature. The Conservative View: Leontiev, Rozanov, Shestov*, trans. and with an Introduction by Spencer E. Roberts (Athens: Ohio University Press, 1968).

torn between very strong sexual desires and an unusually morbid sense of sin and guilt.[15] Toward the end of his life he finally took monastic vows and died at the Trinity Monastery near Moscow. Aside from his critical writings, he has left us some minor fiction and a collection of essays, *Russia, the East, and the Slavs.*

I have called Leontiev an Orthodox critic because one of the chief criticisms he levels, for example, against Tolstoy's magnificient *War and Peace* is the absence in the novel of "the clear contours of dogmatic Christianity" (elsewhere he refers to monasteries as "those salutory repositories of Christian tradition"). He also severely criticizes *Anna Karenina* for being "insufficiently religious, insufficiently Orthodox." Here, while praising the gods that Tolstoy was *not* "sufficiently Orthodox" (he was, in fact, excommunicated from the Church), we are unhappily reminded of an orthodox Marxist critic anathematizing a passage in Zamyatin or Pilnyak as lacking ideological clarity or reflecting "an unfortunately objective view of reality."

Still, despite the narrowness of Leontiev's views and the infelicities of his style, one must, after a careful reading of his criticism, recognize that he was a critic of considerable ability. Thus there is reason for Mirsky's stating that one of Leontiev's works ("Analysis, Style, and Atmosphere in the Novels of Count Tolstoy," 1890) is the "masterpiece of Russian criticism." Although it would be difficult to agree with this superlative evaluation, anyone who reads Leontiev will realize that we have in him something rather unusual on the Russian scene—a descriptive critic. Whether or not we agree with his charges, major and minor, against Tolstoy and aside from all the irritants we are exposed to in reading him, it is refreshing to encounter a Russian critic who cites chapter and verse, analyzes a passage word by word and phrase by phrase, and enlivens his close reading with pointed analysis and easy erudition.

Leontiev has the good sense to recognize that when Natasha, toward the end of *War and Peace,* appears in a living room with her baby's diapers and explains that the stains are now no longer green but yellow, the scene, though it may seem coarse to some, is relevant: Russian women (like all women, even countesses), as Leontiev notes, tend to grow a little careless after marriage and childbirth and to for-

15. Leontiev reminds one in many respects of Tolstoy. Leontiev once wrote a novel, *A Husband's Confession,* in which a middle-aged husband, unable to satisfy his young wife, urges her to have an affair with a younger man. Leontiev later rejected the novel as immoral.

get that medical details concerning their children may not really interest others.[16] But Leontiev objects to Tolstoy's psychological "eavesdropping" (*podgljadyvanie,* literally *peeping*)—when, for example, Tolstoy remarks that General Kutuzov, while speaking with an Austrian general, "listened to his own voice with pleasure." He also dislikes the nonce-formations, quaint distortions, and onomatopoetic words that occur from time to time in Tolstoy; he seems especially irked by Tolstoy's *ozhig-zhig-zhig* (to indicate the sound of a sword being sharpened) in *War and Peace.* Of Tolstoy's relentless analysis, Leontiev writes: "Tolstoy's analysis knows no bounds, neither in a character's temperament, age, nor sex; not even in zoological differences—he even shows us what a bull feels, what a dog thinks, and what a horse muses on. One notices that it is perhaps nationality that resists him more than anything else and he analyzes the French in *War and Peace* much less successfully than he does his compatriots."

As for Dostoevsky, Leontiev contrasts him and Tolstoy as has so often been done. He finds the tragedy of *War and Peace* "sober and healthy" but the tragedy in Dostoevsky is "the tragedy of flophouses and brothels." While the tragedy in *War and Peace* inspires military heroism and patriotism, Dostoevsky's tragedy "can possibly only inspire psychopaths living in poorly furnished rooms." Since Mirsky concludes his survey of Dostoevsky with the comment that "the real Dostoevsky is food that is easily assimilated only by a profoundly diseased organism," we may presume that some at least of his high opinion of Leontiev stems from the recognition of a similar judgment of Dostoevsky.

Nikolay Strakhov (1828–96) was a conservative Slavophile critic and a follower of Apollon Grigoriev. He expended considerable pains over a period of three decades in attempting to refute Darwin's theory of evolution (being a disciple in this respect of Danilevsky[17]) and he is the author of an anti-Western classic, *The Struggle with the West in Russian Literature.* Strakhov knew both Tolstoy and Dostoevsky; he collaborated with the latter as co-editor of the short-lived journal, *Time,* and wrote the first biography of Dostoevsky. But he later came to dislike Dostoevsky the man, and some of the harshest judgments we have of the novelist come from Strakhov's pen—that, for instance, Do-

16. Tolstoy writes of babies and children on the basis of extensive experience: he had thirteen children of his own (not counting illegitimate offspring).

17. Nikolay Danilevsky (1822–85), a historian and philosopher, was one of the most fanatic opponents of Darwinism in Russia.

stoevsky was "a malicious, envious, and immoral man."[18] Even worse is the accusation made by Strakhov that Dostoevsky had at one time boasted to a certain Professor Viskovatov that, with the connivance of a governess, he had once raped a little girl in a bathhouse.

4

The great age of Russian realism, primarily an age of prose fiction, was interrupted in the early 1880s by the beginnings of another period, very rich and productive in all the arts in Russia, which is usually and in very general terms called Russian Modernism. This was not at all a phenomenon peculiar to Russia but rather part of a European neo-romantic movement. Within this period, which in Russia extended in free development down to 1917 but which thereafter was more and more curtailed by the exigencies of official Soviet ideology, there were a number of particular literary movements (the age was now primarily poetic), of which Symbolism and Futurism are perhaps the best known. Beginning shortly after the Revolution (and with a vengeance after 1932), there was a return, again in accordance with Soviet literary doctrine, to something that was called realism. A landmark for the beginning of this so-called Silver Age and, more specifically, for its early Symbolist phase is the year 1894, the year in which there appeared a collection of poems entitled *Russian Symbolists* edited by a twenty-year-old student at Moscow University, Valery Bryusov.[19]

The principal literary critics associated with this Modernist period will be discussed in Chapter VII. In the next chapter, however, we must turn our attention to two figures who, while not being professional critics, hold such eminent places in Russian literature that they cannot be ignored. Both Tolstoy and Dostoevsky were, in different ways, extremely conscious of the problems of art and literature, and, like Pushkin, they have left us explicit dicta concerning the meaning or function of a literary work. Tolstoy, who had the "polytropic" mind of an Odysseus, may legitimately be considered at least an amateur critic, having written a minor classic in the field. On the other hand,

18. Turgenev once said that Dostoevsky was "the most vicious Christian" he had ever met.

19. See below, Chapter VII, section 4.

Dostoevsky's influence on literature and the creative arts in general (not to mention Nietzsche and Freud) has been much more significant, and his name, as we shall see, is especially relevant in the context of Modernism.

SUGGESTED READING

Annenkov, P. V., *The Extraordinary Decade*, ed. A. P. Mendel (Ann Arbor: University of Michigan Press, 1968).

Grigoriev, Apollon, *My Literary and Moral Wanderings*, trans. by Ralph Matlaw (New York: Dutton, 1962).

Roberts, Spencer, ed., *Essays in Russian Literature: The Conservative View* (Athens: Ohio University Press, 1968), contains Leontiev's study of Tolstoy.

Ivask, George, ed., *Against the Current* (New York: Weybright & Talley, 1969), contains a few selections from Leontiev's critical articles.

Gifford, Henry, ed., *Leo Tolstoy* (Harmondsworth: Penguin Critical Anthologies, 1971), contains two brief excerpts from articles by Strakhov on Tolstoy.

Gerstein, Linda, *Nikolai Strakhov* (Cambridge: Harvard University Press, 1971).

Wellek, René, *A History of Modern Criticism: 1750–1950* (New Haven: Yale University Press, 1955–65), Vol. IV, Chapter 12.

Mirsky, D. S., *A History of Russian Literature* (New York: Alfred A. Knopf, 1949), Book One, Chapter 7.

VI TOLSTOY AND DOSTOEVSKY

1

Tolstoy was, to use Burckhardt's phrase, one of the "*terribles simplificateurs*" in European thought (nowhere can we see a better example of Russian "maximalism" than in his notorious essay, *What Is Art?*); and it is remarkable that, following the slight *détente* provided by the conservative critics, we should not only find an ethical Civic view again expressed in the late writings of this enigmatic count (Lenin once called him "the mirror of the Revolution") but find this view reduced to its extreme, its ultimate form. Yet the intensity of Tolstoy's moral vision has its affiliations not so much with his Civic predecessors as with the French *Éclaircissement*. Even if Sir Isaiah Berlin had not pointed this out for us in his brilliant essay, "Tolstoy and Enlightenment,"[1] one familiar with Tolstoy's writings could not read very far, for example, into Peter Gay's *The Enlightenment: An Interpretation* without recognizing some striking parallels. For example:

> The philosophes' attack on fancy was not an attack on imagination but on thought ungrounded in life.
>
> I call the Enlightenment's realism *moral* because whatever channel of expression it used—anticlerical mockery or political polemics—its vital center was a moral vision of the world. "The truth I love," wrote Rousseau in 1761, in harmony on this point with all the other philosophes, "is not so much metaphysical as moral."[2]

1. This essay is included in *Tolstoy: A Collection of Critical Essays* (Englewood Cliffs, N.J.: Prentice-Hall, 1967).

2. *The Enlightenment: An Interpretation* (New York: Random House Vintage Book, 1968), p. 179. Tolstoy thought highly of Rousseau and, when he was young, used to wear a medallion with a picture of Rousseau around his neck.

Tolstoy's own concern with moral truths culminated in 1880 in the form of his *Confession,* a work which Mirsky, using the Thucydidean tag, calls a *ktēma es aei* ("a possession for all time"). This magnificent composition, one of the great confessional documents in a notable European tradition, generally serves as a convenient dividing point in much Tolstoy criticism between the "two" Tolstoys—Tolstoy the artist and Tolstoy the preacher (although the division is by no means so clear cut). Some seventeen years after the *Confession,* in 1897, there appeared the essay with which we shall be primarily concerned in this section—*What Is Art?* This work is again the culmination of the author's long years of preoccupation with, specifically, the morality of art and literature. It is a work, aside from the influence of French Enlightenment thought or of Rousseau or of anyone else, that stands squarely in the Platonic tradition. "As Tolstoy is going to find later," Vernon Hall writes, "Plato found that he had to betray his own art because he discovered something he believed to be greater."[3]

The most striking (for some readers, the most horrendous) aspect of *What Is Art?* is the brutal decimation of practically all that readers and critics of the most diverse persuasions have, down through the years, considered to be great and lasting works of art. Here, too, Tolstoy is the inveterate *netovshchik* or "nay-sayer" (the word is Vyazemsky's), the fierce debunker of accepted standards. He dismisses, amongst others, Aeschylus, Sophocles, Euripides, Aristophanes, Dante, Tasso, Shakespeare, Milton, Goethe, and all the moderns—Zola, Ibsen, Maeterlinck, Verlaine, Mallarmé, and so on (he is particularly hard on the Symbolists). Among the painters, Tolstoy condemns as spurious art the works of Raphael and Michelangelo, for instance, as well as the paintings of such admittedly lesser men as Puvis de Chavannes and Boecklin. Beethoven, Bach, Brahms, Berlioz, Liszt, and Wagner (to cite only the more notable names) are also summarily repudiated as great artists. All critics are excoriated, upon their heads being laid, mercilessly, the chief blame for the general perversion of taste. What then *is* great and authentic art for Tolstoy? He singles out the following works of literature as examples of the highest art: Schiller's *Die Räuber,* Hugo's *Les Pauvres Gens* and *Les Misérables,* Dickens' *A Tale of Two Cities* and *A Christmas Carol,* Harriet Beecher Stowe's *Uncle Tom's Cabin,* George Elliot's *Adam Bede,* and Dostoevsky's *Memoirs from the House of the Dead.* As representatives of merely

3. *A Short History of Literary Criticism* (New York: New York University Press, 1963), p. 1.

"good" art he further cites *The Pickwick Papers* and *David Copperfield, Don Quixote,* the comedies of Molière, and several stories by Pushkin, Gogol, and Maupassant. Several examples of primitive and popular art—the Biblical story of Joseph, Russian folk songs, and the "theater" of the Voguls (a Siberian tribe)—are also rated highly. Since Tolstoy was quite insensitive to poetry (the conventions of verse struck him as especially artificial and affected), the poets are virtually ignored. Finally, Tolstoy condemns, along with so many works of others, all his own fiction—including the two great novels—with the exception of two stories, *God Sees the Truth and Waits* and *A Captive in the Caucasus.*

A glance at the names of those many artists and works rejected and those few accepted will give only a vague idea of the actual criteria used by Tolstoy in making his resolute judgments; yet we can note one or two common features. Tolstoy here, as elsewhere in his widely ranging thought, seems to be observing the dictum, *simplex signum veri,* and equating the "true" with greatness in art. But it is exactly here that we must, while concurring with some of his inclusions and exclusions, strongly disagree on the whole. We no longer look for "truth"—much less "*the* truth"—in art, and we feel that much great art is valuable precisely because it deals with and reflects the complexities of reality and especially the complexities of the human psyche. We also note in Tolstoy's selections the compelling influence of the "repentant nobleman" theme[4] and, in general, a predilection for works showing compassion for human suffering. But here again, although we recognize the importance of and necessity for compassion, we do not set it up as a criterion for greatness in art or literature. Indeed, not only do we feel that there is something maudlin and quite irrelevant in such "criticism," but we have now become diabused of the idea that the reading of humanitarian, compassionate, and even religious literature makes men better.

Tolstoy believed further that the best and highest art derives from a "love for God and man." But this view, too, is dogmatic and one-sided. There is a dark side and there is evil, and these, too, are the material of art. Unlike Dostoevsky, Tolstoy lacked what Keats called the poet's "negative capability"—the willingness of the writer or artist to entertain or tolerate uncertainties, perplexities, and doubts. And as for tragedy, even the residual Christianity which Tolstoy pre-

4. The phrase "repentant nobleman" was given currency by the critic Mikhaylovsky. See below, section 4.

served was enough, it seems, to rule out not only a tragic vision of life but any appreciation of literary tragedy as well. Christianity—like communism—is quite inimical to tragedy; as one critic has written:

> With its emphasis on the moral order of the world, on Original Sin, and the Last Judgment, on submission and humility, Christianity is in every sense antagonistic to the spirit of tragedy. Tragedy, as it represents the struggle of man with Fate, and as it often expresses vividly to our eyes inexplicable evils and undeserved sufferings, has always something profane and blasphemous in it.[5]

The religiosity of Tolstoy, as we see it in *What Is Art?*, although we may sympathize with his attempts (utterly futile as they have always been) to live by the radical Christianity of the Sermon on the Mount, is quite different from the religiosity of the artist as expressed by D. H. Lawrence (in a letter to Ernest Collins): "One has to be so terribly religious to be an artist. I often think of my dear St. Lawrence on his gridiron when he said, 'Turn me over, brothers, I am done enough on this side.'" But I. A. Richards has, with respect to the question of belief and disbelief and its literary relevance, expressed a point of view which many of us share today, regardless of our personal theology: "The question of belief or disbelief, in the intellectual sense, never arises when we are reading well. If unfortunately it does arise, either through the poet's fault or our own, we have for the moment ceased to be reading and have become astronomers, or theologians, or moralists, persons engaged in quite a different type of activity."[6]

Tolstoy stressed the importance of the simple man, the "man of the people," in the judgment of art. Great art cannot appeal only to a clique but must be comprehensible to the masses; and it is one of the functions of art, Tolstoy claims further, to unite. *First* Tolstoy decides what is great art and *then* he glibly concludes, "it cannot be said that the majority of people do not have the taste to esteem the highest works of art. The majority have always understood and understand now what we, too, recognize as the very best art: the story of Genesis, the Gospel parables, folk legends, fairy tales, and folk songs are understood by all." Tolstoy put great store by the taste of the common man *par excellence,* i.e., the peasant—man still uncontaminated (he would have us believe) by the over-sophisticated and corrupt man-

5. Chu Kwang-tsien, *The Psychology of Tragedy* (Strasbourg, 1933), p. 236.

6. *Practical Criticism* (New York: Harcourt, Brace, 1956), p. 277.

ners and tastes of urban Western culture. Here again D. H. Lawrence speaks to the point:

> We know now that the peasant is no better than anybody else; no better than a prince or a selfish young army officer or a governor or a merchant. In fact, in the mass, the peasant is worse than any of these. The peasant mass is the ugliest of all human masses, most greedily selfish and brutal of all. Which Tolstoy, leaning down from the gold bar of heaven, will have had opportunity to observe. If we have to trust to a *mass,* then better trust the upper or middle-class mass, all masses being odious.[7]

Great art must also, Tolstoy tells us, be sincere. And it is here, in connection with this doctrine (hardly a unique one), that the most interesting aspect of *What Is Art?*, from the "technical" point of view, comes to the fore. If a work of art is really sincere, it will immediately communicate this to the reader (or listener or viewer); rather, in Tolstoy's terminology, it will "infect" him. Though this notorious "infection (*zarazhenie*) theory" of art is most often associated with Tolstoy, the latter adopted it from *L'Esthétique* (1878) of Eugène Véron (*"l'artiste vraiment ému n'a doue qu'à s'abandonner à son émotion pour que son émotion devienne contagieuse"*). This emotionalist theory of art seems at first a strange product of a rationalist mind; yet we may recall the explicit ambivalence of Tolstoy's idol, Rousseau, in this respect—"My rule to trust sentiment rather than reason is confirmed by reason itself." It is still interesting, however, that the whole theory, such as it is, has been given a sort of physiological or "fleshly" basis, reminding us of the famous "catharsis" theory of Aristotle.

The conclusions reached in *What Is Art?* served as the theoretical foundation for another work by Tolstoy published in 1906 (an English translation appeared in the same year). This was the essay, "On Shakespeare and on the Drama," in which Tolstoy gives vent to his longstanding dislike of the Bard, a dislike which he had earlier expressed on many occasions and which grew deeper as time went on. "Several times," he wrote, "I read the dramas and the comedies and the historical plays, and I invariably experienced the same feelings: repulsion, weariness, and bewilderment." This reaction on the part of Tolstoy

7. From Lawrence's Introduction to Verga's *Cavalleria Rusticana,* quoted by Donald Davie, ed., *Russian Literature and Modern English Fiction* (Chicago: University of Chicago Press, 1965), p. 146.

stands in striking contrast to the overwhelmingly favorable and enthusiastic reception of Shakespeare in Russia, from the seventeenth century down to and including the Soviet period. Some of Tolstoy's charges and methods remind us of those of Voltaire, who ridiculed Shakespeare—as has been a common practice in France—on the basis of arch-conservative classicist criteria. Tolstoy seems to be most irked by the lack of simplicity of language and the absence of religious and moral didacticism in Shakespeare. But he also dislikes the "unnatural" events and speeches, the contrived and "artificial" situations, the vulgarity of the language, and the unfavorable portrayal of the lower classes as well as the demeaning names that Shakespeare gave to such characters (Starveling, Grindstone, Shallow, etc.). He has, in general, *very* little good to say of Shakespeare (he thought, however, that Falstaff was a good character and that *Othello* was the "least bad play by Shakespeare"), and there is no doubt that some of his judgments were the results simply of insufficient acquaintance with the English language or of basing stylistic evaluations on translations. Thus Tolstoy shows no appreciation whatsoever of Shakespeare's puns and metaphors, and he makes the almost incredible statement (one that has been made of Tolstoy himself) that all of Shakespeare's characters speak the same language.

In a masterly essay (already referred to) by Sir Isaiah Berlin, "The Hedgehog and the Fox," the author, on the basis of a Greek proverb (which may be translated "The fox knows many things, but the hedgehog knows one big thing"), divides writers, artists, and thinkers into two categories: those who relate everything to a single central vision and those who, spurning any overall unifying belief, pursue many ends. In the first category we would include such men as Plato, Dante, and Dostoevsky amongst others; in the second, Aristotle, Montaigne, and Pushkin. As we might expect, Sir Isaiah places both Shakespeare and Tolstoy in the latter category, both being "foxes." But the burden of the essay is that Tolstoy, though a "fox" by nature, sought all his life—and most desperately toward the end—some unitary, simple, and fundamental Truth; that he wanted, in short, to turn himself into a "hedgehog."

Though nothing will diminish the lasting appeal of Tolstoy the "seer of the flesh," of his great novels, and of his infinite variety (which embraces *What Is Art?*), and though we can understand and sympathize with his search and even agree, in part, with some of the basic premises of his aesthetic theory, the extreme conclusions he reached in his late years are frankly absurd and repugnant. Perhaps the best comments on *What Is Art?* and such an equally notorious work as *The Kreutzer Sonata,* as well as the late didactic stories, are two statements found in the ninth chapter of Longinus' *On the Sublime:* "Homer shows that when a great genius is falling into decline, it is a characteristic of his old age that he should be fond of fables," and "I have digressed in this way in order to demonstrate how a great spirit in his decline may very easily be misled into writing nonsense."

2

Dostoevsky never summarized in one work, as did Tolstoy, his overall aesthetic and critical doctrine, but he has left us, in letters, diaries, and notes, many *obiter dicta* expressing both theoretical and practical opinions. In general, except for some early, very idealistic reflections on the Good and the Beautiful (where we see the influence of Schiller), his aesthetic views follow those of Grigoriev, especially in the emphasis on organicism. But regardless of certain changing views (notably with respect to Schiller[8]), he stood firm in opposing and rejecting the utilitarian view of art as advanced by the Civic critics.

Though a character like Myshkin in *The Idiot* remarks that "Beauty will save the world" and though the cult of the Good and the Beautiful is severely belabored in *Notes from Underground,* it is quite impossible to draw any general conclusions from such passages. Unlike Tolstoy, in whose fiction we can clearly distinguish between characters who are voicing "sensible" opinions shared by the author, and characters—they usually talk nonsense—who express concepts repugnant to the author, in the fiction of Dostoevsky there is no such overall clarity.[9] Distinctions, especially between good and evil, are blurred. This feature of Dostoevsky's fiction, along with many other features, makes him quite unacceptable in the Socialist Realist tradition of Soviet Russia: in this tradition, first and foremost, an author must make unambiguously clear the distinction between good and evil (in the special Marxist sense of these words) and must leave no lingering doubts as to exactly where his sympathies lie. It must also be kept in

8. See above, Chapter III, section 3, on Belinsky.

9. See below, Chapter IX, section 6, on Bakhtin and his term "polyphonic" as applied to Dostoevsky's novels.

mind that very often Dostoevsky's literary and aesthetic judgments were in great part prompted by other than objective evaluation; this is paricularly true of his opinions of Turgenev, man and writer, whom he heartily despised.[10] It is also true of his fulsome eulogy of Pushkin in his famous "Pushkin Speech" of 1880.

The most interesting and perhaps the most important aspect of Dostoevsky's criticism is his practice and theory of realism, and it was in this area that he noted a major difference between his own fictional style and those of his predecessors and contemporaries. Dostoevsky uses the noun *realist* in two ways: as applied to his contemporaries, it is used pejoratively and deprecatingly, as if the word were indeed in quotes or preceded by "so-called"; and as applied to himself in another sense that he makes quite clear. Thus, in an oft-quoted letter to A. Maykov in 1868, he wrote: "I have completely different ideas about reality [*dejstvitel'nost'*] and realism [*realizm*] than do our realists and critics. My idealism is more real than their realism. Good Lord! If one simply recounted everything that all of us Russians have experienced in the past ten years in our spiritual development, would not the realists shout that this was fantasy? And yet this was pure, authentic realism! *This* is what realism is, only deeper, but they merely skim the surface." In the following year, in a letter to N. Strakhov, he wrote: "I have my own special view of reality in art and what most people call almost fantastic and exceptional sometimes constitutes for me the very essence of what is real." Finally, in his *Diary of a Writer* for 1873, Dostoevsky wrote: "They say that we must represent reality as it is; but there is simply no such reality at all and never has been, since the essence of things is inaccessible to man, while he perceives nature as it is reflected in his idea after it has passed through his senses. Therefore we should give more leeway to the idea and not fear the ideal."

Although other writers and artists, at other times and in other countries, have expressed similar ideas (we note especially the Kantian epistemology in the last quotation), one thing is clear: Dostoevsky, like Belinsky in his earlier quoted definition of *realism*, is enunciating not so much a purely literary technique as a philosophical or metaphysical approach, and he is obviously using the word *realism* (as applied to his own method) in a sense very close to that of "Platonic realism" or idealism. In other words, Dostoevsky's realism

10. One of the cruelest portrayals of one writer by another is found in *The Possessed* where Dostoevsky caricatures Turgenev in the figure of Karmazinov.

is almost the opposite of traditional literary realism (as defined, for example, by Engels: "To my mind, reality implies, in addition to truthful detail, a truthful reproduction of typical circumstances"). This is made even clearer by another statement by Dostoevsky as reported by Strakhov: "I am called a psychologist. Not true. I am rather a realist in a higher sense—that is, I depict all the profundities of the human soul." The ultimate source of this theory is very probably Plato, via the German idealistic thought so prevalent in Russia since the thirties of the nineteenth century, but it involves concepts which might very well have been reached independently. In any case, it was this "idealistic realism" (the Germans call it *Idealrealismus*) in Dostoevsky, along with his tendency to blur distinctions in an implicit rather than explicit context, that attracted later Russian Symbolist theoreticians and commentators on Dostoevsky such as Vyacheslav Ivanov. It is, by the way, of interest that Dostoevsky's favorite Russian poet was Tyutchev and that Ivanov, in tracing the sources of Russian Symbolism, takes us back precisely to Tyutchev.

But the whole problem of realism in literature is a knotty one, and a great deal has been written on the subject.[11] We can overlook the various sub-classes of realism which have proliferated in the Russian critical literature to an alarming degree (radical realism, critical realism, *byt*-realism, manor realism, etc.). Perhaps the most troublesome term is "romantic realism," the awkwardness here being due, however, to a largely false opposition of romanticism versus realism. Harry Levin speaks of the realism of the romanticists as having its dialectical counterpart in the romanticism of the realists and Jacques Barzun has some provocative comments on the development of realism *out of* romanticism.[12] Donald Fanger has written a convincing study of this problem in connection with Dostoevsky—*Dostoevsky and Romantic Realism* (1965).

In line with his own conception of the "real," Dostoevsky was highly critical of the literary realism of Goncharov: it was too static, too much preoccupied with the minute, the banal, and the particular. It lacked movement, action, and the dramatic, even melodramatic, qualities that Dostoevsky admired and favored—notoriously, one might

11. Good summaries and discussions may be found in Wellek's essay, "The Concept of Realism in Literary Scholarship" (in *Concepts of Criticism*) and Levin's "What Is Realism?" (in *Contexts of Criticism*).

12. *Classic, Romantic, and Modern* (New York: Doubleday Anchor Book, 1961), Chapter IV.

say—in his own novels. He greatly admired Gogol (he is said to have claimed that Russian writers since Gogol came from beneath *The Overcoat*) and, of course, Pushkin. Dostoevsky never met Tolstoy, but he had great respect for him as an artist, although he disapproved of the "manor" or "landowner" realism in *War and Peace* and the great attention paid to the nostalgic details of an earlier and irretrievable age. He praised the poetry of Victor Hugo and he was ecstatic in his admiration of Balzac whose novels, he claimed, were the product of a "universal mind."[13] Scott he read from childhood, and he felt an affinity with Dickens, an affinity which has been noted by subsequent critics. Unlike Tolstoy but like most Russian men of letters, he loved Shakespeare. He literally worshipped Schiller when he was young, later became disenchanted (after his arrest and deportation), and then later became again a devotee of the German poet. Nor can we forget Dostoevsky's love of the Bible (his favorite was the Book of Job) and his extensive reading of the lives of the saints and the works of St. Dmitry of Rostov (seventeenth century) and St. Tikhon of Zadonsk (eighteenth century).

In the history of Russian criticism, however, Dostoevsky is perhaps not so important in his own right as he is an inspirer of other, later critics and as providing an especially rich mine of material for critical interpretation. Dostoevsky's name, as we shall see in the following chapter, is remarkably prominent in the writings of the next generation of critics.

3

The fame of Ivan Turgenev (1818–83) as a novelist has been eclipsed by that of Tolstoy and Dostoevsky. But he was, of the "great three," the most European in his sympathies and tastes, both literary and otherwise, and he was the first major Russian novelist to be appreciated and to exert influences in the West. The reason for this is that he had fewer extreme views and less of the peculiarly Russian genius, with its particular extravagances and religiously held opinions, than did either Tolstoy or Dostoevsky. He also had, despite the cruel and quite unfair

13. Dostoevsky's first literary venture was a translation of Balzac's *Eugénie Grandet* in 1844.

caricature of him in Dostoevsky's *The Possessed,* a rather modest opinion of his own virtues as a writer. Thus he once wrote (and this is a good example of auto-criticism): "When I do not have to deal with concrete figures, I am completely lost and do not know where to turn. It always seems that I might just as well have said the opposite of what I said. But if I am talking about a red rose and blonde hair, then the hair is blonde and the rose is red—no amount of thinking will change that."

Dostoevsky, as was noted, despised Turgenev for a number of reasons: his religious agnosticism, his wealth and freedom to travel extensively, his admiration of Western Europe, and his cavalier and ironic attitude toward Russia, her problems, and her destiny. Tolstoy did not think much of Turgenev's literary style, and their relationship was often touch-and-go. Tolstoy once called Turgenev a scoundrel, and Turgenev once referred to Tolstoy's *Lucerne* (1857) as "a mixture of Rousseau, Thackeray, and the Shorter Orthodox Catechism." In 1861 they had a furious quarrel in the house of Fet, and Tolstoy challenged Turgenev to a duel, but apologies on both sides prevented an actual confrontation. Years later, Turgenev, who was, like many others, much concerned with Tolstoy's growing preoccupation with extraliterary pursuits, wrote him a famous letter, urging him to return to literature.

Unlike both Tolstoy and Dostoevsky, Turgenev loved the West and spent a good deal of his time abroad, joining freely in literary gatherings, and he was on intimate terms with many of the famous writers of France—Hugo, Flaubert, Zola, Daudet, and Edmond de Goncourt. Turgenev revered the masters of French prose but did not think much of French poetry, with the exception of Leconte de Lisle: he once remarked to the Russian poet Fet that de Lisle, "although a Frenchman," was a real poet. The English in particular have always been partial to Turgenev (they like especially *A Huntsman's Sketches*), and John Galsworthy, as a fascinating essay by Ford Maddox Ford tells us, was quite enraptured by Turgenev.[14] In 1879 Oxford University conferred an honorary doctorate upon Turgenev. American writers also interested the Russian novelist, and he had compliments for Hawthorne, Longfellow, and Howells. He also admired Walt Whitman and made plans to translate some of his poems but nothing came of these. Although the poetic and lyrical qualities of Turgenev's prose have often been commented upon, he himself was rather heavy-handed

14. This essay is reprinted in Davie, cited above in note 7.

with the actual techniques of versification; thus he once edited some of Tyutchev's verses and "corrected" the poet's amphibrachic feet.

In striking contrast to Tolstoy's severely moral involvement in literature and Dostoevsky's ardent nationalism and intensely serious theory of realism is Turgenev's typically offhand remark (recorded in the Goncourt Journal) to the effect that, since the Russians are a lying people, the natural result of centuries of slavery, they like truth and realism in art! Though, as he admits himself, Turgenev was not strong in abstract analysis and interpretation, he did write a rather important typological study which is especially relevant in Russian literature. This is his essay entitled "Hamlet and Don Quixote" (1860) in which, like so many other thinkers in so many similar essays,[15] Turgenev divides mankind into two broad categories: the skeptics whose interminable rumination and hesitation prevent resolute action; and those naive idealists who dare to take action, but often in ludicrous ways. Turgenev also popularized the phrase "superfluous man" through his *Diary of a Superfluous Man* (1850), although it was Dobrolyubov, as mentioned earlier, who elaborated on the literary significance of the type.

There is some criticism—again quite offhand—in Turgenev's *Literary Reminiscences*,[16] but not much; there are, however, some important comments on Belinsky. Thus Turgenev tells us how enraptured the St. Petersburg reading public was in 1836 when some verse by Vladimir Benediktov appeared, and how infuriated this same reading public was by Belinsky's negative evaluation of the poet. Turgenev, too, was enraged, but he admits that he had a sneaking suspicion that Belinsky was, after all, right. "A short while passed," Turgenev wrote, "and I no longer read Benediktov. Today who does not know that the opinions expressed by Belinsky at that time, opinions which struck us as blasphemy, are now accepted by all as, as the English say, a 'truism'? Posterity has corroborated that verdict as it has many others reached by that judge."

15. Cf. Heine's "Hebrews and Hellenes," Coleridge's "Platonists and Aristotelians," Berlin's "Hedgehogs and Foxes," etc.

16. See *Turgenev's Literary Reminiscences*, trans. by David Magarshack (New York: Minerva Press, 1968).

4

Ivan Goncharov (1812–91) was one of the major Russian novelists of the nineteenth century and especially famous as the author of *Oblomov,* a novel which has stimulated the writing of many a controversial essay, including Dobrolyubov's "What is Oblomovism?" mentioned earlier in Chapter IV. In his youth Goncharov, who spent most of his life in the civil service, was sympathetic to the ideas of Belinsky but remained throughout his later life a "liberal conservative," primarily interested in describing reality rather than in altering it. In addition to his several novels, he wrote a number of critical essays, the best known of which is his study of Griboedov's comedy, *Wit Works Woe,* entitled "A Million Torments" (*Mil'on terzanij,* 1872), a minor classic in Russian criticism. Griboedov's comedy (which is written in verse) is a marvelous creation and has with justification been lavishly praised by both Russian prose writers and poets: thus Blok called it "perhaps the greatest work in our literature" and a play "unique in world literature." Goncharov, who was especially interested in literary types (he once criticized in a letter to Dostoevsky the latter's "improbable" characters), is also liberal with his praise. He has some succinct comments on the spontaneity, wit, and satire of Griboedov's "colloquial verse" in which the author has managed to capture the lively Russian intelligence as a wizard might enchant and lock up a spirit in a castle.

Goncharov argues that, for all of Pushkin's and Lermontov's genius, their famous characters, Onegin and Pechorin, have become history and grow "petrified in immobility like statues on tombs." No longer, he writes, do we find traces of these personalities in the present age, although they will endure in literature. But Griboedov's play, although it appeared earlier than Onegin and Pechorin,[17] has outlived these heroes: "It passed unscathed through the Gogolian period, . . . is still living with vigor unabated," and will never lose its vitality. Goncharov devotes considerable attention to Chatsky, the principal character of the comedy, who suffers the "million torments" in his

17. The comedy was completed in 1824 but was not approved by the censor. Fragments were published in 1825 and a heavily censored text appeared in 1833. The full text of the play was not printed until 1861.

bouts with a philistine society and its fatuous denizens; here Goncharov's interest in Chatsky, "one of the most un-Oblomov-like figures in Russian literature" (R. Poggioli), is itself noteworthy. Acknowledging the sketchiness of Chatsky's characterization as a mere apparent shortcoming due to the fact that "the strict objectivity of the dramatic form does not permit that sweep and fullness of the brushstroke that we find in the epic form" (he is referring to Onegin), Goncharov repeats that Chatsky's nature is inexhaustible. With this we cannot argue, since it has in fact traditionally allowed the part of Chatsky to serve as a touchstone for Russian actors: "Great Chatskys are as rare and as highly valued in Russia as are great Hamlets" (Mirsky).

5

Alexander Ostrovsky (1823–86) was a major Russian dramatist, and his name has already been mentioned in preceding chapters in connection with the criticism of Dobrolyubov and Grigoriev. In addition to his many plays, he also wrote folklore fantasies such as *The Snow Maiden* (*Snegurochka*) which has become well known in the form of Rimsky-Korsakov's opera of the same name; and he is often rightfully acknowledged as the first modern stage director in the Russian theater. As a critic, Ostrovsky noted (in 1850) an anomalous situation in Russian literature: whereas in the other European literatures critical and—to use his term—"accusatory" fiction was apt to be of secondary importance, in Russian literature the reverse was true. The Russian reading public expected that the best art should be primarily critical, condemning contemporary faults and shortcomings in society. For Ostrovsky himself, the more aesthetically satisfying a work of fiction is, the more "accusatory" elements it will contain and the more national it will be. This, almost a classical statement of what Russian "realism" is or should be, reminds us of the criteria used today by not only dissident and expatriate Russians in evaluating such a writer as Solzhenitsyn but also by Marxist critics in judging Soviet works. But the particular critical elements that are acceptable in each case are, as we shall see, quite different.

Mikhail Saltykov (1826–89), who wrote under the pen-name of "N. Shchedrin" and who is generally referred to as Saltykov-Shchedrin, was primarily a satirist. The author of numerous satirical sketches and stories, he is also famous for at least two longer works, *The History of a Town* (1870) and *The Golovlev Family* (1880). The latter novel, a minor classic, contains a striking account of the decline and fall of a family of provincial gentry and a relentless portrayal of one of the "great" hypocrites of Russian literature, Porfiry Golovlev. Saltykov knew Russia and the Russian bureaucracy very well, having risen in the civil service (despite a period of exile resulting from his criticism of social iniquities) to the rank of provincial vice-governor.

Like Mikhaylovsky (see below), Saltykov adhered rather closely, from the forties to the seventies, to the radical critical tradition of Belinsky and Chernyshevsky. He was an outspoken critic of both the doctrine of "art for art's sake" and the naturalism of such popular French writers as Zola and the Goncourt brothers. Having himself developed a theory of "positive types" which drew heavily on Chernyshevsky's novel, *What Is to Be Done?,* he criticized Goncharov's last novel, *The Precipice* (1869) as representing a decline in "realistic" art in contrast to the same author's earlier *Oblomov.* Saltykov, who was for several years co-editor of two radical journals, *The Contemporary* and *Fatherland Notes,* also engaged in polemics with Dostoevsky who, with his brother, briefly edited the conservative journal *Time.* Saltykov attacked Dostoevsky on two notable occasions. The first was in an article entitled "Presumptuous Fedya" to which Dostoevsky, who seldom let criticism go unanswered, replied by a parody of Saltykov in *The Idiot.* In 1864, following the publication of Dostoevsky's *Notes from Underground,* Saltykov again bitterly attacked the author in an article, "To the Swifts: A Message to the Chief Swift, Mr. Dostoevsky." Referring to the *Notes* as "Notes on the Immortality of the Soul," Saltykov obviously takes delight in making fun of the rambling style of Dostoevsky's work ("The world is in chaos, Dostoevsky has a pain in the back, all men are good-for-nothing scoundrels," etc.) and claims that Dostoevsky gets his arguments mainly from St. Thomas Aquinas but leads his readers to believe that these are his own.

Saltykov-Shchedrin also disliked Tolstoy's *Anna Karenina* which he described by using an expression, as one modern Russian critic (Weidlé) puts it, "we can only translate politely as a 'gynecological novel.'" Finally, Saltykov added to Russian critical terminology by introducing the term "Aesopic language" (*èzopovskij jazyk*). This refers to the use of a highly allusive language, a language of significant but indirect and oblique statement (often, as in the case of some of Saltykov's own writing, requiring a commentary) designed to allow seditious, blasphemous, and iconoclastic ideas to bypass the censor. Dissident Soviet writers have also used this device, although they are up against censors with the accumulated expertise of almost two centuries.

Nikolay Mikhaylovsky (1842–1904), born into an impoverished noble family, was a "repentant nobleman" (*kajushchijsja dvorjanin*—the phrase is his own) and a radical journalist. He holds a rather important position in Russian political thought, and his influence on the Russian Populist movement and the Social Revolutionaries was considerable. Mikhaylovsky was a continuator of the Civic tradition in criticism, emphasizing the writer's service to society and constantly searching for a "message." His name is most notably associated with that of Dostoevsky. In an essay entitled "A Cruel Talent" (1882) he sets the tone for a good deal of subsequent Dostoevsky criticism by noting the novelist's preoccupation with suffering, pain, and humiliation. Mikhaylovsky finds this preoccupation morbid and sadistic, quite outweighing any elements of compassion and sympathy. Not only, he claims, does Dostoevsky torture his characters, but he torments his readers as well! Yet Mikhaylovsky does not really come to grips with the "dark" side of Dostoevsky or the problem of evil nor does he have any conception of Dostoevsky's "negative capability." On one occasion, in discussing *The Brothers Karamazov,* Mikhaylovsky refers to Dostoevsky as a "digger of treasure"; Lev Shestov (see the following chapter) later suggested that here Mikhaylovsky came close—but only close—to an understanding of the real Dostoevsky.

He criticizes the novelist (as Dobrolyubov did earlier) for having all his characters speak the same language, and, like Belinsky, he objects to the atypical characters in Dostoevsky's works—Raskolnikov, for example, or the conspirators in *The Possessed.* But, reading this novel in America of the seventies, we are struck precisely by the verisimilitude and typicality of these figures. On aesthetic grounds he finds fault with the lack of proportion in Dostoevsky's fiction, with the exception of a few short stories and—most notably—*Memoirs from the House of the Dead.* Yet one cannot help but suspect that his criteria here, too, are more Civic in nature than aesthetic.

A key term in Mikhaylovsky's criticism of Dostoevsky is the word *causelessness* (*besprichinnost'*). Thus he finds no satisfactory reason for the appearance of the second Golyadkin in *The Double* aside from merely providing a "second level of suffering" for Golyadkin, i.e., to afford the author further opportunities to indulge his penchant for depicting humiliation and anguish. As for Dostoevsky's *Notes from*

Underground (and Mikhaylovsky was the first to note and comment upon the central importance of this work in any attempt to understand Dostoevsky as a whole), the critic again sees no connection, either logical or artistic, between the first and second parts, a view which reveals his almost perverse blindness when it comes to Dostoevsky.

Mikhaylovsky has a higher opinion of Tolstoy, whom he visited on numerous occasions. He was impressed by Tolstoy's wit and urbanity as well as by his sincerity, although he was somewhat taken aback by the Count's rejection of the aristocratic traditions of his own class, and he was in sympathy with and defended Tolstoy's pedagogical theories.[18] It is to Mikhaylovsky's credit that he was able to detect at an early date the signs of the crisis of conscience toward which Tolstoy was moving and, in effect, to predict his development after 1880. He noted, too, the essentially anarchical nature of Tolstoy's thought and set forth his comments in what is now a minor classic of Tolstoy criticism, "The Left and Right Hands of Count L. N. Tolstoy" (1875). Yet this essay, interesting as it is in many details, is only one of a large number of studies concerned almost solely with the psychology of Tolstoy rather than with his fictional works and his formal achievements as a creative writer.

As for Chekhov, Mikhaylovsky, always judging literature on the basis of rigorously stringent moral ideals, at first was repelled; he had noticed an "evil fire" in Chekhov's eyes and even warned Russian readers of the moral perils immanent in the Chekhovian "poetry of hopelessness." Still, he recognized Chekhov's talent, but only in the short forms; he thus criticized *The Steppe,* one of Chekhov's longest stories, as being "shapeless," without, it seems, any real understanding of the author's intentions—and success—in the treatment of the themes of emptiness and death.

Nikolay Shelgunov (1824–91), a prominent radical critic associated with the monthly *Russian Thought,* was also a Populist and spokesman for moral or "subjective" socialism and Saint-Simonian ideas. Like many another Russian critic before and since, he was interested in the problems of realism and representative types, as shown by his article, "Russian Ideals, Heroes, and Types" (1868). In the sixties and seventies he was quite frank in his opinion that literature

18. Tolstoy's pedagogical writings are often quoted, and it is not surprising to find some of his "terrible words" on this subject in Lawrence Durrell's *Justine* (Part IV).

should be the arena of ideological struggle and that writers should be primarily the propagandists of ideas. But he is perhaps most important for having given currency to the term "popular realism." For Shelgunov, this species of realism, as exemplified in the novels of Reshetnikov and other so-called radical realists of the period, stood in opposition to the "manor" or "aristocratic" realism found in the works of such writers as Turgenev, Goncharov, and Tolstoy. Soviet critics occasionally like to refer to Shelgunov's "popular realism," with its Populist and radical overtones, as a forerunner of their own "socialist realism," although the comparison, as is true of most Soviet assertions, is specious and misleading.

6

Not only were the works of Anton Chekhov (1860–1904) the subject of many Russian critical studies in the late nineteenth and early twentieth centuries,[19] but he himself was an occasional critic whose observations on literature (most of which occur in letters) are important in their own right. Trained as a physician, Chekhov was quite irreligous, and his clinical objectivity, his skeptical irony, and his outspoken materialism have often been stumbling blocks for theistically oriented Russian readers and critics. He himself acknowledged the influence of medical training on his own literary activity: "My acquaintance with the natural sciences and the scientific method has always kept me on guard and, wherever possible, I have tried to conform to scientific facts. . . . I am not one of those literary men who disapprove of science and I would not like to be among those who approach everything with their intellect." Following a brief interest in the ethical views of Tolstoy, he soon (after 1890) became disabused of these; in an oft-quoted letter to Suvorin he writes that prudence and justice have convinced him that there is more love for humanity in electricity and steam than in chastity and vegetarianism.[20]

19. There is a good collection of essays on Chekhov (including several by Russian critics) in *Chekhov: A Collection of Critical Essays* (Englewood Cliffs, N.J.: Prentice-Hall, 1967).

20. Chekhov would have agreed with Lecky (*History of European Morals*): "It

Chekhov had, however, the highest regard for Tolstoy the writer. So long as Tolstoy lived, he wrote in a letter, such things as poor taste in literature and sentimental banality would be "hidden in the shade." The influence of Tolstoy on Chekhov as well as various similarities between the two writers have often been treated in articles and books.[21] Especially apparent in both men is a kind of pagan delight in the flesh rather than any Dostoevsky-like spiritual searching. "My holy of holies," Chekhov wrote in another letter, "is the human body, health, intelligence, talent, inspiration, love, and the most absolute freedom." Chekhov did not believe that it was the function of art to answer narrowly delimited questions, although he stated that he would never deny the right of literature to deal, as life itself must, with the major problems of human existence. He especially admired the way, to his mind, the early Tolstoy posed his problems; thus, in another well-known letter to Suvorin, he writes: "In *Anna Karenina* and in *Eugene Onegin* not a single problem is solved, but they satisfy you completely because the problems posed in these works are basically correct. It is the duty of the judge to put the right questions to the jury, and it is the duty of the jury members to reach their own decisions."

Like Tolstoy, too, Chekhov came more and more, as his writing career progressed, to appreciate the advantages—and the challenges—of anecdotal brevity: "It is strange, but nowadays I have a mania for everything that is short . . . nothing seems short enough to me." He advised young writers, when they finished a story, "to fold it over and then tear up the beginning."

As one might well infer from what has been said, Chekhov also thought highly of Flaubert, whose name appears frequently in the letters. Chekhov's view that the artist should be, insofar as possible, a dispassionate witness; that he should avoid lyricism and romantic sentimentality; that when he describes coldness, the reader should "feel" the coldness of the page; and that even such a trifling object as an ashtray might serve as the starting-point for a work of fiction—all these remind one of Flaubert. But Chekhov's clinical probing as well as many of his epistolary dicta ("For chemists there is nothing unclean. . . . The writer also must be objective like the chemist") reflect his

---

is probable that the American inventor of the first anaesthetic has done more for the real happiness of mankind than all the moral philosophers from Socrates to Mill."

21. See, e.g., L. Speirs, *Tolstoy and Chekhov* (Cambridge: Cambridge University Press, 1971).

interest in both Zola's *Le roman expérimentale* (1880) and Claude Bernard's *Introduction à la médicine générale* (1865). In addition, he showed a fondness for Charles Darwin's methods and theories, and some critics (notably Grossman) have pointed out the relevance of Darwin's basic concepts to recurrent themes in Chekhov's fiction.

Besides his predilection for Tolstoy, Flaubert, and Zola, Chekhov also admired Maupassant, while the Formalist critic Eykhenbaum[22] noted his esteem for the fiction of Pisemsky and Leskov. Eykhenbaum also mentions Chekhov's amazingly wide grasp of the variety of Russian life and compares him with Leskov in this respect. Leskov is famous in Russian literature for his use of the so-called *skaz* (or idiolect) technique (i.e., characterization through lexical peculiarities), and Chekhov's own skill in this area has often been commented on.

7

Of considerable interest and importance are the writings of two men whose contributions were only fully appreciated at a later date. These are Alexander Potebnya (1836–91) and Alexander Veselovsky (1838–1906). Potebnya, a philologist, drew upon the theories of Wilhelm von Humboldt (who distinguished between language as work, *ergon,* and language as activity, *energeia*) to elaborate his own theory of poetic language, a subject that was to intrigue later Russian critics (especially the Formalists) and poets (especially the Symbolists). Potebnya held that the study of literature must be, first of all, a study of language—a refreshing change of emphasis in Russian criticism. Second, he felt that such study must necessarily begin with a distinction between the functions of prose (*ergon*) and poetry (*energeia*). Potebnya's view of poetry as dynamic activity directed at upsetting and disturbing conventional language is echoed in Roman Jakobson's definition of poetry as "organized violence committed on ordinary speech."[23] But Potebnya was himself conventional in returning to metaphor as the real basis of all poetry, an opinion corroborated, however, by many of the great poets. It is interesting that René Wellek writes of Potebnya that "in his general outlook he harks back to German romantic

22. See below, Chapter VIII, section 4.

23. On Jakobson, see Chapter VIII, section 4.

linguistics"; this is an important point and more will be said of it in Chapter VIII.

Alexander Veselovsky, one of the greatest literary scholars of the nineteenth century, through an interest in the social sciences, *Völkerpsychologie,* and comparative folklore, came to view the study of themes, motifs, and plots (their origin, evolution, and migration) as the primary subject of literary and critical scholarship. Though Veselovsky frequently deals with highly speculative theory (e.g., an original, undifferentiated oral poetry is posited, on analogy with the comparative philologists' proto-Indo-European language, as the *Urstoff* of European literature), he is significant in regarding the individual artist's creative role as being severely limited—limited, that is, to merely modifying an inherited "matter," the language and formal conventions being "given." Hardly concerned with aesthetic values and an exponent of nineteenth-century scientism, Veselovsky inspired the later Formalists in thir marked concern for "thematics" and their interest in comparative literature. Indeed, the contributions of Potebnya and Veselovsky allowed these Russian critics, reacting against both the excessively ethical tradition of Russian literary criticism and the vagueness and religiosity of the Symbolists, to analyze form and content on the basis, as they saw it, of more objective criteria.

During the period covered roughly by this and the following chapters, there were of course many critics in Russia writing quite conventional criticism. Some of this was academic and more nearly literary history than criticism; some of it was oriented in particular directions. Just as the overwhelming mass of poetry and prose fiction written in any given period is apt to be inconsequential and of no real value, so the great bulk of literary criticism in any age and country is, frankly, worthless and well deserving of oblivion. In point of fact, any readable history of a country's criticism, as in the case of a country's literature, is actually—as this account is—a survey of a relatively few outstanding or particularly interesting figures, with little attention paid to the vast mass of critical writing or to the minor critics. In a more elaborate study of Russian criticism many names, omitted in this volume, might well be mentioned. Here, however, we shall refer briefly to two men whose names are often linked together in what is called the "Pypin-Skabichevsky" cultural-historical school of criticism.

Alexander Pypin (1833–1904), an Anglophile and a positivist, was a cousin of Chernyshevsky, the Civic critic. He wrote a biography of Belinsky, a four-volume *History of Russian Literature,* and a history of Russian ethnography. His many monographs and studies touch on a great variety of topics (the majority of them only peripherally connected with literature), including Russian folklore, the influence of Montesquieu, Herder, and Bentham in Russia, and Russian Freemasonry. Pypin generally sees in literature a reflection of social thought and "folk" consciousness, and he is concerned primarily with the ideological interpretation of texts and with the history of ideas. Although he was opposed to doctrines of "pure art," he also rejected extremes in both criticism and politics. Because he did not sympathize with the revolutionary movements of the later nineteenth century and, despite his interest in literature as a mirror of the history of thought, because he ignored the class struggle, the Soviets today speak of him condescendingly as a critic who "remained at the level of philosophical positivism and liberal bourgeois enlightenment."

Alexander Skabichevsky (1838–1910) was, like Pypin, a liberal and, like Mikhaylovsky, a Populist. He is occasionally referred to as the foremost critic among the Populists, and he played a leading role in the early phase of what is called the "Sunday-school (*voskresnye shkoly*) movement"—an attempt on the part of repentant intellectuals to bring the benefits of education and learning to the masses through free part-time instruction. Skabichevsky's name was well known at the turn of the century because of his very popular *History of Russian Literature* (1892); but it is in his many other works that we see him both at his best and his worst. For Skabichevsky, as for most of the Populists (and indeed for the majority of Russian critics down to the present time), literature is a moral force. But he rejects radical realism, claiming that it is not the purpose of art to reproduce external reality but rather to reflect the world as it appears to us; art is in effect the expression of subjective impressions. He further makes the point that the radical critics, despite their ostensibly scientific approach, actually did not keep abreast of the latest findings in such areas as psychology and physiology.

Skabichevsky also criticizes the concept of types in literature. Though science moves from the particular to the general, such a logic is misleading in literature, since it results in abstract generalizations and ignores real life with all its color and variety. In this connection, he finds a regular pattern in European thought of movements passing through two phases: the abstract (or philosophical) and the practical. The 1860s represented the abstract, philosophical stage in Russian thought, while the practical stage was reached in the following decades with, especially, the emergence of Populism. Though he had frequent polemics with the early decadents and Symbolists, Skabichevsky seemed to see in these figures as well a manifestation of the "practical" stage. He finds that some of Turgenev's stories of the sixties already show a greater affinity with decadence and Symbolism (as arts of nuance and suggestion) than with traditional realism. Even more striking is his language (reminiscent of Longinus or Pater or Grigoriev) in discussing the emergency of a new romanticism when he speaks of life "afire with a bright flame," the sudden revelation of distant perspectives, and rare moments of spiritual exaltation. Yet of the poet Tyutchev, traditionally—and quite correctly—a forerunner of the Symbolists, he wrote that one can read him only with difficulty and that he is only esteemed by "zealous aesthetes." Tolstoy's *War and Peace* reminded Skabichevsky of stories of war experiences told by talkative and rather simpleminded non-coms in remote Russian villages, an interesting effect, here seemingly generalized, of Tolstoy's mode of "defamiliarization." Most surprising is Skabichevsky's reaction, similar to that of Mikhaylovsky, to some of Chekhov's early stories: Chekhov was clearly for him an author who would die unknown, "like a drunk in a ditch."

Brief mention should also be made here of Sergey Andreevsky (1847–1920). He was a lawyer by profession and wrote some poetry that is very seldom read today; but his name will at least be footnoted in the annals of Russian poetry for the fact that he was instrumental in reviving an interest in the poetry of Baratynsky. Andreevsky was the author of a number of critical studies of several Russian writers, including Lermontov and Dostoevsky. In the case of Lermontov, he finds the reason for the poet's pessimism in strength and pride rather than in a sense of impotent despair. But Andreevsky's style is impressionistic and rhetorical, and one all but gags after a while on passage after passage like the following: "It is quite impossible to compare them [i.e., Pushkin and Lermontov], just as it is impossible to compare dreams and reality, the starry night and bright noon." Andreevsky is often given credit for having been the first critic, as Mirsky puts it, "to give Dostoevsky his due place." The reference here is to an essay (1888) on *The Brothers Karamazov;* but the great mass of subequent Dostoevsky criticism has almost fully eclipsed this work, and no great loss is involved. Andreevsky, who lived to see the rise and decline of Russian Symbolism, was amused by the poetic lexicon of the Symbolist poets; his criticism elicited at least one rebuttal from the poet, Bryusov. Victor Erlich, however, in his history of Russian Formalism, makes passing mention of Andreevsky as one of the few critics writing at the turn of the century who discussed such matters as the structure of Pushkin's verse.

SUGGESTED READING

Tolstoy, Leo, *What Is Art? And Essays on Art,* trans. by Aylmer Maude (New York: Oxford University Press, 1962).

Duffield, H. G., and Bilsky, M., eds., *Tolstoy and the Critics: Literature and Aesthetics* (Chicago: Scott, Foresman, 1965).

Gibian, George, *Tolstoj and Shakespeare* (The Hague: Mouton, 1957).

Christian, R. F., *Tolstoy: A Critical Introduction* (Cambridge: Cambridge University Press, 1969), Chapter 9.

Hall, Vernon, *A Short History of Literary Criticism* (New York: New York University Press, 1963), Chapter 26.

Wimsatt, William, and Brooks, Cleanth, *Literary Criticism: A Short History* (New York: Alfred A. Knopf, 1962), Chapter 21, p. 462 ff.

Magarshack, David, ed., *Dostoevsky's Occasional Writings* (London: Vision Press, 1964).

Jackson, Robert, *Dostoevsky's Quest for Form: A Study of His Philosophy of Art* (New Haven: Yale University Press, 1966).

Linnér, Sven, *Dostoevskij on Realism* (Stockholm: Almqvist & Wiksell, 1967).

Proctor, Thelwall, *Dostoevskij and the Belinskij School of Literary Criticism* (The Hague: Mouton, 1969), contains a chapter (VI) on Mikhaylovsky.

Turgenev, Ivan, *Hamlet and Don Quixote,* trans. by Robert Nichols (London: Hendersons, 1930).

Magarshack, David, ed., *Turgenev's Literary Reminiscences* (New York: Minerva Press, 1958).

Field, Andrew, ed., *The Complection of Russian Literature* (New York: Atheneum, 1971), contains excerpts from Goncharov and Andreevsky.

Gifford, Henry, ed., *Leo Tolstoy* (Harmondsworth: Penguin Critical Anthologies, 1971), contains several excerpts from Chekhov on Tolstoy.

Wellek, René, *A History of Modern Criticism: 1750–1950* (New Haven: Yale

University Press, 1955–65). Vol. IV, Chapter 12 (on Dostoevsky, Tolstoy, Potebnya, and Veselovsky).

Mirsky, D. S., *A History of Russian Literature* (New York: Alfred A. Knopf, 1949), Book One, Chapters 6–8, Book Two, Chapter 1.

Seduro, Vladimir, *Dostoyevski in Russian Literary Criticism 1846–1956* (New York: Octagon Books, 1969), Part I, p. 28 ff. on Mikhaylovsky.

VII THE MODERNISTS

1

In the preceding chapter we mentioned some of Dostoevsky's views on literature. But, however interesting or even provocative these views may be (and they are mainly so because of, or in addition to, Dostoevsky's importance as a creative writer), they do not—just as Pushkin's do not—constitute an organized body of literary criticism; nor did Dostoevsky, as did Tolstoy, ever bring together in one work his literary theory or give a formal treatment to the end result of his thinking along these lines. Yet despite the fact that Dostoevsky died almost two decades before the end of the nineteenth century and Tolstoy at the end of the first decade of the twentieth, the writings of the former have had an immensely greater impact on modern thought than those of the latter. To say this is, of course, not necessarily to say that Dostoevsky is the greater writer of the two; but when one reads Tolstoy one is carried into the past,[1] whereas the reader of Dostoevsky is constantly struck by the essential contemporaneity of theme and situation. In *The Possessed,* for example, we even meet "non-student" protest leaders, "traveling from one university town to another to participate in the tribulations of poor students and urging them to protest." This contemporaneity is especially familiar to us through the association between Dostoevsky and Existentialism as well as through such graphic examples as Max Ernst's painting (1922) showing the painter and Jean Paulhan seated on Dostoevsky's lap.[2]

There is an odd though quite natural reversal of the situation in the Soviet Union. There Tolstoy is, so to speak, "up to date" in the

1. I refer to Tolstoy's fiction; in his expository and polemical works his doctrine of nonviolence has very clear relevance to our times.

2. The original painting is now in Cologne (Wallraf-Richartz-Museum).

sense that he was, as Lenin put it, "a mirror of the Revolution" (i.e., a critic—one of the most virulent—of almost all facets of the *ancien régime* in general and of his own class in particular) and also because of his rationalist leanings. (Sometimes, in view of what has happened and what is happening in the Soviet Union, we must be reminded that Marxism-Leninism and the entire Soviet system claim actually to be rational and scientific.) Although, like Marx himself, Tolstoy would be one of the first, were he alive, to castigate this infamy and dissociate himself from it, he is now, together with almost all of his writings (some ninety volumes), *persona grata* in Russia, and his works (with certain minor exceptions) have always been published in vast editions. But the anti-scientific Dostoevsky, the irrationalist, the religionist, and the reactionary, is another matter. His writings have always been suspect and the printings of his works quite rigidly controlled.[3] Some works, such as *The Possessed,* are, from the Soviet point of view, simply impossible: how embarrassing it is to have the cruelest mockery of socialism come from the pen of one of Russia's greatest writers! In the thirties Ilya Erenburg (now dead) wrote the following of Dostoevsky, managing, in his clever way, both to condemn him and to emphasize his greatness: "It is a truth which is undeniable and deadly. One cannot live with it. It can be given to the dying as formerly they gave last rites. If one is to sit down at a table and eat, one must forget about it. If one is to raise a child, one must first of all remove it from the house. . . . If one is to build a state, one must forbid even the mention of that name."[4]

Dostoevsky's connection with the age of Modernism in Russian literature and criticism is especially important and noteworthy. This period, extending from about 1880 (Dostoevsky died in 1881) until the Revolution,[5] was part and parcel of a European romantic revival. It was essentially a neoromantic movement, a reaction against certain aspects of the preceding age of realism. Its early stage was markedly decadent (*fin de siècle*), while its later stage was strongly Symbolist; indeed, the whole neoromantic movement (in the pan-European sense)

3. There seems to have been some relaxation in recent years. See "Moscow Summer" by Mahajlo Mihajlov in *The New Leader,* 29 March 1965, p. 8 ff.

4. Quoted in J. Billington, *The Icon and the Axe* (New York: Random House Vintage Book, 1970), p. 415.

5. A more inclusive *terminus ad quem* is the year 1932, the year in which the Party turned its full attention to literature and the arts. On the art of the period, see Camilla Gray, *The Great Experiment: Russian Art 1863–1922* (New York: Harry N. Abrams, 1962).

is perhaps best known as the Age of Symbolism. From the official Soviet point of view, however, this entire Silver Age is considered decadent and shameful. It was Gorky himself who once called the brilliant years 1907–17 "the most shameful decade in Russian literature." It is passed over hurriedly in official histories, and many of the most important figures in the movement (a good number of them managed to emigrate but many more remained either to perish, to finish their lives in ignominy, or to compromise) are not even mentioned in Soviet compendia of currently acceptable information. And yet all scholars familiar with early Soviet literature are agreed that the best writers of this period, despite all the clumsy and absurd attempts to produce cadres of "proletarian" writers, were those whose literary styles had been formed during the prerevolutionary Silver Age.

2

But in criticism we shall begin with something less than the best. Harbingers of the new age were Y. Yasinsky (1850–1930) and N. Vilenkin (1855–1937) who wrote under the pseudonyms, respectively, of M. Belinsky and N. Minsky. The former, one of the first non-party intellectuals to join the Bolsheviks in 1917, was a third-rate "naturalist" who treated the subject of sex somewhat openly (for his time) in now long-forgotten works. In several critical articles published in the 1880s, however, protesting against didacticism in literature, he advocated increased individual expression as well as greater artistic freedom. He was a spokesman, in effect, of autotelic art (i.e., "art for art's sake") and he foreshadowed, by vaunting the claims of the poet as a superior being, one of the major doctrines of the later Symbolist poets, a doctrine anticipated by Friedrich Schlegel when he wrote of poets: "They are Brahmins, a higher caste, made noble not by birth but by free self-dedication."

Vilenkin (or Minsky)[6] also decried utilitarianism in the arts and urged that the readers of poetry look only for aesthetic pleasure and delight, not instruction and moralizing. Minsky also claimed that art was superior to science, since the former is synthetic and the latter

6. According to Mirsky, "the first full-blooded [!] Jew to win a reputation in Russian letters."

merely analytic. The idea of the artist's creating not only something "new" but also whole new worlds has, of course, often been expressed. Aristotle's concept of *mimesis* is, in this sense, "creative," while Schleiermacher's view is almost solipsistic: "Whenever I gaze upon my inward self, I am immediately in the realms of eternity. I behold the activity of the spirit which no world can change, which time cannot destroy, which itself creates both world and time."[7] Minsky himself, in a philosophical tract published in 1890, again expressed the arch-romantic and aestheticist opinion that art, like everything else in life, is motivated by egoism. Such a view becomes a commonplace, as we know, throughout most of Europe and England beginning in the 1890s.

It may well be noted here that there was a typically inherent contradiction in the aesthetic concepts held and preached by these two critics. On the one hand there was a clear-cut antipathy toward didacticism and utilitarianism in literature (especially poetry) and an emphasis on the poet's freedom and individualism as well as on the intrinsic aesthetic value of a work of art. On the other hand, however, there were at first intimations and then later declarations of the function of the artist-poet as superior being, seer, and prophet. But if the poet is a superior being and if he is a veritable magus, then it behooves us to heed his words—and we are, before we know it, back to poetry as instruction. It was not, in fact, long before these two aspects of early neoromanticism developed into an actual schism in Russian literature: between the defenders of "pure" poetry, as represented by Bryusov (see below, section 4), and the "religious Symbolists" represented by Vyacheslav Ivanov (section 6).

Somewhat more important than either Yasinsky or Vilenkin was A. Volynsky (1865–1926), the pseudonym of A. Flekser. Toward the turn of the century Volynsky was even more outspoken in his opposition to positivism and the entire Civic tradition and for this reason was himself severely castigated by Mikhaylovsky, a staunch defender, as we have seen, of Belinskian radical criticism. He had no cogent theory behind him but only a vague philosophical idealism, drawn in part from Kant and his followers. Somewhat later (in 1900) Volynsky defined Symbolism as the union in art of the world of appearances and the divine or transcendental world. Although his critical efforts were

7. Quoted in O. Walzel, *German Romanticism* (New York: Putnam's, 1932), p. 50. Cf. John Donne's definition: "Poetry is a counterfeit creation, and makes things that are not, as though they were."

eclipsed by later and more important figures (who were often at the same time creative artists of note), Volynsky was acknowledged by the very important writer, Bely, as one of his teachers, while Mirsky, in his literary history of the period, calls him a "martyr."

We see in Volynsky something that was to grow increasingly dominant in later Russian Modernism—namely, the marked metaphysical and religious tone in both the actual Symbolist poetry and art and in critical theory. As a matter of fact, at least one of the major critics to be discussed below was as much a philosopher as he was a critic. Not too much, obviously, can be said here about the almost bewildering proliferation of "isms" and esoteric beliefs of the period, but adequate accounts are available elsewhere.[8] (The most important name in this respect is Vladimir Soloviev, who will be discussed below.) Another point worth mentioning in connection with Volynsky is the importance in Russia at this particular time, as in Western Europe, of the periodical press.[9] Volynsky was closely involved with the *Northern Herald* (*Severnyj Vestnik*) which, from its founding in 1885 until its demise in 1898, gave needed recognition to the early Symbolists. Again little attention can be paid to this aspect of the age, but we will say something later about one of the most famous of these periodicals, *The World of Art.*

Some brief remarks must be made here concerning Innokenty Annensky (1856–1909). Annensky was a professor of Greek, a classical scholar, and the translator (into Russian) of the plays of Euripides. In Russian literature he is known primarily as a poet, and, as such, he had a marked influence on the later Acmeist poets. As a critic, however, his remarks seem either incongruous today (e.g., that Gorky, after Dostoevsky, was the most clear-cut Symbolist!) or commonplace (e.g., that the musicality of verse serves to create a mood). But occasionally his observations are more significant and even provocative: thus he notes (writing in 1903) that the "new poetry" of the Symbolists, instead of "inventing emotions," "seeks exact symbols for feelings," a statement that is reminiscent of Eliot's concept of the "objective correlative."

8. E.g., in O. Maslenikov, *The Frenzied Poets* (Berkeley and Los Angeles: University of California Press, 1952).

9. There is a survey of the Symbolist press in Russia in G. Donchin, *The Influence of French Symbolism on Russian Poetry* (The Hague: Mouton, 1958), Chapter II.

3

Occasionally the Russian Modernist period (in particular, its early "decadent" phase) is considered to have begun with the publication in 1893 of Merezhkovsky's "On the Present Condition of Russian Literature and on the Causes of Its Decline." Dmitry Merezhkovsky (1865–1941), poet and novelist as well as critic, was one of the leading figures in the "Religious and Philosophical Society" (founded in 1901), the aim of which was to inspire a mystical spirituality among members of the new literati. Merezhkovsky's political stands were extremely varied put not unusual for the time: at first a liberal, he next became a supporter of theocratic autocracy; then, at the time of the 1905 Revolution, he attacked the tsarist regime so openly that he was compelled to flee abroad, and he lived in France for a number of years before returning to Russia in 1912. By this time the radicals of various persuasions had little sympathy with any sort of religious mysticism, and Merezhkovsky, together with his very talented and beautiful wife, Zinaida Gippius (a poet in her own right), having lost his revolutionary ardor as well as his hope for a "religious" revolution, again left Russia in 1919, now an almost fanatical opponent of Bolshevism.

Merezhkovsky also shifted in radical fashion his poetic style. Before the advent of Modernism (which, to a great extent, meant the advent of French Symbolist poetics), he had been a poet, promising but not remarkable, in the moribund Civic tradition of Nadson. His Symbolist poetry (appearing in the 1890s) is no great improvement, but provides a useful casebook, so to speak, of stock "decadent" themes. After the turn of the century, however, it was Merezhkovsky's prose, represented chiefly by his historical trilogy, *Christ and Antichrist* (1896–1905), which brought him some short-lived fame abroad. In the early 1900s in America, to be reading Merezhkovsky's *Leonardo da Vinci* along with the then quite *risqué Sanin* of Artsybashev and *Yama* of Kuprin, was evidence of a sophisticated and exotic taste.

Perhaps the most striking feature of both Merezhkovsky's prose style as well as his method of reasoning (if it may be so dignified) is the inordinate use of, and variations on, all the devices of antithesis and contrast. Everything has its polar opposite and, as one reads him, one can anticipate not only that a reference to the flesh will certainly be followed by a reference to the spirit but that (and I exaggerate) a mention of fish will be followed by a mention of fowl. "From about 1905," writes Mirsky, "he developed a sort of verbal hysteria that has made all he wrote after that date utterly unreadable. Every one of his books and essays is a seesaw of mechanical antithesis sustained from beginning to end in the shrillest of hysterical falsettos." But this almost pathological development in Merezhkovsky's prose is simply a variety of the *faisandé* style that we commonly find elsewhere at about the same time—in, for instance, Swinburne or Pater in England.

Time has dealt sternly with Merezhkovsky. As a poet, he has been cast into the shadow by many of his contemporaries, including his own wife (it is not uncommon to hear Merezhkovsky referred to as the "husband of Zinaida Gippius").[10] As a novelist, he is very seldom read, forgotten in the West, and condemned as a decadent reactionary in Soviet Russia. What, then, is his reputation as a critic? Here his name is at least still current in the West—few commentaries on Dostoevsky or Tolstoy omit mention of him and quite often reprint portions of his well-known study of these two novelists. The collection of essays mentioned at the beginning of this section on Merezhkovsky, given special prominence because Mikhaylovsky deigned to review it (quite harshly) and because it was a kind of Symbolist manifesto, called for a rejection of traditional socio-literary criticism in favor of what we would now call impressionistic or aesthetic criticism, something rather different from the so-called aesthetic criticism of A. Grigoriev, to be sure, but still a criticism not purely aesthetic (or even objective), since, as we shall see, Merezhkovsky's literary views are strongly colored by non-literary prejudices.

Merezhkovsky's immoderate use of antithesis, mentioned above, is a very characteristic feature of his critical articles as well. Most familiar in this respect are his descriptions of Dostoevsky and Tolstoy as, respectively, "seer of the spirit" (*tajnovidets dukha*) and "seer of the flesh" (*tajnovidets ploti*). These famous and oft-quoted phrases are from his study, *Tolstoy and Dostoevsky* (1901–1902). These key terms are, admittedly, quite appropriate, but they merely sum up, after all, diverse aspects of the two novelists that have been noted by most intelligent readers, since Tolstoy and Dostoevsky, so different in so many

10. In his recent anthology, *Modern Russian Poetry* (New York: Bobbs-Merrill, 1967), V. Markov includes twenty-two poems by Gippius but none by her husband.

respects, lend themselves very readily to antithetical descriptions. Merezhkovsky's criticism, however, is vitiated by at least two major defects. In the first place, the basic contrast he posits between Dostoevsky and Tolstoy is, with a good deal of what can only be called sophistry, extended and generalized, *a priori,* to support absurd conclusions. The picture we get, then, of Dostoevsky is of a novelist who ignores vulgar, external reality and who describes all but disembodied spirits. It is quite true, as we have noted, that Dostoevsky had a more metaphysical concept of realism than many other novelists; but we cannot overlook the importance of the physical, urban setting in his works nor the specific reflection in these works of the author's intense interest in, for example, newspaper accounts of the details of crimes and murders.

The second defect is an undisguised bias in favor of Dostoevsky. The "fleshly" Tolstoy is a "pagan," in contrast to Dostoevsky the "great Christian." I suppose, as it has often been remarked, that all readers of Dostoevsky and Tolstoy who are not imbeciles will eventually gravitate, according to their age, their upbringing, and other factors, to either one or the other of these writers. And there is no reason why the situation should be different for a critic; but in Merezhkovsky's case there is more than a preferential bias, since he brings in again (the study was written during the author's "rightest" phase) that old bromide, the "messianic mission" of Russia, associating this with Dostoevsky's spirituality. Thus, despite the fact that Merezhkovsky, like the majority of early Symbolists, was a man of wide reading and considerable erudition and despite his own recognition of the decadents as the first truly European Russians, we find here once more the intrusion of an essentially nationalistic prejudice, decked out, as such views usually are, with religious trappings. Apocalypticism, however, was rife at the time Merezhkovsky wrote his study (his brand was what is sometimes called "Third Testament Christianity") and was by no means a unique feature. But Merezhkovsky does not—as we might imagine him doing—summarily dismiss Tolstoy. He likens him and Dostoevsky to two great columns in an unfinished temple, the temple being that of "Russian religion which, I believe, will be the future religion of the entire world."

Merezhkovsky comments in his study on the language of the various characters in both novelists. Although he agrees that Tolstoy differentiates between the language of the gentry and the language of the "common people" (by, for instance, introducing gallicisms in the speech of the former and proverbs in the speech of the latter), he accuses Tolstoy of having all his characters in *Anna Karenina* and *War and Peace* speak the same language: "Levin uses exactly the same language as Pierre Bezukhov or Prince Andrey, Vronsky, or Pozdnyshev; Anna Karenina uses the same phrases as Dolly, Kitty, or Natasha. If we did not know who was talking, we would not be able to distinguish one person from another by the language they use or the sound of their voices with, so to speak, our eyes closed. . . . In essence, the language of all the characters in Tolstoy is the same—or all but the same. It is colloquial parlance, the sound, as it were, of Lev Tolstoy himself, whether in peasant's or gentleman's dress." Of Dostoevsky, however, he says that it is impossible *not* to recognize a character at once by the words he or she speaks. In the case of Dostoevsky, Merezhkovsky is correct, but his penchant for antithesis (and perhaps his own prejudice) has seriously misled him in the case of Tolstoy. Here, for example, is what Mirsky writes of Tolstoy's idiolect technique:

> The speech that Tolstoy lends his characters is something that surpasses perfection. In *War and Peace* he attains for the first time to a complete mastery of this medium. It gives the reader the impression of actually hearing the different individual voices of the characters. You recognize the voice of Natasha, or Vera, or Boris Drubetskoy as you recognize the voice of a friend. In this art of individualized intonation Tolstoy has only one rival—Dostoevsky.[11]

Though one often has the impression that Merezhkovsky's literary essays are to be chanted or intoned as liturgy rather than read as elucidation, *Tolstoy and Dostoevsky* (especially the first two parts) is probably the most readable thing he wrote and it can still be read with pleasure. Merezhkovsky has some wonderful—and valid—remarks on many examples of sheer clumsiness in Tolstoy which are often quoted, as well as extensive passages dealing with the same writer's technique of characterizing through the cumulative effect of the recurrent mention of physical traits or features: Vereshchagin's "long, thin neck," for example, or General Kutuzov's corpulence and slow-moving stolidity in contrast with the energetic and self-confident Napoleon.[12]

11. *History of Russian Literature*, p. 259. See also the comments on Tolstoy's language in R. Christian, *Tolstoy: A Critical Introduction* (Cambridge: Cambridge University Press, 1969), p. 139 ff.

12. There are selections from *Tolstoy and Dostoevsky* in *Russian Literature and*

Tolstoy and Dostoevsky first appeared in installments in what was perhaps the most famous publication of the period, *The World of Art* (*Mir Iskusstva*). This lavishly printed and illustrated literary and art review was founded in 1899 in St. Petersburg by a group of artists—their group bore the same name as the publication—under the patronage of Countess Tenisheva and S. Mamontov, a rich merchant. Later the Tsar, Nicholas II, having become interested in the group when he sat for a portrait by Serov, provided funds from his privy purse. The editor was Sergey Diagilev, famous as the brilliant but notorious impresario of the Russian ballet which had a fabulous premiere in Paris in 1909. Diagilev was also an art critic and was awarded a prize by the Imperial Academy in 1902 for his study of the painter Levitsky. The "Yellow Book" and decadent atmosphere of *The World of Art* is made clear by the fact that, interspersed amidst the text of Merezhkovsky's installments were reproductions of Aubrey Beardsley's erotic line drawings.

Zinaida Gippius (1867–1945), Merezhkovsky's wife (she continued to use her maiden name, of Swedish origin), is known primarily as a poet. Her poems, though superior to those of her husband, are replete with the standard decadent themes—*ennui,* loneliness, death and evil. As the "*grande dame* of Russian Symbolism" (Victor Erlich's phrase), she maintained an influential salon in St. Petersburg from about 1905 to 1917, and as a critic she wrote a number of interesting but often acidic pieces under the pseudonym of "Anton the Extreme" ("*Anton Krajnij*"). She contributed articles to several publications, including a series in French on Russian symbolism for *Mercure de France,* but she allied herself mostly with *Vesy* ("Scales"). This publication supported the "conservative" branch of Symbolism, with a greater emphasis on the formal and aesthetic aspects of poetry, as opposed to *Zolotoe Runo* ("The Golden Fleece"), which came to represent the national elements in art as well as the voices of the so-called mystical anarchists. Gippius, in addition to writing many invectives against *Zolotoe Runo,* also expressed in her articles and prefaces her pro-French and Mallarméan leanings, especially with respect to music. "Poetry in general," she writes, "and prosody and verbal music in particular, constitute one of the forms that prayer takes in the human soul."

In her articles published in *Mercure de France,* she complains

---

Modern English Fiction, ed. D. Davie, and in *Tolstoy: A Collection of Critical Essays,* ed. R. Matlaw.

that Russia, until the advent of Symbolism, lacked an authentic literature, not to mention literary schools, in the European (especially French) sense, and she ascribes this deficiency, this lack of tradition, to the long years of subservience on the part of creative artists to socio-political conditions and exigencies. She emphasizes the vitalizing force of Symbolism which brought the Russian Modernists into closer contact wth the artistic cultures of Europe and the world. This accent on cosmopolitanism is, of course, one of the most notable features of the Symbolist and Impressionist movement throughout Europe: we need only recall the employment by European poets of such "exotic" verse-forms as the Malayan pantoum (René Ghil) or the Persian ghazal (V. Ivanov), or the interest in Japanese prints (Whistler) and Indian literature (Balmont's adaptation of Kalidasa's *Shakuntala*).

4

Valery Bryusov (1873–1924), the son of a merchant and grandson of a serf, first came into contact with French symbolist poetry in 1892. His reading of the poems of Mallarmé, Verlaine, and Rimbaud was a revelation, and subsequently, through his translations, his own poetry, and his critical articles, he became the prime intermediary between French and Russian poetry in the Silver Age. A French critic, Jean Chuzeville, later dubbed Bryusov "*le plus français des écrivains russes.*" In 1894, in collaboration with a fellow translator, A. Lang, he published his *Russian Symbolists* (followed shortly by two more collections), a brief volume of translations and adaptations from the French as well as contributions by Bryusov himself. But this is not the place to comment on the furor that these booklets caused in traditional poetic circles or to discuss Bryusov's development as a poet and his Parnassian attention to and mastery of form. His devotion to the art of poetry endured, however, to the end of his life. Unlike many of his fellow decadents, Bryusov chose to join the Communists and to remain in Russia after the Revolution; but he died, wisely withdrawn from active engagement, before the Party's actual onslaught on the vestiges—living and dead—of Symbolism began.

As for Bryusov's criticism, this is concerned almost exclusively with poetry. Here we shall refer only to his various pronouncements on Symbolist theory and practice, although his studies of Pushkin are rather important as well—he is often given credit, for instance, for having anticipated later Formalist studies of Pushkin's so-called canonization of eighteenth-century *vers de société*. In his many statements on Symbolist methods, two points are consistently stressed: that Symbolism is purely a literary method (and not a substitute for religion or *ancilla theologiae*) and that the poet must avoid the commonplace and the banal. Many of his articles are but variations on Baudelaire's dictum that "*la poésie n'a pas d'autre but qu'elle même.*" His great concern for form in poetry (he once wrote a "Sonnet to Form") and his Rimbaud-like disdain for meaningful or a least explicit content echo Mallarmé's principle of poetry as being objectless and subjectless. Consequently Bryusov also staunchly defended the "clarist" tradition in poetry and rejected the mystics and their fatuous "myth-making" (*mifotvorchestvo*). But, being a Symbolist in the French tradition, he still advocates a "poetry of suggestion" or of nuances (it was Renan who once wrote that "*la vérité est dans les nuances*"); and he speaks of the hypnotic effect of juxtaposed images. The term "juxtaposition" is perhaps the most important key term in the entire Modernist movement, in Russia as well as elsewhere in Europe. It was the abandonment of familiar transitional devices in all the arts[13] in favor of devices of juxtaposition (or of omission) that provided the artist with new and exciting techniques and resources which have still not been exhausted, although some extremes seem to have been reached. At the same time, consternation and often malevolence have been aroused in the public by the unprecedented demand that the reader or viewer or listener now supply for himself, out of his own (and very frequently inadequate) background, much that had once been so gratuitously provided by the artist.[14]

Like Baudelaire, Bryusov urged the Symbolist poet to avoid the commonplace and constantly to seek the new, the strange, and the previously unvoiced. But this is a very difficult thing to do, to say the least, and in Bryusov's case, as in the cases of many other Symbolists in Russia and abroad, the results amounted largely to shocking the reading public with *outré* (especially erotic and satanic) subject matter and such things as monostichs or one-line poems. Like Baudelaire,

13. E.g., linear perspective in painting, ornate modulations between vertical and horizontal elements in architecture, harmonic progression in music, and the full use of unambiguous connectives in literature.

14. On this subject, see the collection of essays in *Literary Modernism*, ed. I. Howe (New York: Fawcett Premier Book, 1967).

too, Bryusov cultivated a constant search for new sensations, advocated a *carpe diem* philosophy, and practiced a veritable cult of individualism. In none of these respects, however, is he in any way unique or original; rather, he is expressing concepts and preferences common throughout Europe, England, and even America at the time.

Konstantin Balmont (1867–1943), whose name (which is of Scotch origin) is always mentioned in connection with that of Bryusov, was again primarily a poet. His original poetry is outstanding for its musicality, although his use of alliteration is sometimes quite bizarre. His translations of English and American poetry are remarkable, and this is especially true of his translations of Poe. It has been claimed—and the claim is a valid one—that his translation of *The Raven* is superior to the original. His critical views, much more impressionistic than those of Bryusov, are also less valuable. Whereas Bryusov was intimately related, in his poetic practice and critical theory, with French Symbolist thought, Balmont was a prejudiced admirer and fervent propagandizer of English poetry. He believed that, in its essentials, nineteenth-century Symbolism was of Germanic origin and due primarily to English, Scandinavian, and German inspiration. But the real German influence is seen most clearly in the "religious" Symbolists, especially in Ivanov. Perversely and consistently he minimizes the French influence, ascribing this to the superficial effects of French linguistic hegemony—and this in the face of the fact that his own poetry is markedly French in tone. Rather than accept any French origin for the famous "doctrine of correspondences" (which is not French in origin to begin with, although Baudelaire's *Correspondances* is a classical statement in poetry of the doctrine), Balmont cited a poem, "Malaria," by Tyutchev as the starting point. To be sure, the poem does utilize this theme, but the concept can, after all, be traced back to Plato.

Balmont's essay, "Poetry as Magic" (*Poèzija kak volshebstvo,* 1915), outlines an irrational theory of poetry as magic or sorcery, a view very popular at the time, but one again with a very long history (the Greeks had a word for it—*kēlēsis*). The immediate source here may well be Baudelaire (*"manier savamment une langue, c'est pratiquer une espèce de sorcellerie évocatoire"*); but, in conjunction with even more oracular statements by Balmont on the magicality of verse and "the word as miracle," we are reminded of Novalis: *"Die Sprache ist Delphi."*

Balmont left Russia shortly after the Revolution, languished for many years abroad, and died insane in Paris during the German occupation, "a pathetic remnant and a reminder of a forgotten but glorious past" (Slonim).

5

Bryusov and Balmont were poet-critics, and their major accomplishments are contained in collections and anthologies of Russian poetry rather than in histories of criticism. The three men we shall discuss next—Rozanov, Shestov, and Berdyaev—were philosopher-critics, and their works are to be found, for the most part, in anthologies of prerevolutionary Russian religious thought and commented on in histories of Russian philosophy. But all of them wrote on various aspects of Russian literature and all were attracted in particular to Dostoevsky. Rozanov remained in Russia after the Revolution but died in poverty in 1919; both Shestov and Berdyaev emigrated and subsequently became important figures in French existentialism. Brief mention should be made here, too, of Vladimir Soloviev (1853–1900), the son of a distinguished Russian historian, who was also a religious philosopher of very wide influence and the "spiritual father" of many of the metaphysical and mystical tendencies in later Russian Symbolism. His other-worldliness was offset, however, by a keen sense of humor, and he wrote the best parodies we have of early Russian "decadent" Symbolist verse. He was also a serious poet in his own right, being the author of the most classically Platonic poem in Russian ("Friend Beloved"). The name of Soloviev (like Rozanov, Shestov, and Berdyaev, he was an outspoken irrationalist) is also closely connected with that of Dostoevsky, but it is a matter in this case of the influence of the mystic on the novelist, a subject which cannot concern us in this book. Soloviev did occasionally comment on literature and, in particular, on Dostoevsky (he disliked Tolstoy), but his remarks are of little critical value.[15]

15. Selected philosophical works of Soloviev, Rozanov, Shestov, and Berdyaev may be found in volumes II and III of *Russian Philosophy,* ed. Edie, Scanlan, Zeldin, and Kline (Chicago: Quadrangle Books, 1969). No mention of these names will be found in histories of Western philosophy, however, and what Mirsky says of Soloviev applies equally to the others: "He cannot in any sense be put on a level with the world's greatest philosophers, and in a universal history of philosophy he may be overlooked."

Vasily Rozanov (1856–1919) is best known as a critic for his "The Legend of the Grand Inquisitor" (*Legenda o velikom inkvizitore,* 1894), a study of what is often, but erroneously, considered to be the most enigmatic portion of not only *The Brothers Karamazov* but of all the other major novels as well. Actually it is one of the poorest studies of Dostoevsky ever written. Rozanov here claims, in a manner that remands one of Blake's famed comments on Milton, that Dostoevsky reveals to us in the monolog of the Grand Inquisitor his true affiliations and sympathies; that Dostoevsky is in fact on the side of the Grand Inquisitor and that the words of Alyosha to Ivan—"And you are with him"—apply equally to the author. Although, surprisingly, a number of writers and critics (among them, D. H. Lawrence) have agreed with Rozanov, in the context of the novel such a view is quite untenable. Nor is it of any consequence to refute the Grand Inquisitor's argument as being invalid; it is, on the contrary, perfectly valid and perfectly logical. And that is precisely the point: the truth lies, for Dostoevsky, not on the side of logical demonstration but on the side of the "humiliated and the injured" and on the side of Christ's kiss. Nowhere else does Dostoevsky make so clear his opinion of the vast abyss that separates the religion of the Western Church from that of the Eastern Church. Rozanov went to great lengths to penetrate the "mysteries" of Dostoevsky, and in 1880 he even married Polina Suslova, Dostoevsky's former mistress.

Rozanov's interpretation of Dostoevsky can be better understood in the light of his contemptuous view of Christ and the New Testament, and his Nietzschean evaluation of Christianity as a "religion of death." Though he called Judaism a "religion of life" mainly because of the absence of asceticism and its saner view of sex, he himself was a political reactionary, a Slavophile, and an anti-Semite. He wanted to create, it seems, a new "phallic" Christianity in which the act of sexual intercourse would be the central rite. Needless to say, his name is anathema to Orthodox Russians. But Rozanov's life as well as his writings are characterized by paradox (the favorite device of the irrationalists); before his death he had priests from a monastery administer Extreme Unction and had the prayers for the dying read over him three times.

Of more value as criticism are Rozanov's essays dealing with Gogol.[16] Rozanov was the first Russian critic to react emphatically

16. Two of these, "Pushkin and Gogol" and "How the Character Akaky Akakiye-

against the generally held opinion that Gogol was a realist (in the traditional, "conservative" sense); he argues that Gogol's characters come not from everyday Russian life, not from amongst the poor, the oppressed, and the downtrodden, but rather that the gallery of grotesque figures in Gogol is the figment of—to say the least—a troubled mind. In fact, he goes further and says that Russians, in reading Gogol, began to lose their sense of reality and gained an aversion to it. In all this, Rozanov is quite modern, his interpretation of Gogol now being the one generally accepted in the West. Although he complicates the "naturalism/realism" terminology by calling Pushkin the "real father of the Natural School," unlike Vladimir Nabokov who will later refer to Gogol's prose as "four-dimensional" in contrast to Pushkin's "three-dimensional" prose, Rozanov correctly emphasizes the versatility and many-sidedness of Pushkin as opposed to Gogol who "moves in only two directions." Rozanov admits the genius, odd and enigmatic as it is, of Gogol, but his comparison is vitiated by the assertion that Gogol was the real progenitor of the ironic mode in Russian literature.

Earlier we saw how Belinsky and some of his successors—especially Dobrolyubov and Mikhaylovsky—lauded the creation of "types" in literature and how they favored "typical" characters. It is interesting, therefore, to hear Rozanov reverse this view and call the literary type a defect. A type, for Rozanov, is a generalization and therefore a distortion of reality. In this connection, he praises Pushkin for the individuality and atypicality of his characters. But Gogol's characters are more than mere types; they are bizarre wax figures that live and move in a different world entirely.

Rozanov's own highly unconventional prose style, replete with striking stylistic and typographical novelties, reflects a characteristic modernist tendency observable in all the arts: to suggest, and thereby to communicate more effectively, the paradoxical and fragmentary nature of modern thought through the medium of juxtapositional rather than transitional devices. Mirsky's statement, however, that Rozanov "was the greatest writer of his generation" can only be explained by a rather uncritical tendency to exaggerate.

Lev Shestov (1866–1938), the pen name of Lev Shvartsman (Schwarzmann), was born into a wealthy Jewish merchant family of Kiev.[17] He studied law but, since his doctoral dissertation at Kiev

---

vich Originated," may be found in *Essays in Russian Literature*, ed. Spencer Roberts (Athens: Ohio University Press, 1968).

17. Due to Shestov's long residence in France and his close association with

on the touchy subject of the Russian working class was considered "revolutionary," he never received his degree. He served briefly in his father's textile firm, but after 1895 he turned to more intellectual and artistic pursuits. His early desire to be a singer was, for several reasons, frustrated, and what Plato called "the highest music," i.e., philosophy, eventually became his primary concern. But this is another story, readily available in the introductions to the many works of Shestov now in English translation.[18] Of all the writers mentioned in this chapter, by the way, it is very clearly Shestov, because of his Nietzschean, Dostoevskian, and existentialist sympathies, who is most popular in the West. This popularity is much more a comment, however, on the irrationalist tendencies of our age than on the genius of Shestov.

Here we shall consider four critical works by Shestov. In the first, *Shakespeare and His Critic Brandes* (1898), Shestov takes a strongly idealist position (which he was later to abandon) and attacks the positivism, rationalism, and skepticism of the Danish critic. Georg Brandes, whose original surname was Cohen, was a literary scholar and critic of wide-ranging erudition who took the whole of European literature, ancient and modern, for his province. His name is especially important in connection with studies of Kierkegaard, Ibsen, and Strindberg, and he may be said to have "discovered" Nietzsche. One of the first literary historians in the West to write on Russian literature, Brandes admired Lermontov most of all (presumably for the poet's romantic pessimism), but much preferred Turgenev, Tolstoy, and the Russian realist tradition in general to Dostoevsky, of whom he makes no more than the "standard" remarks: that Dostoevsky was a "poet" but a "repulsive person," a Christian but a sadist, and an advocate of "slave morality." Despite his rationalism and positivism, however, Brandes shows his true literary predilections in his admiration of Lermontov and adulation of the French romantics. In his study of Shakespeare (1896), Brandes is constantly searching for Shakespeare's "personal" voice and claims to have found it in the speeches of Troilus and Timon. But Shestov sees in the Brutus of *Julius Caesar* the embodiment of a moral optimism greater than death.

French thought, his name is often encountered in the French spelling—Léon Chestov.

18. E.g., *Chekhov and Other Essays* (Ann Arbor: University of Michigan Press, 1966); *Athens and Jerusalem* (New York: Simon & Schuster Clarion Book, 1968); *A Shestov Anthology* (Athens: Ohio University Press, 1970).

In *The Good in the Teaching of Count Tolstoy and Friedrich Nietzsche* (1900) we see not only the catalytic influence of Nietzsche but also the beginnings of Shestov's own mature metaphysical stance—that of a paradoxically argued irrationalism. Shestov in this book rejects Tolstoy's homiletics, moralizing, and rationalized Christianity in favor of the passionate Nietzschean cry: "Woe to those who live and know no love better than pity. . . . We must seek that which is above pity and above the Good—we must seek God." In *Dostoevsky and Nietzsche: The Philosophy of Tragedy* (1903),[19] Shestov emphasizes the apocalyptic, irrational, and catastrophic in Dostoevsky and discounts his prophetic pretensions. Pointing out that Nietzsche and Dostoevsky (whom Thomas Mann linked together as representing disease) were kindred spirits, a fact which Nietzsche himself had noted, Shestov writes that Dostoevsky's regeneration of his convictions (the agonizing break with his early ideals) was the equivalent of Nietzsche's "revaluation of all values" and that *Notes from Underground* represents a "public, although veiled, renunciation" of the author's past. In the manner of Rozanov, Shestov attempts to demonstrate that Dostoevsky, without being fully conscious of his intention, is really on the side of the doubting and godless heroes in his novels—men like Shatov and Kirilov in *The Possessed* or Ivan in *The Brothers Karamazov*.

Shestov is a most clever rhetorician who has a knack for summing up unresolved problems in the form of paradoxical and hence eminently quotable dicta, leaving one with the impression that the last word has been said. Though his language has been exorbitantly praised, Shestov has an irritating defect characteristic of didactic criticism (reminding us unpleasantly of the Civic critics): the habit of repeating certain key phrases—often in Latin—over and over again. It is quite apparent, too, that Shestov is as little concerned with literature *qua* literature as the great majority of earlier and later Russian critics. Indeed, for Shestov, with his quaint mixture of Judaism and Christianity, art must yield (as must every other human activity) to the priority of religion and faith, just as aesthetic values had to bow before social values for the Civic critics and as they must take a secondary place in Marxist criticism. Reading Shestov, one is reminded constantly of Miguel de Unamuno and his *The Tragic Sense of Life* (*Del Sentimiento Trágico de la Vida*): here is the same preference

19. This work may be found in *Essays in Russian Literature*, cited in note 16, above.

for the irrational and contempt for empirical knowledge, the same intensity and elegance of style, the same Latin quotations from Tertullian, and even the same predilection for quotations in Greek (seriously botched, by the way, in the English versions of both writers). We can easily imagine Shestov agreeing with Unamuno when the latter writes, "The Church defends life. It stood up against Galileo and it did right." Though Unamuno does not mention Shestov, he does quote Soloviev; and Salvador de Madariaga, in his introductory essay, likens Spain to Russia and calls Unamuno the Spanish Dostoevsky.[20]

References to Dostoevsky are found in many of Shestov's other works. A few of these contain salutary advice ("Woe to him who would order his life according to Hegel, Schopenhauer, Tolstoy, Schiller, or Dostoevsky"—*The Apotheosis of Groundlessness*); many are platitudinous ("When Dostoevsky rudely mocked the claims of reason and its universal and mandatory truths, he was only following the Bible"—*Athens and Jerusalem*); and a good number are debatable ("Dostoevsky understands nothing, nothing whatsoever, about politics"—"The Gift of Prophecy"). But all of Shestov's comments (strangely categorical for one who regularly attacks positivism), whether they concern Dostoevsky or Nietzsche or Kierkegaard, indicate one thing quite clearly: that, as Berdyaev notes, Shestov is actually more interested in his own ideas than in the writers he discusses. In brief, we learn more about Shestov in reading Shestov than about anything else. In this sense, he is—or at least comes dangerously close to being—an autotelic critic.

Bunin, amongst others, has called Shestov's essay, "Creation from Nothing" (*Tvorchestvo iz nichego,* 1905),[21] the best thing ever written on Chekhov. It is, more likely, the worst. Many critics have expounded the view that Chekhov was a pessimist and have emphasized his "tragic" and "melancholy" aspects (we know, incidentally, what Chekhov thought of Stanislavsky's attempts to turn his "comedies" into "tragedies"), but Shestov goes beyond them all. He calls Chekhov the "poet of hopelessness" and interprets him, in effect, as a destructive writer, a writer who attained virtuosity in killing, "by his mere touch, breath, or glance, everything by which men live and in which they take pride." "In Chekhov's hands," Shestov writes, "nothing escaped death." We can, of course, understand Shestov's reaction to a writer

20. *Tragic Sense of Life* (New York: Dover, 1954), p. xxxi.

21. Available in *Essays in Russian Literature* and *Chekhov and Other Essays,* cited in notes 16 and 18, above.

who had little use for transcendental beliefs and who once said (as noted in Chapter VI), "Prudence and justice tell me that there is more love for humanity in electricity and steam than in chastity and vegetarianism." But our real objections are more technical—that Shestov too literally identifies Chekhov with his fictional characters and that he too boldly generalizes on the basis of purposely limited and selected works. Yet how does one go about refuting a philosopher-critic who believes that philosophy is an "art which aims at breaking the logical continuity of argument and bringing man out on the shoreless sea of imagination, the fantastic tides where everything is equally possible and impossible"?[22]

Many of the writings of Nikolay Berdyaev (1874–1948) have long been available in English translations. The great majority of these works, however, deal with metaphysics and Russian socio-political thought and, interesting and provocative as they are, we must pass them over here. As mentioned earlier, Berdyaev settled in France after the Russian Revolution and became closely associated with religious existentialism. But there is one work by Berdyaev that will serve as an adequate example of his literary criticism, such as it is. This is his study of Dostoevsky entitled *The World View of Dostoevsky* (*Mirosozertsanie Dostoevskogo*), published in Prague in 1923.[23] Like Shestov, Berdyaev uses the Dostoevskian texts more for an exposition of his own ideology than as matter for literary analysis and evaluation. But whereas Shestov's didactic and protreptic criticism revels in the mysteries of paradox, Berdyaev's study, which exalts Dostoevsky, as René Wellek remarks, "to dizzying heights," might well be cited as an example of hyperbolic criticism. This aspect of Berdyaev's study manifests itself most clearly in the concluding paragraph, where the author announces that to have produced Dostoevsky is sufficient justification for the existence of the Russian people!

Berdyaev does, however, occasionally refer to literary matters. Thus, in connection with the place of love in Dostoevsky's novels, he expatiates on the absence in the Russian literary tradition of courtly love and an age of chivalry—an absence noted in dozens of histories of Russian literature. But his actual discussion of love in Dostoevsky is solely on a metaphysical level; even the scenes of sensuality and

22. Quoted by Bernard Martin in his Introduction to *A Shestov Anthology*, cited in note 18, p. xi.

23. An English translation of the French version of this work is available, entitled *Dostoevsky* (New York: Meridian Books, 1957).

references to debauchery in the novels are phenomena, according to our critic, "of the metaphysical and not of the physical order." There is also a good deal of attention paid to Dostoevsky's theodicy (probably the best part of the book) and a multitude of references to matters which are quie incomprehensible—e.g., the "structure of the Russian soul." The difference between the art of Tolstoy and the art of Dostoevsky is expressed in Spenglerian terms as Apollonian versus Dionysian art. Berdyaev errs seriously when he attempts, with specious and pompous metaphor, to set Tolstoy and Dostoevsky too neatly at polar extremes in almost every respect. We must certainly disagree, for instance, when he calls Tolstoy a "portrayer of static things" (Tolstoy thus becomes a sort of Parmenides among novelists!) in contrast to Dostoevsky in whom he finds (as we hope there is in every novelist) "something of the spirit of Heraclitus."[24]

Despite the rather harsh comments made here concerning Rozanov, Shestov, and Berdyaev as critics, it must nevertheless be admitted that their works—especially those on Dostoevsky—make rather unusual and, at times, even fascinating and stimulating reading. Certainly they deserve the serious attention of students interested in gaining as complete a picture as possible of the multifarious responses to Dostoevsky's unique genius.

6

Vyacheslav Ivanov (1866–1949) was one of the major figures among the later Russian Symbolist poets. Selections from his verse are regularly anthologized, new editions of his poetry are being prepared, and considerable attention is given to his creative achievements in histories of modern Russian poetry. Here, however, we will discuss him solely as a literary theoretician and critic. In this area, as well, he is important, notably in two respects: as a commentator on Dostoevsky and as a spokesman for Russian "realist" Symbolism. Available in English is his *Freedom and the Tragic Life: A Study in Dostoevsky*[25] and

24. Cf. George Steiner, *Tolstoy or Dostoevsky* (New York: Random House Vintage Book, 1961), p. 102: "Tolstoy is the Heraclitus among novelists."

25. Trans. by Norman Cameron (New York: The Noonday Press, 1957). The passages quoted below are from this edition.

there has recently appeared in England a study of Ivanov and Russian Symbolism.[26]

By professional training, Vyacheslav Ivanov was a classical scholar, having at one time studied under the famous Mommsen at the University of Berlin. His poetry and prose are replete with classical allusions, and the titles of many of his poems are in Latin—one of his major collections of verse is entitled *Cor Ardens.* Ivanov was also, like Nietzsche, particularly interested in the ancient cult of Dionysus, and he wrote a number of monographs in this field. But he seems to have been too much preoccupied with the "dark side" of Greek religious thought, an aspect of Hellenism hardly well documented with texts and one which invites speculation rather than rigorous scholarship. With all due respect to his sincerity, it must be acknowledged that, so far as professional classical scholarship is concerned, the bitter epithet which the great Wilamowitz-Möllendorff applied to Nietzsche's *Die Geburt der Tragödie,* viz., "*Zukunftsphilologie,*" applies equally well to the corpus of Ivanov's studies of Dionysus. His sympathies for the Western classical tradition no doubt played a part, too, in his eventual conversion from Russian Orthodoxy to Roman Catholicism. Ivanov's poetry is metaphysical, esoteric, and extremely ornate. One gets the impression, in reading his verse, of a strange and somewhat tasteless mixture of Alexandrianism, eroticism, Christian hymnology, and German mysticism. As for Ivanov's prose, Shestov once remarked (in an essay entitled "Vyacheslav the Magnificent," 1916) that this always reminded him of the prose of Schiller: "If I believed—as, apparently, V. Ivanov now and then believes—in the transmigration of souls, I would conclude that, a hundred and fifty years ago, V. Ivanov lived in Germany, wrote *Don Carlos, The Song of the Bell,* and *The Cranes of Ibycus,* and that he corresponded with Goethe." But the pervasive influence of German romantic thought in all its varieties (from Boehme through Novalis to Nietzsche) is very nearly everywhere manifest in Ivanov and he refers to Goethe as the early "father" of Russian Symbolism.

Ivanov's study of Dostoevsky, referred to above, is perhaps the ultimate in the metaphysical or anagogic interpretation of the novels. Though he discusses Dostoevsky under three aspects—the tragedic, the mythological, and the theological—the principal thesis of the book is that Dostoevsky's major works are "novel-tragedies." In effect, he reads

26. James West, *Russian Symbolism: A Study of Vyacheslav Ivanov and the Russian Symbolist Aesthetic* (London: Methuen, 1970).

the novels as if they were some sort of Greco-Christian tragedies. Now the dramatic—or melodramatic—qualities of Dostoevsky's novels are, to be sure, quite apparent, and his works lend themselves readily to dramatization (witness Camus's *Les Possédés*); but to find laws of "epic rhythm" and "agonistic development" in Dostoevsky—although all this may be a welcome relief from the frequent references today in Dostoevsky criticism to the more pedestrian "gothic" background—seems a little far-fetched. One might at first assume that Ivanov had the classical scholar's natural predisposition to bring "order and decorum" into the rebellious novel by finding there structural or mythic affinities with Greek tragedy. But actually Ivanov was not at all "classical" (in the sense, that is, of one who advocates understatement and the sacredness of traditional forms or one who scorns all modern literature); he was, in fact, one of the leading figures in a neoromantic movement, had himself written "revolutionary" poetry, and had shocked the public with such oddities as his *Veneris Figurae*. Ivanov's interpretation of Dostoevsky rather represents a Russian counterpart of the modern "anthropological" school of classical scholarship, most familiar through the names of Jane Harrison, Frazer, Murray, and Cornford (who read the history of Thucydides as Greek tragedy), and concerned with ritual origins and vestiges. The name of Dionysus appears again and again in Ivanov's study and the author even refers to the novel as a "Dionysiac form of art."[27] "After all," he asks, "why shouldn't the new chariot of Dionysus make its entry along the crowded highway of the novel?" But especially incongruous is the admixture of Christian theology. We cannot help being suspicious of the scholarship—not to mention the critical judgment—of a man who discusses Greek tragedy in terms of the Christian dispensation. And unless one can close one's mind to a large area of experience (as Dostoevsky himself did in his "Pushkin Speech"), it is difficult to understand how Ivanov can use the term "epic"—much more apposite with respect to Tolstoy's prose—in any meaningful way in connection with the narrative action in Dostoevsky's novels.

There are also far-fetched and excessively mythic interpretations of particular novels. Thus Ivanov reads *The Possessed* (*Besy*) as an especially deep and profound work in which Dostoevsky shows how the "eternally feminine principle in the Russian soul" must suffer violence from the Demons who contend against Christ for domination of the "masculine principle in the people's consciousness."

27. Gorodetsky has a poem, "To Vyacheslav Ivanov, Priest of Dionysus."

Very often Ivanov is inordinately abstract and, in direct violation of the norms of good criticism, not so much illuminating as obfuscating—witness this passage from the chapter entitled "Daemonology":

> Since, however, hypostatic unity is the characteristic of absolute Being, whereas Evil, in its ontological nullity, simultaneously denies and imitates true Being (otherwise it would have not even the appearance of a positive content, without which its existence would be impossible), it follows that both these two patterns of an entity that is no true entity appear in separation and mutual negation. Neither of them, however, can achieve an original self-determination each on its own behalf, and both are compelled to seek their substance—as they find to their horror—each in its counterpart, reproducing each in itself the other's abysmal depths, like two empty mirrors confronting one another.[28]

Still, he has from time to time managed to sum up cogently if not always concisely certain striking features of Dostoevsky the novelist. Thus, as it was said of Turner that he "invented" the London fog and caused people, for the first time, to really see it, so Ivanov writes that it was Dostoevsky who revealed to us (and thereby in a sense "invented" for modern man) the labyrinthine depths of the human psyche. Continuing the graphic metaphor, he likens Tolstoy's prose to the sun-filled canvasses of the Impressionists and Dostoevsky's to the paintings of Rembrandt with their dark shadows and chiaroscuro.[29] In Ivanov's opinion, Dostoevsky sometimes so complicated his novels, became so involved in such problems as teleology and theodicy—in short, "dropped anchor in such depths"—that he often found it impossible to provide an artistically satisfying closure ("to clear his vessel, he had to cut more than one cable"). Ivanov's fondness for metaphor is, of course, an indication that his criticism is strongly Impressionistic and, in this respect, it has much in common with the literary criticism of the Symbolists both in Russia and in Western Europe and England. Here is a *locus classicus* of this species of criticism in which certain *general* features of Dostoevsky the novelist have inspired, so to speak, in Ivanov an almost poetic (especially in the original Russian) response:

28. *Freedom and the Tragic Life*, p. 120.

29. Diderot had earlier compared the "dark" prose of Tacitus to the paintings of Rembrandt.

> Direct experience tells us, as soon as we have traversed a great work by this epic poet-tragedian, that our tender hearts have not been stung in vain; that some inerasable mark has been left upon us; that we have become somehow different; that, indeed, a quite inconceivable and nevertheless joyful confirmation of the meaning and value of life and suffering has begun to shine like a star in our souls, which have been ennobled by the secret sacrifice of a shared renunciation, and blessed and redeemed by the painful gift of spiritual parturition.[30]

But there is more than Impressionism that is at fault in Ivanov. It is, for instance, irritating and distasteful to find seriously considered in this erudite and "European" critic a theme—or rather a perversity—that has appeared again and again in Russian thought from the earliest times: the light-bringing destiny of Russia. Today such prognostications and visions have, understandably, an embarrassingly ironic if not a comic ring to them. For example, in the chapter entitled "Hagiology" and while discussing *The Brothers Karamazov,* Ivanov writes the following:

> Holy Russia will not allow the besieging darkness of Ahriman to sweep over her; not only will Ahriman's triumph he swept away by the dynamism of the Luciferian Russia, as the fancies of winter are swept away by the hot sunshine of the brief northern summer; but Holy Russia will herself send out her champions into the midst of the civilization dominated by Lucifer, and will permeate it with the invisible rays of a Thebaid that works by stealth.[31]

It will be noted here that the *literary* qualities and features of Dostoevsky the novelist have been completely lost sight of (and such passages often extend for several pages in Ivanov), while the literary text is being used solely as a springboard for learned disquisitions upon sundry non-literary topics. Though the criticism of Ivanov (and of many of his contemporaries) is a far cry from that of the Civic critics, this criticism has obviously not come far at all in resisting the

30. *Freedom and the Tragic Life,* p. 13.

31. *Ibid.,* pp. 164–65. It is interesting to note the similarity, in many instances, between such passages in Ivanov and the less controlled and "vatic" passages in Arnold Toynbee.

temptation—seemingly endemic in Russia—to interpret works of art as sociological or religious documents.

Beneath Ivanov's rich and exuberant metaphor, his esoteric allusions, and his metaphysics, we see clearly a line of thought, however, that links him with many of the other Russian critics considered in this chapter as well as with an oft-noted tendency in modern European thought as a whole. I refer to irrationalism which, in Ivanov, is usually related, in one way or another, to Dionysus. Speaking again of Dostoevsky, Ivanov writes:

> Like the ancient Greek dramatists, he remained true to the spirit of Dionysus. He would not accept the optimistic view that "the good" could be demonstrated by proofs, or that right knowledge alone could make mankind good. On the contrary, wholly inspired by Dionysus, he repeatedly proclaims: "Seek ye exaltation and ecstasy; kiss the earth, and learn from it that each is responsible for all, and shares in all guilt. In the joy of this exaltation and this understanding, ye shall find redemption."[32]

Yet this statement is, after all, a commonplace, and it refers to an aspect of Dostoevsky's fiction recognizable by any intelligent sophomore who has read *The Brothers Karamazov*. What Ivanov has done here, as he does so often elsewhere, is to take a commonplace observation and then to express this in a highly worked, metaphorical, and allusive language. It is as if someone were to take one of Aesop's fables and express the moral by expanding and restating it in terms, say, of Hindu philosophy. One wonders, incidentally, whether Dostoevsky was ever conscious of being inspired by the "spirit of Dionysus" or what he might have thought about this particular allusion.

As a spokesman for Russian Symbolist theory, Ivanov was the author of a large number of critical articles, most of them written in the early 1900s.[33] As in the case of much Russian criticism, these essays often concern themselves more with philosophical than with literary matters; but many of them, unnecessarily abstruse though they may be, are good examples of theoretical criticism. Ivanov's main concern was with expounding and explaining the nature of what he called

32. *Freedom and the Tragic Life*, pp. 27–28.

33. One of the best collections of essays is *Borozdy i mezhi* ("Furrows and Boundary Markers," 1916), not yet available in English translation.

"realist symbolism." In this phrase, the word *realist* is used (as in the phrase "realist metaphysics") with reference to Platonic "realism" ("*universalia ante rem*"), where the meaning of this latter word is almost the opposite of its meaning in the phrase "literary realism." Whereas the concept of conventional "literary realism" is ultimately of Aristotelian origin (*mimesis*), Ivanov's "symbolic realism," while stemming originally from Platonic theory, is actually derived from more immediate sources—German romantic theory and the writings of Vladimir Soloviev. Ivanov calls Soloviev a "Symbolist" because "everything in nature and the spirit is atremble for him with the intimate breath of a hidden life and tells him of the essence concealed behind the veils of the divine symbolism of the visible world" (*Furrows and Boundary Markers*).

In an essay entitled "On the Limits of Art" Ivanov elaborates in considerable detail on just how the poet mediates between the suprasensible world and this inferior world. Ivanov divides the making of a work of Symbolist art into two stages: the ascent (*voskhozhdenie*) of the artist, through an ecstatic Dionysiac vision, to what is essentially the Platonic world of ideas; and his descent (*niskhozhdenie*) as a creator. "Many," he writes, "are those who ascend, but few are those who know how to descend"—a statement with which it is difficult to disagree. As for the reader of a Symbolist poem, his soul is led (to use Ivanov's oft-quoted Latin phrase) *a realibus ad realiora*—"from the real to the more real."[34] This essay is particularly interesting because of the use of diagrams. Actually, though these may give the impression of occultism (Ivanov uses such symbols as the triangle and the inverted triangle merging to form a hexagram), they are, in relation to the text, quite as relevant as I. A. Richards' now famous and much-ridiculed "psychological" diagram in *Principles of Literary Criticism.*

Despite the fact that both his poetry and his criticism were not only quite incomprehensible to the masses but were even inaccessible to the average member of the intelligentsia, Ivanov still insisted that the artist should embrace the masses and that art must reflect the spirit of the people. Such a striking contrast between the nature of Ivanov's art and the idealistic, almost Populist, view of the presumed innate capabilities of the people elicited (as did many other opinions of Ivanov) acid comment from contemporaries. The writer D. Filosofov called Ivanov and Blok (see below) proponents of a "naive up-

34. In his study of Dostoevsky, Ivanov relates this Symbolist principle with Dostoevsky's reference to his own "realism in a higher sense."

side-down populism," while the poet Ellis (L. Kobylinsky) spoke scornfully of Ivanov's preachments as mere ivory-tower verbiage. The problem of the ever-widening gap between popular appreciation of the arts on the one hand and the constant and often radical experimentation by artists on the other became critical in the Modernist period.[35] But it seems clear that Ivanov was especially concerned, not only because he had "inherited," so to speak, the Russian tradition of the social responsibility of the artist, but also through the influence, again, of German romantic theory. As we know, organic, unifying concepts were always part of this theory; and nowhere is this quality more manifest than in the writings of Friedrich Schlegel. For Schlegel (who was, like Ivanov, a convert to Catholicism), a reconciliation or union would eventually occur between classic and romantic, i.e., romantic poetry would ultimately become a "*Universalpoesie*": all artificial differences such as those between poetry and prose or between poetry and philosophy would disappear and even life and society would become "*poetisch.*" That we should find in the theorizing of Vyacheslav Ivanov a sort of aesthetic meliorism (with respect to the relationship between artist and audience) which reminds us of a similar concept in Soviet Russian "proleterian" literary theory is therefore not at all surprising, since both meliorisms stem largely from the same source.

7

Ivanov, together with Alexander Blok and Boris Bugaev (better known by his pseudonym, Andrey Bely), were the three major figures in the later stage of Russian "religious" Symbolism, so clearly different in many ways from the earlier, so-called decadent, stage (Bryusov, Balmont, and others). All three were deeply involved, as men, poets, and critics, with religion or mysticism. Ivanov once said that poetry constituted a "religious act and sacerdotal deed"; Blok wrote that the Symbolist poet is first and foremost a "theurgist" and possessor of oc-

35. "The symbolist tradition from Baudelaire to surrealism produced much of the greatest poetry of our time. It is a pity that this poetry should remain unintelligible to the society that unintentionally produced it," W. Tindall, *Forces in Modern British Literature* (New York: Vintage Books, 1956), p. 20.

cult knowledge; and Bely was for some time associated with Rudolf Steiner and his anthroposophy movement. Unlike their "decadent" colleagues who wrote mainly under the influence of French Symbolist models, these three writers were, in varying degrees, influenced by German thought which reached them either directly or through the already pervasive presence of German aesthetics and metaphysics in the Russian tradition. Blok is surely the greatest figure of the three and one of the two or three greatest Russian poets; Ivanov the most eloquent spokesman for Symbolist theory as well as a major Symbolist poet; and Bely—poet and novelist as well as critic—was, as we shall see, extremely influential (much more so than either Blok or Ivanov) on subsequent developments in Russian literature and criticism.

The life Alexander Blok (1880–1921) is clearly separated into two periods. The first period, one of extreme idealism and involving especially a passionate interest in Soloviev's concept of Sophia, the feminine principle of Divine Wisdom, lasted until shortly after his marriage, in 1903, to a daughter of the famous Russian chemist Mendeleev. The second period, beginning with Blok's very early disillusionment with married life, was one of constantly growing despair, gloom, pessimism, and chronic melancholy right up until his death. Here we must ignore his magnificent accomplishments as a poet as well as his somewhat less important contributions as a Symbolist playwright in order to limit ourselves resolutely to his criticism. As in the case of Pushkin, Blok did not sum up in any formal critical study his overall poetic or aesthetic views, and we must seek out his opinions in these areas in a number of articles he wrote on various occasions. Furthermore, the criticism in these articles (consisting largely of an exposition of an almost mystical poetic doctrine) is chiefly valuable for understanding Blok's own poetry and is actually of very little value for general critical purposes. Since Blok was very nearly a "pure" poet, his verse seems spontaneous and unaffected (much like that of Pushkin's) in contrast to the often labored striving for effect in men like Bryusov and Ivanov; but he was so much the pure poet that his criticism itself is apt to be more poetry than analysis. Thus, in his critical review of a Symbolist and very poetic novel by Bely, he quite frankly makes no effort at all either to analyze, interpret, or elucidate, and his "review," probably one of the strangest ever written, is essentially a lyrical evocation, a poetic response to poetry.[36]

36. A passage from this review is quoted by O. Maslenikov in his *The Frenzied Poets*, pp. 156–57.

What were Blok's opinions concerning poetry? Basically, aside from his early idealistic views, these revolved around two central themes: the utter devotion of the poet to his art and the seminal importance of music. In his "Letters on Poetry" (1908), the emphasis is on the self-sacrifice of the poet and on his veritable "immolation": only poetry that has resulted in the poet's "burning himself to ashes" can truly be significant or great. As for Blok's high regard for music (and his own verse is almost magically musical), this was a subject that intensely interested Symbolist poets throughout Europe (although perhaps the names of Verlaine and Mallarmé are most important in this connection); and Bely was later to attempt more technical studies in this area of poetics. In the case of Blok, the influence of Nietzsche is very apparent, and in the Preface to a collection of essays published in 1918 Blok speaks of Russia as the incarnation of the "spirit of music." It will be noted here that Blok, like Ivanov and so many other Russian writers and thinkers, is messianic and apocalyptic. On a later occasion he expressed the view that Russia, free of the humanistic and individualistic traditions of the West, would eventually bring about a new man and a new society—key concepts, of course, in later Marxist-Leninist theory.

Blok's view of the importance of the theater and especially his hope that through the theater a lost "wholeness" of life might be restored, with mass audiences participating in something that would be a once art and ritual, also remind us of later, more nearly contemporary thought in this connection (T. S. Eliot). Blok also felt, without giving the word *realism* its technical philosophical meaning, that his age was characterized by a merging of traditional Russian literary realism, with its marked social orientation, and Symbolism with its "other-worldly" preoccupations. This is not a notably clever conclusion but one which anticipates Zamyatin's similar view of the prose of his time as being a "neorealism," the dialectic synthesis of realism and Symbolism.

The Symbolist period in Russian literature was rich in major and minor literary and philosophical squabbles, often involving a good deal of heated debate, invective, and animosities. As many of Ivanov's vatic utterances elicited harsh replies, so Blok's opinions very frequently stirred the ire of other poets and critics. Zinaida Gippius, especially, expressed what can only be called contempt for Blok's cryptic pronouncements. Much more serious was the break between Blok and Bely caused (amongst other things) by a favorable review which the former wrote of a mediocre novel by the "radical" realist Stepan Petrov. Bely felt that Blok was trying, dishonestly, to ingratiate himself with the traditional realists (the forerunners of Soviet "Socialist Realists"); but the fact was that Blok, completely disillusioned with ideology and frantically searching for something to believe in or some movement to throw himself into, had, like Ivanov, come to an almost Populist and revolutionary stance. He defended Gorky and wrote a series of articles in which he lamented the growing schism between Russian intellectuals (especially the Symbolists) and the Russian masses. Blok now felt that the ivory-tower world of the Symbolists, with their learned and subtle discussions and their esoteric literature, was doomed and that Russia had to undergo a test of fire. Blok was largely inspired here by his association with the so-called Scythian movement led by the minor critic Ivanov-Razumnik (see below). The Scythians were a major "fellow-traveler" group which rejected Marxist communism but accepted and welcomed the Revolution as a bloodbath that would sweep away the harmful effects of years of European influence, allowing Russia to follow her "true destiny." But the Revolution of 1917 and its aftermath were hardly what Blok and the Scythians had envisioned them to be. Although Blok saw through the press just before he died a republication of his earlier essays on Symbolism, he had by this time long ceased to write poetry and had grown more and more apathetic to the world around him. Lev Trotsky, writing in his *Literature and Revolution* (1923), says of Blok: "To be sure, Blok is not one of ours. But he reached out towards us and, in doing so, collapsed."

8

Andrey Bely (1880–1934), the son of a famous mathematician, had early intended to make science his career. But after reading Schopenhauer and Nietzsche, he turned more and more toward the study of philosophy. Under the influence of the Soloviev family, this interest broadened, and it was Mikhail Soloviev (the brother of Vladimir) who encouraged Bely to publish his earliest poetry. As a poet, Bely is always mentioned, along with Blok and Ivanov, as a leading "second-generation" Symbolist. But his poetry never, for various reasons, became popular (even amongst the *literati*), and it is as a Symbolist novelist and "poet in prose" that Bely is best known in the annals of Russian literature. One of his novels, *St. Petersburg*, is perhaps the closest approach in Russian literature to something like Joyce's *Ulysses* in English.[37]

But here we must consider Bely solely as a critic and literary theoretician. In this domain the bulk of his work is concerned with poetry—more particularly, with the mechanics of versification and prosody and especially with the problem of verse rhythm. Of course Bely frequently spoke, as a ranking Symbolist poet, in a highly romantic fashion and in general terms of art ("All art—of the present, of the past, and of the future—is symbolic") and of the "magic of words." Indeed, the concept of the "word" and of poetic language (the gist of the idea was presumably drawn from the writings of Potebnya) is paramount in Bely's thinking, and it is no doubt the original of the later Futurists' "self-sufficient word" (*samovitoe slovo*). But Bely's real importance as a critic lies precisely in his turning the attention (partially at least) of his followers away from abstract, ideological content and in directing this attention toward the formal aspects of poetics. In an early work in this field, "Lyric Poetry as Experiment" (1910), Bely refers to his attempts at a "comparative morphology of rhythm"; he also studied, drawing up his own statistical tables, the development of the iambic tetrameter in Russian poetry from Lomonosov to his own day. Bely's particular interest lay in the way Russian poets—especially Pushkin—made use of what he called "half-stresses" (*poluudarenija*) for the purpose of subtly varying the rhythm in lines of metrical verse.[38] The stress pattern of a line of such verse or the rhythm—that is, the alternation of stresses (tonic accents) and unaccented syllables (the situation is peculiar in Russian verse due to the "free accent" in the language)—constituted for Bely, as noted by Erlich, a "triumph over meter" and the primary problem of poetic art. At about the same time Bely founded the "Rhythmics Society" (*Ritmicheskij kruzhok*) for promoting the study of the formal elements of Russian poetry. Later, in 1929, he wrote a book entitled *Rhythm as Dialectic* in which he tried, somewhat unhappily, to combine his poetic theory with Marxism. But by this time his early pio-

37. This novel (written in 1913) is available in an English translation by the late John Cournos (New York: Grove Press, 1959).

38. Vladimir Nabokov, in his excursus on prosody in his edition of Pushkin's *Eugene Onegin* (now available in a separate Bollingen Series paperback), refers to Bely's "admirable work." Nabokov has coined his own term—"scuds"—for Bely's "half-stresses" (i.e., the unaccented syllables in various metrical feet).

neering experiments and studies had already laid the foundation for important areas of Formalist poetics (see the following chapter).

Though he was principally interested in poetry, Bely also devoted attention to the study of Russian prose, notably that of Gogol. As early as 1910 he had written a brilliant study of Gogol's prose style, and his further work in this field culminated in what is now considered a classic of Gogol scholarship—his *The Craftsmanship of Gogol* (*Masterstvo Gogolja*, 1934). This is another brilliant work of analysis, often erratic and arbitrary, but one that, along with Bely's own works of fiction, exerted a palpable influence not only on young literary scholars but also on many writers (such as Pilnyak) whose experiments could still be tolerated in the early Soviet period. Gogol was the master of what is technically referred to in Russian literature as "ornamental prose" (Mirsky, using Formalist language, calls Russian ornamentalism the "declaration of the independence of the smaller unit"), and Bely the novelist was Gogol's greatest and most successful epigone. His interpretations of the imagery in Gogol are very frequently cited almost as "standard" ones: the symbolism of the wheel—and rotundity in general—in *Dead Souls* and the interpretation of that elaborately described traveling-case or box which Chichikov so solicitously cares for as the "wife" of its owner.

Almost as valuable as his more technical critical works are Bely's memoirs and reminiscences. We may legitimately object to "artiness" in critical prose, but the presence of the "ornamental" style in these late writings of Bely adds to their evocative qualities as the author recreates for us, with a good deal of pungent satire and scintillating language, the very spirit of the intellectual and artistic circles of a remarkable age.

9

Although the writings of Mikhail Gershenzon (1869–1925) are mainly concerned with the history of ideas in nineteenth-century Russia and although he himself took an active part in the development of the now almost forgotten movement known as Solidarism, he did find time to deal with literature on several levels. His *The Moscow of Griboedov* (*Griboedovskaja Moskva*, 1916) provides us with a scholarly study of

Moscow society in the time of the playwright Griboedov. More important is his classic study, *The Wisdom of Pushkin* (*Mudrost' Pushkina,* 1919), a work replete with acute observations but vitiated by excessively subtle and strained interpretations. Gershenzon also seems to have been the first scholar to note that Pushkin's story, "The Stationmaster," is actually a parody of the biblical parable of the Prodigal Son. In an essay entitled "The Poet's Vision" (*Videnie poèta,* 1918), Gershenzon, while arguing for the close reading of texts and for scholarly methods in criticism, still emphasizes the need for "integral knowledge." This is a laudable desideratum, and yet, despite the fact that much of his work reminds us of Formalist concentration on the text, there are still slightly irrational—almost mystical—overtones to some of his analyses.

This irrational side of Gershenzon is seen even more clearly in a work which has made his name familiar to many who might not ordinarily have heard of him; I refer to the "Correspondence Between Two Corners," a series of letters which Gershenzon and Vyacheslav Ivanov wrote each other in 1920 while resting in the same room of a home for "workers" in science and literature near Moscow.[39] Gershenzon, who had, like the Scythians, welcomed the Revolution as a cataclysm that would free man from the awful burden of the past, wanted a Tolstoyan "simplification of things" and a return to a sort of Rousseauan primitivism (anticipatory, we presume, to starting all over again). He emphasized the personal as opposed to the communal, the new against the old, and he believed that the full significance of *Hamlet* or of the Sistine Madonna occurred only once—at the moment of its creation by the artist—and thereafter the work of art became a mere text for annotators or a museum piece. Ivanov, on the other hand, urged respect for the past, defending cultural traditions and conservatism. Thus, as Helen Muchnic writes, "it was, curiously enough, the 'difficult' poet who spoke for humanity and the quite understandable historian who insisted on the exclusive validity of personal experience."[40]

R. V. Ivanov-Razumnik (the pseudonym of R. V. Ivanov, 1878–1946), mentioned earlier in connection with Blok and the Scythians, was a mystic and a socialist as well as a critic. He greeted the Revo-

39. The "Correspondence" has been translated into many languages; an English version appeared in *Partisan Review* for September, 1948.

40. *From Gorky to Pasternak* (New York: Random House, 1961), p. 416.

lution and believed that Russia and the Russian people were destined to lead the world forward to a new historical era (he was later arrested by the Cheka and spent many years in prison and exile). In 1918 Yevgeny Zamyatin (see below) wrote an article in which he subjected Ivanov-Razumnik's Scythianism to harsh criticism and demonstrated the utter fatuousness of his political views. As a critic, Ivanov-Razumnik has been called "second-rate," and Viktor Shklovsky, whom we shall discuss in the next chapter, listed him among the Russian critics he despised. But his name crops up quite regularly in various accounts of the Symbolist period, and he took part in numerous polemics. Using Horatian tags, he once distinguished between the early Symbolists or decadents and the Symbolists proper (i.e., V. Ivanov, Blok, and Bely) by stating that poets like the former "are made" (*fiunt*), while poets like the latter "are born" (*nascuntur*). He also recognized the greatness of Bely's novel, *St. Petersburg,* calling it the masterpiece of his generation.

In a collection of critical articles published in 1922, Ivanov-Razumnik points out the danger of hasty evaluations of contemporary writers; has some perceptive comments on Gorky (praising his tales but condemning his tendency to philosophize); expresses his low opinion of Artsybashev's "decadent" novel *Sanin;* recognizes Kuprin as a second-rate author despite much contemporary acclaim; and remarks of Blok that all his poetry is a "combination of the black rose of amorousness and the bright cross of suffering." The most significant comments in the collection have to do with Ivanov-Razumnik's distinction between the true artist who "demonstrates" (or "renders") reality and the inferior artist or belletrist who merely "narrates" his observations of reality.

10

There is good reason to consider Yevgeny Zamyatin (1884–1937) one of the very best literary critics that Russia has ever produced. Here is a Russian critic, all but completely free of dogmatic aesthetic, metaphysical, religious, or socio-political allegiances and the accompanying verbiage, who displays a keen, discriminating, and cosmopolitan taste together with an enviable erudition and an extensive acquaintance with Russian literature, past and contemporary. Hardly less important, he has a fine style—almost classically clear, concise, and cogent—and is a superb master of irony. He is also a master of prose fiction, having gained worldwide fame through his dystopian novel, *We,* and he has won a solid and lasting place in Russian literature with his many tales, stories, and novellas. All this is not to imply that Zamyatin is faultless: one may well object to his strange (but unobtrusive) penchant for the Hegelian dialectic and certainly his regard for Anatole France seems excessive. But there are in this critic remarkably few of the shortcomings and little of the capriciousness which we so often encounter in even first-class critics, Russian or non-Russian.

Although by professional training a naval engineer, Zamyatin had rather early in life (in 1911) come into contact with the tsarist police because of his connections with the Social Democratic Party; and this led directly, as he tells us in his autobiography, to his avocation as a writer: "If I have any significance in Russian literature, I owe this all to the Petersburg Secret Police."[41] Later, during World War I, Zamyatin spent a year and a half in England supervising the building of Russian icebreakers (he referred to naval engineering as his "lawful wife" and to literature as his "mistress"); his sympathies for English life and manners are manifest (he himself was nicknamed the "Englishman from Moscow" by Blok), even though he did not spare his satire in the wonderful short novel, *The Islanders.* In 1921 Zamyatin, whose reputation as a leading writer was now well established, was instrumental in the coming together of a somewhat heterogeneous group of writers (Fedin, Lunts, Zoshchenko, and others) into a loosely-knit organization calling itself, from the title of a story by E. T. A. Hoffmann, the "Serapion Brothers." This was another "fellow-traveler" group whose fond hopes that, following the Revolution, Russian writers would at long last enjoy full creative freedom were very soon to be shattered. But in no sense did it represent the beginnings of a "literary school," since a basic tenet of the society was that every writer should be able to write exactly as he pleased, regardless of government or Party dictates. This was a concept of incredible boldness, given the Russian tradition, but one that echoed Zamyatin's words: "True literature can exist only where it is produced by madmen, hermits, heretics, visionaries, rebels, and skeptics." Even more extraordinary, however, is the letter that Zamyatin wrote to Stalin in 1931, asking for permis-

41. For this and other details, see Alex Shane, *The Life and Works of Evgenij Zamjatin* (Berkeley and Los Angeles: University of California Press, 1968).

sion to leave the country. He explained to the dictator his sundry vexations and emphasized the fact that, because of his "death sentence" by the Russian Association of Proletarian Writers, it had become utterly impossible for him to continue in his profession as a writer; that, further, he had some unfinished business abroad and that he might even be able to find there a cure for his chronic colitis. Stalin, surprisingly, granted Zamyatin's request, not of course because of any compelling arguments on the writer's part, but rather, it seems, through the intercession of Gorky, whose own time was fast running out. Zamyatin was granted one year of leave abroad, but he never returned and settled in France. That even as late as 1934 the Soviets were still expecting him to return is indicated by his election that year to membership in the newly founded Union of Soviet Writers.

Zamyatin is the great spokesman of continued revolution in literature and of the value of the heretic: "The world is kept alive only by heretics—the heretic Christ, the heretic Copernicus, the heretic Tolstoy. Our symbol of faith is heresy."[42] For Zamyatin, there is no final revolution in any area of human thought, and, without being explicit, he means that the Russian Revolution of 1917 is no more final than any other: revolutions are infinite. In what is perhaps his best-known essay, "On Literature, Revolution, and Entropy" (1923),[43] Zamyatin makes effective metaphorical use of the physical concept of entropy—a concept which has appealed to a number of Russian thinkers (Berdyaev uses it as well as the theologian Pavel Florensky):

> The law of revolution is red, fiery, deadly; but this death means the birth of a new life, a new star. And the law of entropy is cold, ice blue, like the icy interplanetary infinities. The flame turns from red to an even, warm pink, no longer deadly, but comfortable. The sun ages into a planet, convenient for highways, stores, beds, prostitutes, prisons: this is the law. And if the planet is to be kindled into youth again, it must be set on fire, it must be thrown off the smooth highway of evolution: this is the law.
>
> The flame will cool tomorrow, or the day after tomorrow (in the Book of Genesis days are equal to years, ages). But someone must see this already today, and speak heretically today about

42. Quoted in *A Soviet Heretic: Essays by Yevgeny Zamyatin,* ed. and trans. by Mirra Ginsburg (Chicago: University of Chicago Press, 1970), p. 51.

43. The full text of this essay will also be found in *Literary Modernism* cited in note 14, above.

tomorrow. Heretics are the only (bitter) remedy against the entropy of human thought.[44]

Zamyatin's trenchant style is splendidly evident in this oft-quoted passage from the same essay:

> When the flaming, seething sphere (in science, religion, social life, art) cools, the fiery magma becomes coated with dogma—a rigid, ossified, motionless crust. Dogmatization in science, religion, social life, or art is the entropy of thought. What has become dogma no longer burns; it only gives off warmth—it is tepid, it is cool. Instead of the Sermon on the Mount, under the scorching sun, to up-raised arms and sobbing people, there is drowsy prayer in a magnificent abbey. Instead of Galileo's "But still, it turns!" there are dispassionate computations in a well-heated room in an observatory. On the Galileos the epigones build their own structures, slowly, bit by bit, like corals. This is the path of evolution—until a new heresy explodes the crust of dogma and all the edifices of the most enduring stone which have been raised upon it.[45]

The view of literature as a goad is another favorite theme as exemplified by this passage from Zamyatin's essay on Sologub:

> The whip has not yet been given its full due as an instrument of human progress. I know of no more potent means than the whip for raising man from all fours, for making him stop kneeling down before anything or anyone. I am not speaking, of course, of whips woven of leather thongs; I am speaking of whips woven of words, the whips of the Gogols, Swifts, Molières, Frances, the whips of irony, sarcasm, satire.[46]

Zamyatin attributes the presence of irony and satire in Russian literature to influences from the West; in an essay on "The New Russian

44. *A Soviet Heretic,* p. 108. Zamyatin wrote a biography of Julius von Mayer, a pioneer in thermodynamic theory, and was struck by the analogies between Mayer's exposition of entropy in physics and roughly similar phenomena in society.

45. *Ibid.,* p. 108.

46. *Ibid.,* p. 221.

Prose" he says that the "rapier of irony" is a "European weapon" and that few Russians, so used to the cudgel, as yet know how to handle it effectively.

In striking contrast to Zamyatin's enthusiastic comments on "revolution," "heresy," and "irony" are his acid remarks on the pedestrian quality of the "proletarian" literature being produced immediately after the Revolution. The "Victorious October Revolution," he writes succinctly, "has not escaped the general law on becoming victorious: it has turned philistine." He then goes on in a passage so strong in its condemnation that it could only have appeared when it did, in 1918:

> What the priest in the purple cassock hates most of all is the heretic who does not recognize his exclusive right to bind and to permit. What Mrs. So-and-So with her hair curlers hates most of all is the Fair Lady who does not recognize her sole right to the prerogatives of love. And what every philistine hates most of all is the rebel who dares to think differently from him. Hatred of freedom is the surest symptom of this deadly disease, philistinism.
>
> Shave all heads down to the skin; dress everybody in the regulation uniform; convert all heretical lands to your own faith by artillery fire. This was how the Osmanlis converted the giaours to the true faith; this was how the Teutonic Knights saved heathens from eternal flames—by the sword and by temporal flames; this was how dissenters, sectarians, and socialists were cured of their errors in Russia. And it is not the same today? Konstantin Pobedonostsev is dead—long live Konstantin Pobedonostsev![47]

Elsewhere Zamyatin writes that there will be no genuine new Russian literature so long as the Russian people are treated as children whose innocence must be protected and that, in the meantime, the only future Russian literature has is its past. He is highly critical of certain experiments in proletarian art theory and refers ironically to a Moscow symphony orchestra that has rejected the single authority of its conductor and now conducts itself "collectively"; and to a new proletarian symphony performed solely on factory whistles. As for the "new" criticism, Zamyatin likens Russian literature to Peter Schlemihl who lost his shadow (i.e., the critics), claiming that what criticism there is (aside from the Formalists, who still continue to "dissect corpses") acts the part of a male nurse to Russian literature.

47. *Ibid.*, p. 23. Pobedonostsev was a notoriously conservative Procurator of the Holy Synod, i.e., lay head of the Church.

In the area of literary theory, Zamyatin devotes considerable attention to his theory of Neorealism or Synthetism. He considers this movement—of which he himself is a part—to be the synthesis, in Hegelian terms, of traditional literary realism (thesis) and Symbolism (antithesis). He recognizes the contributions of the Russian Symbolists (they created a "science of verbal music") but they erred in trying to cope with the tragedy of life through religion (Zamyatin is relentlessly agnostic, to say the least), while the Neorealists represent an antireligious trend and make intensive use of irony. He notes, too, the marked tendency of the Neorealists to be much bolder in their use of metaphor than antecedent prose writers as well as their essentially impressionistic style. Whereas a great deal of earlier Russian realistic prose had a rural setting and whereas the Symbolists were notably urban in their proclivities, Neorealists like Pilnyak turned again to the country, to the deep provinces and godforsaken regions. Zamyatin makes one especially interesting point, something noted by other and later critics. Writing again of the Neorealists, he asks:

> Have you ever had occasion to examine a tiny piece of your own skin under a microscope? If you ever do, you will probably be startled at first: instead of your pink, delicate, smooth skin, you will see clefts, enormous bumps, pits; from the pits something rises, as thick as a young lime tree—a hair; next to it is a huge boulder—a speck of dust.
>
> What you see will bear little resemblance to the usual appearance of skin; it will seem incredible, like a nightmare. Now ask yourselves: which is more real—this smooth, pink skin, or that one, with the bumps and clefts? After some thought, you will have to say: the real thing is that incredible skin we see under a microscope.[48]

Compare this comment made several years ago by René Huyghe:

> Take one of the modern works that claim to be non-figurative, a product of Abstract Expressionism, for example, and compare it with a scientific photograph, which, through the use of the electronic microscope or Wilson chamber, enables us to perceive the structure and motion of matter. We are immediately aware of disturbing coincidences. The normal appearance of reality is

48. *Ibid.,* pp. 41–42.

> no longer there. But art is still an investigation of reality, at a level where we can penetrate the inmost secrets of matter and perceive the energy that is at its source.[49]

Zamyatin also remarks that life in Russia had become "Americanized" by the time the Neorealists appeared; again one is reminded of Pilnyak who once exclaimed, not long before his arrest and disappearance, "Revolutionary romanticism is out! We are entering an era of Soviet Americanism: technique and practical soundness!"[50]

So far as theory is concerned, Zamyatin also has some stimulating (but not terribly original) ideas on plot development. He finds two principal types—inductive and deductive—which he defines and illustrates with examples drawn from contemporary writers. Much more effective, however, are Zamyatin's analyses and his judicial criticism. The dynamic quality of the new writers (Neorealists) is due largely to the closeness of their language to living speech; their language is non-rhetorical, "uncorseted," paratactic, and it shuns participles. Though folk speech cannot be used everywhere, it is still the well of language, and Zamyatin reminds Russian writers that the purest Russian is to be found in the north (Olonetsk and Archangel regions). The old palette of color-adjectives is neither adequate nor suitable for capturing the hues, actual and figurative, of a city like Petersburg; the writer must draw on the linguistic legacies of Gogol, Remizov, and Hoffmann. Zamyatin's emphasis on the new, the dynamic, and the bold in language is characteristic: "The old, slow, creaking descriptions are a thing of the past; today the rule is brevity—but every word must be supercharged, high-voltage."[51]

Of Vsevolod Ivanov's tendency to exaggerate folk speech, he remarks that it is quite unnecessary, in order to convey the sounds of a village morning, to put a live rooster next to the violins. He praises Babel's skill in reproducing, in an aesthetically satisfying manner, the syntactic oddities of colloquial language: one always feels, in reading Babel, that the author not only has acute perceptive faculties but a brain as well. Of Pilnyak, he notes with satisfaction the compositional device of "suddenly shifting planes" (simply one variety of Modernist juxtapositional technique), but he objects to the inappropriate "Karam-

49. *New York Times,* 17 January 1960.

50. Quoted in Victor Serge, *Memoirs of a Revolutionary* (Oxford: Oxford University Press, 1967), p. 269.

51. A *Soviet Heretic,* p. 111.

zinian syntax" and the often incongruous typographical caprices. He has a sympathetic essay on Gorky (whom he once referred to in an article published in France as *"le papa de la littérature soviétique"*[52]) which obviously errs on the side of leniency. He speaks of the official use made of Gorky in terms reminiscent of Pasternak's comment on Mayakovsky—that he was propagandized as potatoes were under Catherine II. In an excellent essay on O. Henry, Zamyatin makes it clear that he finds in the American writer many of the qualities he has been advocating. "It is wrong," he writes, "to say that the cinema was invented by Edison: the cinema was invented by Edison and O. Henry. In the cinema, the most important thing is motion, motion at any cost. And in O. Henry's stories the most important thing is dynamics, motion."[53] He finds a device in O. Henry for which he coins a new term—the device of the "integrating image": thus, in "The Defeat of the City," the coolness and inaccessibility of Miss Van Der Pool are likened to the Matterhorn, and this image of the mountain is further developed in the course of the story. But this is exactly the technique that Zamyatin uses extensively in his own fiction, and the influence of O. Henry on Zamyatin's prose style has often been commented on. Still, O. Henry's work is uneven ("the same carbon produces both graphite and diamonds"): he wrote too much and the endings of his stories are repetitious in manner—the "chronic surprise ending" tends eventually to pall.

In his essay on H. G. Wells (1922), Zamyatin gives us one of the finest appraisals ever written of the British author. Keeping his obvious personal sympathy under strict control, he recognized that the Wellsian fiction was to a great extent of only contemporary significance (it is to the credit of Wells that he recognized this himself—in 1917 he said to Arnold Bennett, "My boom is over. I'm yesterday"). Zamyatin notes the similarities in basic motifs between Wells's "urban fairy tales" and other fairy tales—the cap that makes one invisible, the metamorphoses, the flying carpet, and the man-eating monsters. He analyzes the convincing scientific "matter" in Wells' fantastic stories as well as the striking prophetic qualities of many of the stories and novels. But it is Wells the "sociofantasist" whom Zamyatin admires most of all and he expatiates upon Wells's socialist theory and his humanism. Yet Wells's socialism is not a "party" socialism: "if any political party should attempt to use Wells as a rubber stamp for its

52. In the article *le papa* appeared inadvertently as *le pape*.

53. A *Soviet Heretic*, p. 111.

program, it would be much like attempting to affirm Orthodox Christianity by reference to Tolstoy or Rozanov."[54] Zamyatin also notes that Wells, like the majority of contemporary British prose writers, pays much more attention to plot than to language and style; it is clear that Zamyatin misses the typically Russian concern for the word, the careful attention to subtleties of phrasing and sound that he so eagerly appreciates in the Neorealists.

Although Zamyatin was never officially connected with the Formalists, he was quite favorably disposed toward their methods (his own criticism is, after all, seriously concerned with the objective analysis of "devices") and he gives us a short but sympathetic account of their origin and aims. To be sure, he is sometimes sarcastic, especially with reference to Shklovsky (but the Formalists—and Shklovsky most of all—often invited sarcasm): thus, in commenting on how much of contemporary fiction begins well but ends badly, Zamyatin likens his day and age to a novel, the close of which "not even Shklovsky can compute with his arithmetic."

Both Lev Lunts and Veniamin Kaverin (pseudonym of V. Zilberg) were associated with the Serapion Brothers. Lunts (1901–24), a promising young playwright and critic, wrote the brash "manifesto" of the Brothers, complaining of the stiffness and commonplaceness of Russian literature, eulogizing the rich fantasy of Hoffmann, and urging that the works of Russian writers be, if nothing else, organic. And in order for Russian prose to be organic, mastery of plot construction must catch up with mastery of ornamental prose. Lunts studied in seminars conducted by the Formalists Shklovsky and Tynyanov and in 1923 published an essay, "To the West!" in which he recommended that Russian writers turn again to the masters of fiction and plot in the West and relearn their craft. This "cosmopolitan" advice, together with Lunts's fervent belief in the purposeless nature of art and his apolitical views in general (Trotsky complained that the Serapions "gloried in their lack of principles"), naturally called forth angry attacks from hack Marxist critics who as yet, however, were not in sole control of literary production.

Kaverin (born 1902), the author of a good early Soviet novel, *Artist Unknown* (1931), was enthralled by the fantasy as well as the structural devices of Sterne and the German romantics. Like Lunts, he was particularly concerned with the study of plot development and with prose fiction in which plot is the chief preoccupation of the au-

54. *Ibid.*, p. 268.

thor (*sjuzhetnaja proza*[55]). His own early fiction, however, of almost bewildering fantasy, does not show mastery of plot, a fact noted by his friend Lunts.[56] Like many modernists, Kaverin urged—and practiced in his own fiction—experimentation with the categories of time and causality and the purposeful disruption of chronological sequences. Kaverin has also left us an important work of literary scholarship in his study of "Baron Brambeus" (pseudonym of Osip Senkovsky, a literary figure of the age of Pushkin).

11

There were two major post-Symbolist movements in Russian poetry, both reacting in their own ways against the vagueness and mysticism of the religious Symbolists and both producing, in addition to a remarkable body of poetry, some theoretical criticism of note. These were the two groups known as the Acmeists and the Futurists. The Acmeists (this is the more familiar name of the Poets' Guild, founded in 1912) included three major Russian poets, Akhmatova, Gumilev, and Mandelshtam, as well as a minor poet, Gorodetsky. Of these, Akhmatova was silent for many years, "purged" in 1946, and allowed to publish again in the fifties and sixties; Gumilev was executed, and Mandelshtam died in a Soviet concentration camp. Generally speaking, the poetry of the Acmeists is neoclassicist or Parnassian in its tendencies, showing a renewed interest in "Apollonian" clarity of statement, and more reminiscent of French than of German traditions. Anna Akhmatova (1888–1966)—her real name was Anna Gorenko—was the least interested, amongst the Acmeists, in poetic theory, although excellent Formalist analyses of her own verse were later written by Eykhenbaum and Vinogradov. In the twenties, however, she published some important Pushkin studies, including research that demonstrated the dependence of Pushkin's *The Tale of the Golden Cockerel* on Washington Irving's *The Tale of the Arabian Astrologer.* Akhmatova was briefly married to Nikolay Gumilev (1886–1921), who was executed for alleged complicity in an anti-Soviet plot; he was for

55. On the terms *sjuzhet* and *fabula,* see Chapter VIII, section 2, on Shklovsky.

56. In the thirties Kaverin renounced his "Formalist" experimentation and turned to a more conservative style in conformity with Socialist Realism.

long (and still is officially) a "non-person," but his exotic and vigorous poetry seems now to be attracting more and more young readers. In his essay, "The Heritage of Symbolism and Acmeism" (1913), Gumilev pays homage to Symbolism as a worthy predecessor of Acmeism; but the Acmeists reject the cult of individualism and demand a closer relationship between poetry and life. Their ideals are no longer to be found in German mysticism or fantasy. Gumilev mentions in particular the names of Shakespeare, Rabelais, Villon, and Théophile Gautier. "Each of them," he writes, "is a corner-stone of the Acmeist structure." Shakespeare shows us the inner world of men, Rabelais reveals the body and its delights, Villon tells us about life in all its variety, and Gautier's art offers a proper form; to unite these four traditions is the goal of the Acmeists. But the emphasis is on a return in Russian poetry to simplicity and lucidity, while the symbol should be, not the keystone of poetry (as it was for the Symbolists), but only one of a number of "methods of poetic effect." In his "Letters on Russian Poetry" (1923), Gumilev pays homage to Bryusov and the pioneering accomplishments of the Symbolists, notes the predominant "Gallic spirit" amongst the new poets, and everywhere makes clear his "clarist" preferences. But poetry for Gumilev is not a mere vehicle for crystal-clear exposition, since he believes that true poetry, whatever else it might or might not do, must "hypnotize" and enchant.

Osip Mandelshtam (1892–1942?), although primarily a poet, has left us, in addition to his theoretical articles, a fascinating collection of "poetic" prose—*The Egyptian Stamp* (1928). For Mandelshtam (who wrote an Acmeist manifesto, "The Dawn of Acmeism") and for the Acmeists in general, a word is valuable in its own right—for its own meaning, its own sound—and not as a means to any "higher reality." Poetry is no longer "theurgy" but a product, to a very great extent, of craftsmanship. This Acmeist emphasis on craftsmanship and on exactness, concision, and lucidity of statement, as well as the epigrammatic quality of both Acmeist prose and poetry, have led many critics to liken the movement to eighteenth-century neoclassicism, although the term "neoparnassian" is perhaps more fitting. In another essay Mandelshtam notes and objects to the manner in which Symbolist poets such as Balmont treat their readers: they seem to pride themselves on their aloofness from (and sometimes contempt for) their readers, while their "address" has the habit of shooting past the listener like an arrow intent only on its own high goal.

The sensitivity of Mandelshtam as a critic of poetry is especially striking and there is now available, for example, a good translation of an essay of his on Dante.[57] The criticism of Mandelshtam, though replete with illuminating metaphor, is not purely impressionistic by any means. He is thus not averse to using analogies from the natural sciences and likens the *Divine Comedy* to a "strictly stereometric body, one integral development of a crystallographic theme. It is unthinkable that one might encompass with the eye or visually imagine to oneself this shape of thirteen thousand facets with its monstrous exactitude." Of traditional Dante criticism he writes:

> If you give a child a thousand rubles and then leave him the choice of keeping either the small change or the notes, he will of course choose the coins, and by this means you can take the entire amount away from him by giving him a ten-kopeck piece. Precisely the same thing has befallen European Dante criticism, which has nailed him to the landscape of Hell as depicted in the etchings. No one has yet approached Dante with a geologist's hammer, in order to ascertain the crystalline structure of his rock, in order to study the particles of other minerals in it, to study its smoky color, its garish patterning, to judge it as a mineral crystal which has been subjected to the most varied series of accidents.

Mandelshtam notes a special quality of Dante's metaphor, a way of describing a phenomenon so as to "exhaust" it (and he quotes an exemplary passage from the *Inferno*, XXVI, 25–42):

> To do this he makes use of a device which I should like to call the Heraclitean metaphor, with which he so strongly emphasizes the fluidity of the phenomenon and with such a flourish cancels it altogether that direct contemplation, once the metaphor has done its work, is really left with nothing to live on. Several times already I have had occasion to remark that the metaphoric devices of Dante surpass our notions of composition, since our critical doctrines, fettered by the syntactic mode of thinking, are powerless before him.

Like his poetry, Mandelshtam's criticism is extremely rich in allusions to the thought, literatures, and monuments of Western Europe.

57. "Talking About Dante," trans. by Clarence Brown and Robert Hughes, *Delos* (a publication of the University of Texas at Austin), 6 (1971), pp. 65–106. Subsequent quotations are drawn from this translation.

He had an especially intense interest in classical antiquity, and, though he was Jewish, his poetry is shot through with touching reminiscences of Russian churches and Orthodox liturgy. His cosmopolitanism, however, and his Jewishness were both marks against him, reminding us of Khrushchev's later denunciations. But it is also interesting to hear Mandelshtam talk about the poet "thinking in images," albeit in a modern, technological setting:

> As in all true poetry, Dante's thinking in images is accomplished with the help of a characteristic of poetic material which I propose to call its transformability or convertibility. It is only by convention that the development of an image can be called development. Indeed, imagine to yourself an airplane (forgetting the technical impossibility) which in full flight constructs and launches another machine. In just the same way, this second flying machine, completely absorbed in its own flight, still manages to assemble and launch a third. In order to make this suggestive and helpful comparison more precise, I will add that the assembly and launching of these technically unthinkable machines that are sent flying off in the midst of flight do not constitute a secondary or peripheral function of the plane that is in flight; they form a most essential attribute and part of the flight itself, and they contribute no less to its feasibility and safety than the proper functioning of the steering gear or the uninterrupted working of the engine.

Considerable attention is also paid to the auditory effecs in Dante: the "peculiar labial music" of words like *abbo, babbo,* and *gabbo;* the squawk of a "Slavonic duck" in *Osteric, Tambernic, cric;* and the "locust phonetics" of *Mettendo i denti in nota di cicogna.*

Quite naturally—but this is most ironic in view of Mandelshtam's own sad end—he comments on the roles prisons have played in the life of the Italian people. "The *Trecento,*" he writes, "threw men into prison with an amazing unconcern." When and if, however, detailed studies of prisons and the literature of imprisonment are ever written, a separate volume at least will be required to survey the extensive Russian and especially Soviet contributions.[58]

Sergey Gorodetsky (born 1884) showed a special interest in the theater and drama as vitally important forces in bringing together the

58. It has recently been reported that a collection of Mandelshtam's poetry, prepared over ten years ago, has been published in Moscow.

intelligentsia and the people. Like Gumilev, he felt that the Symbolists (including both the early decadents and the later metaphysical poets) had done a memorable service for Russian poetry; but their individualism had gone too far and had eventually separated their art from this world and the masses. Gorodetsky notes that the Acmeists have come to accept the world as it is, with its beauty and its ugliness, and he speaks in pure Parnassian terms when he writes: "Art is solidity, whereas Symbolism has only exploited the fluidity of the world" ("Some Currents in Contemporary Literature"). It was Gorodetsky who provided the most-quoted definition of Acmiesm by pointing out that, whereas the rose was valued by the Symbolists as a symbol of mystical love, the Acmeists valued the flower for itself and its physical qualities.

Although Mikhail Kuzmin (1875–1936) and Vladislav Khodasevich (1886–1939) were not officially connected with the Acmeist group, their views are in many respects similar. Kuzmin, whose predilections again were Mediterranean rather than Germanic, was a poet and a novelist, a master of what Russians call "stylization." His themes were notoriously erotic, although they seem innocuous enough today. Like the Acmeists, Kuzmin was an advocate of clarity and lucidity as well as logic in poetry. Indeed, his best-known article is entitled "On Beautiful Clarity" (*O prekrasnoj jasnosti*, 1910); here he advises poets not only to be logical in their thought and syntax and meticulous with details but also to "love the word as Flaubert did, be economical in means and sparing in the use of words." Then, he says to the poet, "You will find the secret of a marvelous thing—beautiful clarity, which I would call clarism [*klarizm*]." One is reminded here of the stress laid on logic and simplicity by Karamzin and his followers as well as their opposition to the "wild poetics" of men like Lomonosov and Derzhavin. "This heritage of the Karamzinians," writes Krystyna Pomorska, "was taken over by Pushkin, who was considered by the Acmeists their dearest and closest tradition."[59] Khodasevich (whom Vladimir Nabokov ranks surprisingly high as a poet[60]) left Russia at the time of the Revolution. Like the Acmeists, his sympathies were classicist and he himself stands firmly in the Pushkinian tradition. He wrote a study of

59. *Russian Formalist Theory and Its Poetic Ambiance* (The Hague: Mouton, 1968), p. 47.

60. A footnote on p. 33 of his *Notes on Prosody* (New York: Pantheon Books, Bollingen Series LXXIIA, 1964) informs us that "this century has not yet produced any Russian poet surpassing Vladislav Hodasevich."

Derzhavin (1931), a book of literary memoirs (*Nekropol'*, 1935), and a fine essay, in the Acmeist manner, on Pushkin's poetic economy (*Poèticheskoe khozjajstvo Pushkina,* 1929). In addition to his general comments on Symbolism (he stresses the lyrical heritage of Symbolism and its extra-literary involvements), he has some astute remarks on Bryusov and his poetry. He speaks of Bryusov's "intellectual Don Juanism" and notes that, with the Symbolist poets, it is especially difficult to separate the poems from the poet, an observation that is reminiscent of Friedrich Schlegel's view of the poet as Brahmin. Khodasevich, as an *émigré,* thinks little, as one might expect, of Gorky, and his comments on Mayakovsky (that, for example, in his themes he departed considerably from "orthodox" Futurist canons) are hardly unique.

Marina Tsvetaeva (1892–1941) was a poet, the "chief rival and only peer" (Poggioli) of Anna Akhmatova. Having published some poetry in Russia, she emigrated in 1922 and spent some twenty years abroad, mainly in Prague and Paris, where she became one of the leading writers of the emigration. Her husband, Sergey Efron, who was apparently a Soviet agent, later returned to the Soviet Union where he disappeared and is presumed to have been executed. His wife also returned to Moscow in the late thirties but was soon evacuated (or banished) to the provinces; she hanged herself in the town of Elabuga in 1941. In 1956 Ilya Erenburg, the Soviet novelist and journalist, published an article that revealed her tragic death and suggested that, with the "thaw," her poetry would soon appear in print.

Mirsky is gracious enough to comment that Tsvetaeva's verse is "entirely free from the doubtful amenities of 'ladyish' poetry," and Pasternak, in his *Autobiography,* devotes some of his most moving pages to this woman. She is the author of a modern verse classic—*Tsar-Devitsa* ("The King-Maiden")—and her poetry is regularly anthologized abroad. A collection of her prose, including some critical articles, was republished in the United States in 1954; these provide a sensitive insight into the works and personalities of several important figures of the Silver Age—notably Bryusov and Pasternak. Tsvetaeva's criticism is highly impressionistic and has many of the qualities of her richly melodic and "staccato" verse. American readers may now sample her prose in English translation, and there is an excellent study of her art by Simon Karlinsky.[61]

61. *Marina Cvetaeva: Her Life and Art* (Berkeley and Los Angeles: University of California Press, 1966).

12

Russian Futurism, in addition to being, like Acmeism, a post-Symbolist movement (it has been called a "Symbolist heresy"), had affiliations with other earlier and contemporary currents in European thought.[62] It had connections, though tenuous and controversial, with "original" Italian Futurism and was closely related with French (and Russian) Cubist painting and theory. Futurism was, of course, a broad aristic movement, involving or influencing not only literature (especially poetry) but also painting, sculpture, and architecture, the theater and cinema, and even industrial design. It is significant that all three major figures in Russian literary Futurism to be discussed below were in one way or another connected with painting or drawing; and it is now a commonplace to point out how Symbolism was oriented toward music, Futurism toward painting and the graphic arts. There are also subtle associations with new philosophical ideas (e.g., the phenomenology of Husserl, whose works began to appear in Russian translation in 1912) and, more important, with new linguistic and stylistic theory. Though this linguistic and stylistic theory will be more appropriately discussed in the following chapter on Russian Formalism, it should be kept in mind that for a number of years Futurism and Formalism ran concurrently in Russia and both the ideas and personalities of the two movements were closely interrelated.

Marinetti, the spokesman of Italian *futurismo,* vaunted the modern and glorified the advent of a new, dynamic industrial age of stainless steel, glass, and electric power. He also attacked the strongholds of tradition in literature and the arts, urging the adoption of new themes consonant with the times. The Russian Futurists (who called themselves Cubo-Futurists), although notoriously harsh in their condemnation of the old and the traditional, stressed not so much the adoption of new themes as of new forms. Subject matter for them was of secondary importance. Genuine novelty in literature lay not in treating new thematic material but rather in the application of new forms

62. For an account of Russian Futurism in English, see Vladimir Markov, *Russian Futurism: A History* (Berkeley and Los Angeles: University of California Press, 1968).

or, even more important, in a radically new manipulation of language. It goes without saying that the tradition, strong in Russian poetry (and art in general), of meaningful ethical content was rejected: all talk of "content" and "spirituality" represented, for David Burlyuk, a veritable crime against genuine art. Camilla Gray, speaking of Futurism in painting, notes both the international quality of the movement as well as its uniqueness:

> Russia, in fact, became a truly international centre during these next years up to the outbreak of the First World War in 1914: on the basis of this international meeting-ground of ideas, the Cubo-Futurist movement emerged. While intrinsically bound up with, and owing much to, contemporary Western European movements—reflected in its name—Cubo-Futurism was a movement peculiar to Russia and immediately preceded the schools of abstract painting which arose in Russia during the years 1911–21, in which the Russians emerged at last as pioneers in the "modern movement."[63]

Russian Futurism may be said to have officially begun in 1912 when a group of four men—David Burlyuk, Aleksey Kruchenykh, Vladimir Mayakovsky, and Velimir Khlebnikov—issued a manifesto, insolently entitled "A Slap in the Face of Public Taste." Announcing themselves as mouthpieces of "Time's trumpet," they called for nothing less than the scrapping of the entire Russian cultural tradition. "The Academy and Pushkin are," they wrote, "less comprehensible than hieroglyphics. Toss overboard from the steamship 'Modernity' Pushkin, Dostoevsky, Tolstoy and the others. . . . From the top of our skyscraper we look down on their meanness. . . . Even if our writings yet show traces of your 'common sense' and 'good taste,' they still gleam for the first time with the flashes of a new beauty to come." The manifesto also called for an "uncompromising hatred" of traditional literary language and urged that the Russian language be enriched with new words. David Burlyuk, a minor Futurist poet, is best known for having convinced the young Mayakovsky to become a poet rather than an artist. He left Russia in the early twenties, settled in the United States, where he became a well-known painter, and died here in 1967. Although he was a belligerent spokesman and defender of

63. *The Great Experiment: Russian Art 1863–1922* (New York: Harry N. Abrams, 1962), p. 86.

Futurist tenets, Burlyuk was essentially superficial and in no sense a critic.

Viktor Khlebnikov (1885–1922), who wrote under the pen name of Velimir Khlebnikov, was not the greatest of the Futurist poets (this honor belongs to Mayakovsky), but he was the leading figure in the movement insofar as brilliant insights, experimentation, and the elaboration of poetic theory are concerned. Gumilev and Mayakovsky, amongst others, have testified to his originality and genius. Khlebnikov coined the word *budetljanin* as the Russian equivalent of *futurist* and provided, in his own strikingly innovational poetry, a favorite corpus for Formalist analysis. He also coined the phrase *samovitoe slovo* (self-sufficient, or self-valuable, word), which became so popular with the Formalists. Together with Kruchenykh, he devised both the term and technique of "transmental language" (*zaumnyj jazyk*), of which a number of his own poems are "classical" examples. Thus his most famous "*zaum*" poem, "Incantation by Laughter" (*Zakljatie smekhom*), consists entirely of derivatives, newly coined, of the Russian word for *laughter, smekh.* Occasionally some of his poetry is erroneously described as "nonsense verse"; but, while a good deal of his verse is obscure and elliptic, Khlebnikov was never a practitioner of purely "phonic" poetry, since, as Jakobson has pointed out, his basic unit is the morpheme in which there is always a minimum residue of meaning. The Formalist critic Tynyanov, who once remarked that even "nonsense" syllables, once they are set to iambic rhythm, acquire *some* meaning, credited Khlebnikov with bringing about a renewed interest in the nature of meaning in Russian poetry. Khlebnikov, who was quite indifferent to contemporary themes and deeply interested in Slavic mythology and philology, wanted, as Krystyna Pomorska puts it, "to reestablish the lost contact between sign and referent." This was to be done by revitalizing archaic roots with new affixes. "By replacing one sound with another in an old word," he writes, "we immediately make a road from one linguistic valley to another and, like railway engineers, we lay lines of communication in the land of words across the mountain ranges of linguistic silence." A particular form of this interesting but unorthodox philology is Khlebnikov's concept of the "internal declension of words": in this way he considers, for instance, the two Russian words *byk* (ox) and *bok* (side) to be meaningfully related.

The more one reads Khlebnikov, the more one is struck by the strangeness of his ideas in the ambiance of Futurism. There is his almost mystical adulation of the Word, his interest in the ancient

Slavic past and in quaint and fantastic word-lore, and his search for the "philosopher's stone" whereby to transform all Slavic words—in all this there is more that smacks of cabalism than of literary theory proper. There is thus good reason why he has been called both "passéist" and "classicist." It is noteworthy, for example, that his name has been linked with that of Lomonosov (Erlich), that his philology has been likened to that of Vico (Pomorska), and that his obsession with the ancient myth of a universal language and his methods of regaining this have been compared with the work of René Ghil, the French Symbolist (Poggioli). Still, there is, especially in Khlebnikov's poetry, much that puts him securely in the *avant-garde,* and much of his thought, refreshingly free at least of socio-political and religious mumbo-jumbo, looks forward to new and bold horizons: he theorized, for instance, about the future possibilities of using mathematical symbols and "syncretic graphic signs" in verse.

Aleksey Kruchenykh (born in 1886) was somewhat more extreme in his theory and practice of poetry. Kruchenykh began his artistic career as a painter and, when he turned to poetry, expressed a keen desire to emancipate words completely from their "traditional subservience to meaning." He wrote that Russian literature from Pushkin to his own day was never concerned with literature as such but rather with "exorcizing the devil": it was not literature at all but a "rescue society." He claimed that a five-line poem of his own, consisting of true nonsense words, contained more Russian national feeling than all the poetry of Pushkin.[64] In many of his statements there is a clear-cut anticipation of familiar Surrealist views: psychic states may give birth to new and strange combinations of letters, words, and sounds, devoid of articulate meaning. He further asserted that "form determines content" and that new forms automatically produce new content, an idea that was enthusiastically taken up by the Formalists. (For Kruchenykh —and the Futurists and Formalists in general—Cato the Elder's traditional advice, *Rem tene, verba sequentur,* is reversed: *Verba tene, res sequetur.*) Kruchenykh's concept of "transmental language" (*zaumnyj jazyk*) was quite broad, including the use of provincialisms and dialectical stylization (called *skaz* in Russian), and he commented on these linguistic and stylistic features in the prose of Babel and Leonov. He has several interesting short studies—such as "The Texture

64. Trotsky (in *Literature and Revolution*) commented on the bad manners of Kruchenykh and the Futurists, observing that perhaps someone will eventually write poetry in the Futurist key that will be greater than Pushkin's—"but we will have to wait."

of the Word" (*Faktura slova,* 1923) and "The Shiftology of Russian Verse" (*Sdvigologija russkogo stikha,* 1923)[65]—in which there are clever observations on alliteration and on traditional versus modern sound combinations in poetry. Kruchenykh admires the extreme practices and extravagant juxtapositions of the Futurists and other Modernists, and feels that these are what distinguish the language of his own "impetuous age." This constant—and sometimes annoying—Futurist emphasis on the new and on "inventiveness" (*izobretatel'stvo*), as if these qualities represented the sole essence of all great art, is something we shall also find among the Formalists. Kruchenykh was also interested in *avant-garde* theater and his own "Futuristic opera," *Victory Over the Sun* (in which the songs of The Frightened One are entirely in vowels, those of The Aviator in consonants), was considered by the painter Malevich to be the beginning of a new movement —Suprematism.

The name of Vladimir Mayakovsky (1893–1930), although his reputation as a poet seems now well established, still elicits strong reactions amongst many Russians outside the Soviet Union (in Russia a certain side of Mayakovsky and a selected body of his poetry have been "canonized"). On the one hand he is considered a crude and embarrassing interloper in the Parnassus of Russian poetry; on the other, he is admired as, at the least, a refreshing and stimulating voice and, at the highest, as one of the three or four greatest Russian poets. Pasternak, like many other professional poets, speaks highly of him ("Mayakovsky's taste," he once wrote, "was so mature and fully developed that it seemed older than himself"), but recognizes that he was "spoilt from childhood by the future." From a technical point of view, Mayakovsky's poetic language and especially his startlingly new rhymes are at times breath-taking, and Unbegaun rightly calls Mayakovsky "the supreme virtuoso" in this respect.[66]

More than the other Futurists, Mayakovsky is iconoclastic and hyperbolic in his denunciations of traditional Russian poetics; and like them he regards poetry as a craft and poems as products. Scornfully rejecting the notion that poetry must be mellifluous, he prefers difficult, unprecedented sound combinations, striking juxtapositions, and

65. The term *sdvigologija,* coined by Kruchenykh, covers the use and study of all types of "shifts" or "dislocations," i.e., purposeful violation or distortion of traditional meanings, categories, sequences, etc. It should be noted that the terms *faktura* and *sdvig* were borrowed from painting.

66. Boris Unbegaun, *Russian Versification* (Oxford: Oxford University Press, 1956), p. 148.

startling metaphor and simile ("I am as lonely as the only eye of a man going blind"). Still, it is surprising to what an extent this metaphor draws, for instance, upon Russian Orthodox liturgy and ecclesiastical language. Many of his pronouncements, though they might once have sounded outrageously radical, reflect quite traditional romantic views. He rejects, of course, the doctrine of *mimesis* but then adds, in true romantic fashion, that art is the determination to "distort nature in accordance with the latter's reflections in the individual consciousness." Like the other Futurists, the early Mayakovsky upheld the primacy of form: it mattered little, he once wrote, "whether you pour wine or slop into a vase." But such a view had necessarily to be modified in the face of Soviet demands for relevant and dogmatic content. Though Mayakovsky was an extreme romantic and though his true talent lay in the lyric poetry of love and private states of mind, his public pronouncements defend the significance of the social context and vaunt revolutionary themes and slogans. His, indeed, was an exemplary case of a poet valiantly trying to do two radically different things at the same time, and it is no wonder that his life ended in suicide. The personal idiosyncrasies of Mayakovsky were notorious in his day but seem rather tame to us now; yet while these caprices are often exaggerated in books and articles dealing with his life, the fact is often forgotten that he was most seriously interested in his craft of words. "He was present," Erlich observes, "when Jakobson read his paper on Khlebnikov and listened intently to the speaker's abstruse argument in which he examined Russian Futurist verse in the light of concepts derived from E. Husserl and F. de Saussure."[67]

In what is perhaps his best-known technical analysis of poetry and step-by-step description of the genesis of a poem, *How Are Verses Made?* (1926),[68] Mayakovsky tries boldly to state some of the crucial problems of aesthetics and poetics in a simple and down-to-earth language, at the same time treating us to a first-hand account of the creative process. He stresses again and again the view that poetry is "manufacture," that the poet must practice his craft daily, and he even goes into the importance of "tools"—the need, for instance, of a good notebook. He combines with these tenets the Marxist doctrine that the poet must not be apolitical: he should study economics and science, be in the vanguard of his class, help destroy the myth of art for art's sake, etc. But no problems are really solved, and we have no statistics on

67. Victor Erlich, *Russian Formalism* (The Hague: Mouton, 1969), p. 65.

68. Available in English translation (London: Cape Editions, 1970).

how many would-be poets were inspired by Mayakovsky's advice. What is very clear, however, is the unresolved contradiction between the view of poetry as the end product of a complex technical process and the view that the real power of poetry lies in that inexplicable mystery (Mayakovsky uses the word *magic*) of certain words in certain combinations, something the late American critic Richard P. Blackmur called the "synergical influence of words thrown together." On the whole, and allowing for the understandable shift from radical apolitical Modernism to a politically oriented proletarian and utilitarian stance more palatable to the authorities, there is no consistent or even original critical or poetic theory in Mayakovsky. He says much that has been said before in a language that is superficially "shocking" but basically platitudinous.

In 1923 Mayakovsky and a number of other Futurists founded an organization known as LEF (The Left Front of Art), a short-lived attempt to bring about an alliance between Futurism and Bolshevism. After the Revolution, although the Communists early began a campaign to do away ruthlessly with all vestiges of Russia's past, it was not long before signs of a reverse trend were evident; gradually much that was traditional and that had, in fact, been abolished—such as insignia of military rank—began to return, until the Soviet Union eventually became—and remains—one of the most conservative systems in the world. Prior to the Revolution and until the twenties, the radical views of the Futurists, like those of other fellow-traveler groups, had been roughly in line with radical revolutionary doctrine and there was not too much friction. But the extreme Modernism of the Futurists and many other smaller radical movements in art and literature (including the *nichevoki* who wrote nothing and *vsechestvo* or "everythingism"), with their flamboyant behavior, their relentless denunciation of the classics of Russian art and literature, their "high-brow" manipulation of language, and their underlying apoliticism, gradually became distasteful and embarrassing to Party officials. One can imagine, for instance, what Marxists thought of Kruchenykh's "Formalistic determinism." Lenin himself, who loved Pushkin and the Russian classics, said that he could not understand Mayakovsky and he referred disparagingly to the poet's "hooligan-communism." The LEF organization, which preached an "encompassing of the great social theme by all the instruments of Futurism" (Mayakovsky) and advocated the factual reporting of reality ("factography") in lieu of an imaginative literature, ceased to play any effective role by the time of Mayakovsky's suicide in 1930; and by 1932, when the Union of Soviet Writers was established with official Party sanction, the activities of all *avant-garde* groups as well as of more leftist groups (which had tried clumsily and in vain to produce a new "proletarian" literature) were brought to an end. By this time, too, the era of Formalism in Russian criticism had all but ended and a considerable body of Marxist theory had accumulated. In the next chapter, therefore, we shall go back and trace some of the major aspects of Formalist theory; and in Chapter IX we shall consider Russian Marxist-Leninist literary theory and criticism.

SUGGESTED READING

Maslenikov, Oleg, *The Frenzied Poets* (Berkeley and Los Angeles: University of California Press, 1952).

Donchin, Georgette, *The Influence of French Symbolism on Russian Poetry* (The Hague: Mouton, 1958).

West, James, *Russian Symbolism: A Study of Vyacheslav Ivanov and the Russian Symbolist Aesthetic* (London: Methuen, 1970).

Field, Andrew, ed., *The Complection of Russian Literature* (New York: Atheneum, 1971), contains brief extracts from Annensky, Bryusov, Gippius, Ivanov, Blok, Bely, Ivanov-Razumnik, Mandelshtam, Kuzmin, Khodasevich, and Tsvetaeva.

Gifford, Henry, ed., *Leo Tolstoy* (Harmondsworth: Penguin Critical Anthologies, 1971), contains excerpts from essays by Merezhkovsky, Shestov, Berdyaev, and Blok on Tolstoy.

Roberts, Spencer, ed., *Essays in Russian Literature* (Athens: Ohio University Press, 1968), contains essays by Shestov and Rozanov.

Berdyaev, Nicholas, *Dostoevsky*, trans. by Donald Attwater (New York: Meridian Books, 1957).

Ivanov, Vyacheslav, *Freedom and the Tragic Life: A Study in Dostoevsky*, trans. by Norman Cameron (New York: Noonday Press, 1957).

Ginsburg, Mirra, ed. and trans., *A Soviet Heretic: Essays by Yevgeny Zamyatin* (Chicago: University of Chicago Press, 1970).

Oulanoff, Hongor, *The Serapion Brothers* (The Hague: Mouton, 1966).

Raffel, Burton, and Burago, Alla, trans., *Selected Works of Nikolai S. Gumilev* (Albany: State University of New York Press, 1972), contains selections from Gumilev's criticism.

Brown, Clarence, trans., *The Prose of Osip Mandelstam* (Princeton: Princeton University Press, 1965).

Brown, Clarence, *Mandelstam* (Cambridge: Cambridge University Press, 1973).

Markov, Vladimir, *Russian Futurism: A History* (Berkeley and Los Angeles: University of California Press, 1968).

Mayakovsky, Vladimir, *How Are Verses Made?*, trans. by G. M. Hyde (London: Jonathan Cape, 1970).

Brown, Edward, *Mayakovsky* (Princeton: Princeton University Press, 1973).

Seduro, Vladimir, *Dostoyevski in Russian Literary Criticism 1846–1956* (New York: Octagon Books, 1969), Part I, Chapter 2 ("Decadents, Symbolists, and Mystics").

Mirsky, D. S., *A History of Russian Literature* (New York: Alfred A. Knopf, 1949), Book Two, Chapters 2–6.

VIII THE FORMALISTS

1

If, beginning with Lomonosov, we divide the movements in Russian literary criticism into those concerned primarily with form and those concerned primarily with ideas (or content), we observe the following sequence. First, the pseudoclassical critics are almost wholly intent on proper form; second, Belinsky and the Civic critics are almost wholly concerned with ideology; third, the Aesthetic critics, although still very conscious of social implications and relevancies, swing back to an interest in form. This interest in the formal aspects of literature, along with a general disparagement of ideas—especially in poetry—was continued by the early Symbolists of the Modernist period, while the "second generation" of Symbolists again became almost excessively concerned with ideologies of one kind or another. In turn, their epigones—in particular the Futurists—reacted with a vengeance and returned to a very marked interest in form. Subsequently, as we shall see in the following chapter, Marxist-inspired Socialist Realist literary doctrine shows a manifest but often crude return to a preoccupation with social, political, and narrowly ideological content in literature.

Those critics, flourishing more or less contemporaneously with the Futurists and often associated with them, who displayed such a renewed and intense interest in the formal qualities of literature that they were dubbed the Formalists *par excellence,* represent one of the most significant movements not only in Russian literary criticism but in European criticism as a whole. For this reason, and because they have had a good deal of influence on literary criticism (and linguistics) in the West, they deserve particular attention.

The origin of the Formalist school is specifically associated with the formation, shortly before the Revolution, of two groups of linguists, philologists, and literary historians and scholars in St. Petersburg and Moscow. In 1915 a group of students of Moscow University (including the later renowned Roman Jakobson), at first interested mainly in linguistic phenomena but later much concerned with poetics, founded the Moscow Linguistic Circle. A year later there was founded in St. Petersburg an organization known as *"Opoyaz,"* an acronym for (in Russian) the "Society for the Study of Poetic Language." Of the principal names involved in the Society, some were students of language (such as L. Yakubinsky) and some were literary theoreticians (V. Shklovsky, B. Eykhenbaum). But the Formalist school also drew on broader and older traditions. These included the work of Potebnya, discussed earlier, itself based upon German theory; the studies of Bely and the "Rhythmics Society"; and the linguistic and aesthetic theorizing of the Futurists. We can also see the influence of earlier Russian critics as far back as Lomonosov and including men like Leontiev. In addition, we can detect in many of the concepts and pronouncements of the Formalists interesting echoes of much earlier German romantic literary theory, and we can certainly note, in connection with the whole movement, the pervasive influence of German organicist and holistic thought as well as important contributions to modern structuralist theory. In this chapter we shall consider chiefly the works of two of the Russian Formalists, one fairly well known in the West and one who is not too familiar: Viktor Shklovsky, the *enfant terrible* of the group, and Yury Tynyanov. Some attention will also be paid to several other outstanding figures in the movement.[1]

2

Viktor Borisovich Shklovsky was born in St. Petersburg in 1893. Though his father, born a Jew, was later a convert to Christianity, it is tempting to speculate that perhaps much of Shklovsky's radicalism of thought and skepticism with regard to long-accepted and cherished Russian literary gentilities may be ascribed to his paternal legacy. Shklovsky made his debut as a literary theoretician in December of 1913 when, a freshman in the University of St. Petersburg, he read a paper (in a somewhat bohemian café called "The Stray Dog")

1. The definitive scholarly study in English of Russian Formalism is Victor Erlich's *Russian Formalism: History and Doctrine* (The Hague: Mouton, 1969).

entitled "The Place of Futurism in the History of Language." This paper enunciated two principal points, both of which were to be made again and again in Shklovsky's later writings. The first was that, as the Futurists themselves emphasized, the new poetry, "speech-oriented" as it was, by giving often startling primacy to sound over meaning,[2] had begun to free words from their traditional and very frequently trite meanings in verse and to restore to them a sort of "primal" freshness. It should be noted here at once that it was very characteristic of the Futurists, the Formalists, and the various structural linguists descended from or associated with these movements to stress the importance of the spoken rather than the written word, to prefer what the Germans called *Ohrenphilologie* rather than *Augenphilologie*. Indeed, it was out of this background that there eventually came a new emphasis on the "oral/aural approach" in the teaching of languages as well as the tendency, still strong today in linguistic circles, to disparage as old-fashioned and quaint the traditional textual and philological approach.

The second important point made by Shklovsky in this early paper was that it is specifically the function of art to make us *see* things (i.e., words and the illusions they create) rather than merely to recognize them; in other words, it is the function of art to "defamiliarize" the world around us and to counteract the natural tendency for perception to become automatized.[3] But this concept, of central importance in Shklovsky's thought, was later elaborated upon and exemplified in his numerous literary studies; we shall discuss it in more detail below.

In 1914 Shklovsky published his paper under the title "The Resurrection of the Word" (*Voskreshenie slova*)[4] and showed it to one of his teachers at the university, Jan Baudouin de Courtenay. This scholar, a Pole and a descendent of Baldwin I, King of Jerusalem, was the leader of the so-called Kazan school of linguistics but best known today for his formulation of that basic concept in modern linguistics, the phoneme. Professor de Courtenay did not agree fully with all of Shklovsky's ideas (few people have ever agreed with everything he expounded), but he introduced him to other students of language and

2. Tynyanov was later to note that in poetry it is sound that influences meaning, whereas in prose the reverse is true.

3. Some readers may recognize here parallels with ideas set forth by Henri Bergson in his *Le Rire.*

4. The religious and metaphysical connotations of the title did not escape the Communists, and Trotsky has some perceptive comments on this matter in particular (see below).

it was this group which later became the *Opoyaz* referred to earlier in the chapter. Meanwhile, however, Shklovsky enlisted in the army when Russia entered World War I. After assignments in Galicia and the Ukraine, he returned to Petersburg—now Petrograd—in 1916 and resumed his association with *Opoyaz.* But Shklovsky's literary activities were interrupted again by the outbreak of the February Revolution, and Shklovsky has recorded his adventures of the following several years in a book, now available in English translation, *A Sentimental Journey.*[5] The ironic title indicates his very keen interest in Laurence Sterne and we shall have more to say about this later. The book was originally published in 1923 in Berlin whither the author had fled, via Finland in 1922, to escape arrest for anti-Bolshevik activities (he had served as a commissar for the Provisional Government and had taken part in campaigns against both Whites and Reds). But in the fall of 1923 he was granted an amnesty and was allowed to return to Russia.

In 1917 Shklovsky published another article, often called the manifesto of Russian Formalism, entitled "Art as Device."[6] Here Shklovsky begins by criticizing the traditional view of poetry—or art in general—as "thinking in images." For the author, metaphor and imagery are not employed to make the unfamiliar familiar but to do the exact opposite—to make the familiar unfamiliar. Shklovsky's term, *priem ostranenija* (or "device of making strange," i.e., technique of defamiliarization[7]), although always associated with his name in discussions of Formalism and elsewhere, is actually an old idea, first outlined in Aristotle (*Poetics,* Ch. 22, 1458a) but found frequently in neoclassical "baroque" poetics (see above, Chapter I, on Lomonosov) and notably in German romantic literary theory. Thus Novalis (Friedrich von Hardenberg) writes: *Die Kunst, auf eine angenehme Art zu befremden, einen Gegenstand fremd zu machen und doch bekannt und anziehend, das ist die romantische Poetik.* Closely associated with this well-known Shklovskian concept is the general predilection of the

5. Trans. by Richard Sheldon (Ithaca: Cornell University Press, 1970).

6. *Iskusstvo kak priem.* The word *priem* is variously translated as *device, technique,* and *strategy.* This article, along with Shklovsky's stylistic commentary on Sterne's *Tristram Shandy* and two studies by Tomashevsky and Eykhenbaum, is available in English translation in *Russian Formalist Criticism: Four Essays,* ed. L. T. Lemon and M. J. Reis (Lincoln: University of Nebraska Press, 1965).

7. Occasionally the terms "alienation" and "estrangement" are used in English to translate *ostranenie.*

Formalists for what may be called "inventiveness" (*izobretatel'stvo*): that is, for bold innovation, recherché metaphor, and various ways of "toying with the narrative." Hence the Formalists—and especially Shklovsky—were particularly attracted to writers who employed such mannerisms, e.g., Gogol in Russian literature, Cervantes in Spanish literature, and Sterne in English literature. But another Russian writer, not usually thought of as a bold innovator, who provided much grist for Shklovsky's mill was Tolstoy. This writer's ironic manner (and irony must be understood here in the original Greek sense of *eiron*, "one who affects ignorance") with respect to so many aspects of upper-class Russian society lent itself splendidly to Shklovky's analysis; indeed, many modern commentators on Tolstoy now employ Shklovsky's terminology.[8] Tolstoy's works are replete with "classical" examples of what Shklovsky means by "defamiliarization": e.g., the horse as narrator in the story "Kholstomer," the description of the opera in *War and Peace*, or the account of the liturgy in *Resurrection*. Incidentally, a recent novel by William Golding, *The Inheritors*, is a treasure-house of "making strange," and Shklovsky would surely have delighted in it.[9]

Of unusual interest in the essay "Art as Device" is the section devoted to an analysis of passages from what Shklovsky calls "erotic art." Here again he easily finds many examples (in Gogol, Knut Hamsun, Boccaccio, and Russian folk poetry) of his defamiliarization technique in passages which are generally referred to as ironic or euphemistic. The erotic and sexual are seldom touched upon in Russian criticism, and it is typical of Shklovsky that he does not avoid considering this topic. It must be said, however, that he fails to cite some of the most interesting cases of erotic defamiliarization, involving grammatical and rhetorical categories: those in medieval Latin literature and in the Orient.[10] Here and elsewhere, though Shklovsky's brilliance of perception must be granted, erudition and exhaustive scholarship, as Erlich points out, are not his strongest points, and certainly amongst the Formalists he is, with all his reading, the least academic. One thinks of Nietzsche's reference to Sterne and his "*Eichhornseele*."

8. E.g., John Bayley, *Tolstoy and the Novel* (New York: Viking Press, 1967), p. 103 ff. See also R. F. Christian, *Tolstoy: A Critical Introduction* (Cambridge: Cambridge University Press, 1969), p. 144.

9. See an interesting technical discussion of this novel by M. Halliday in *Literary Style: A Symposium* (Oxford: Oxford University Press, 1971), p. 330 ff.

10. See the instances cited by Curtius, *European Literature and the Latin Middle Ages*, Appendix III.

Another technical term introduced by Shklovsky is "defacilitation" (*zatrudnenie*). In discussing this "device," Shklovky criticizes a specific aspect of Western "positivist" thought (exemplified in this case by Spencer), namely that, in accordance with the "law of the conservation of energy," the writer always exerts the least effort in expressing his ideas. Shklovsky says that this may be true of colloquial speech but that it is not at all true in art, and he cites numerous examples drawn not only from Russian literature but also from Russian folk poetry to validate his argument. For Shklovsky and the Formalists, defacilitation refers to ways in which the narrative—or poem—is deliberately, for aesthetic ends, made difficult or impeded, through the use of difficult words and syntax, the absence of a traditional metrical convention, and juxtaposition rather than transition, to name a few devices. Poetry especially employs this approach, since it is, in Shklovsky's words, "a unique kind of dancing of the speech organs" (or, as Erlich puts it, "verbal tight-rope walking"[11]). Closely related to defacilitation is retardation (*zamedlenie*)—a deliberate slowing down of the action; and in his essay on *Don Quixote* Shklovsky finds many examples of anecdotes or interpolated short stories used for this purpose. The works of Sterne and Gogol provide many more examples. Incidentally, Cervantes' novel is for Shklovsky an "open form," corresponding to parataxis on the syntactical level, just as a "closed form" (such as a literary treatment of the Oedipus legend) is analogous to hypotaxis.

At the conclusion of his essay on *Tristram Shandy* (1921), Shklovsky writes the following (and he might well be speaking of *Ulysses*): "The assertion that *Tristram Shandy* is not a novel is a common one. For persons who make this assertion, only opera is music—a symphony is a chaos." Shklovsky has just denied that the forms of art are justified by verisimilitude (or realism)—hence the reference to opera—and here he emphasizes again a basic Formalist tenet, that (as Shklovsky himself says elsewhere) "a work of literature is the sum total of all the stylistic devices used in it." Earlier in the same essay he disposes, in abrupt fashion, of the function of emotion and sentimentality in literature. Art has no mainstay, he states, least of all sentimentality: art is essentially trans-emotional. There are more than faint parallels here with certain pronouncements in the West, notably Eliot's claim that poetry is escape from emotion. But one other remark must be made here. In view of Shklovsky's essay on *Tristram Shandy* and his numerous references to Sterne's technique of the novel and especially

11. *Russian Formalism*, p. 178.

in view of the wide influence exerted by the works of Sterne in Russia, it is most surprising and disappointing not to see in a recent bicentenary volume devoted to Sterne and his influence (including an article on "Laurence Sterne and Japan")[12] a single reference to Russia, Russian literature, or Russian Formalism. It is almost as if one should publish a similar volume on Poe and neglect to mention France.

It will have been noticed in all of the foregoing—and this is another important feature of the Formalist method—that Shklovsky shies away from making value judgments. This "scientific" insistence upon the validity of description and analysis alone, all evaluation being regarded as subjective and unsound, actually culminates later in the writings of Formalists who were more structural linguists than literary critics (e.g., Roman Jakobson). But as we shall see, such literary "objectivity," scientific or not, along with practically all other Formalist tenets, very soon came into conflict with another and very different "objectivity"—Marxist-Leninist theory as applied to the arts.

Appearing in 1925 was Shklovsky's *Theory of Prose.* In his introduction to this collection of essays, Shklovsky explains his principal concern with the "internal laws of literature,"[13] and, in his typically non-academic but effective language, writes: "To use a metaphor drawn from industry, I am not concerned with the world cotton market or the policies of the trusts but only with the count of yarn and the techniques of weaving." In his article on Rozanov (see above, Chapter VII, section 5), he analyzes this writer's use of various modes of defamiliarization to achieve a particularly novel apprehension of reality. In connection with another of his concepts, his "law" of the "canonization of the lesser genres" (e.g., Blok brings into high poetry and makes canonical the themes and rhythms of gypsy songs), Shklovsky mentions Dostoevsky as a novelist who gives literary canonization to devices of the detective story.[14]

Two other important terms (out of many others) associated with Formalist literary analysis might also be mentioned here. One is "laying bare the device" (*obnazhenie priema*), a term applied by the Formalists—and later critics—to rather special cases when a writer re-

12. *The Winged Skull* (Kent State University Press, 1971).

13. Jakobson put this aspect of Formalist doctrine more explicitly when he stated that the subject matter of literary scholarship is not literature as a whole but rather "literariness" (*literaturnost'*).

14. George Moore, the Irish novelist, once dubbed Dostoevsky "Gaboriau with psychological sauce."

veals (i.e., calls attention to) a literary convention or stylistic device. Such a situation (an example would be Sterne's chapter on chapters in *Tristram Shandy*[15]) is clearly one in which form and content assume a special relationship or, as the Formalists liked to believe, content becomes form. In their analysis of novels (most often selected features of novels), the Formalists viewed character development, plot, narrative techniques, and other aspects of the novel as mere pretexts on the part of the author for employing what they called the "unfolding of the verbal material." But any attempt to argue that, for instance, Dostoevsky introduced the "Legend of the Grand Inquisitor" into his *Brothers Karamazov* simply as a pretext for exploiting certain stylistic strategies is as fatuous as it is futile.

Another set of terms used by the Formalists in their literary studies is *fabula* and *sjuzhet,* the former referring to the raw material of the story or narrative (the Russian word *fabula*—in transliteration identical with the Latin word—means simply "story" or "plot"), while the latter term (the French *sujet*) is used to mean the raw material in its artistic arrangement, that is, the aesthetically ordered presentation of the *fabula.* Though this may sound clever to some, it is basically the ancient distinction between *res* and *verba* or, in contemporary terms, between "message" and "code"; and if someone should now assert that the Formalists tried at least to define and particularize some of the essential differences, it might well be argued that the ancient rhetoricians and their successors down through the ages did as good a job. Even if we agree that, as Roland Barthes does, a story can be analyzed like a sentence and that literary study can derive useful concepts from the linguists, we must also agree that, the more rigorously and successfully any critic applies the canons of linguistic analysis to literary texts, the more his performance tends to become something other than literary criticism in the original sense of the word (i.e., as judgment and evaluation), as commented on in the Introduction here. But those of us concerned with poetry and prose literature or with art in general, much as we cherish these areas in which the products of the synthetic imagination reflect the amazing labyrinths of the mind and provide a rich variety of rewards, whether we regard art as a religious undertaking or as a game, must be prepared to see these

15. Cf. the remarks of D. Grossvogel in his *Limits of the Novel* (Ithaca: Cornell University Press, 1971), p. 148: "Structural subtleties that would normally be hidden within the fictional weave of the novel Sterne deliberately exposes for the purpose of turning his book into yet another kind of parlor game which he plays with his reader."

areas more and more subjected to analysis in the light of expanding knowledge in the fields of psychology, linguistics, and communication theory. In this new advance the Formalists were among the pioneers and there is good reason to call them, as Eykhenbaum once did, not critics in the traditional sense but rather "specifiers" (*spetsifikatory*).

The name of Flaubert has not yet been mentioned in this chapter. But those acquainted with his theoretical writings must surely have been struck by certain parallels with Formalist doctrine, especially with some of the dicta of Shklovsky. Thus the latter's disdain for content reminds one of Flaubert's rejection of the importance of subject matter—"*Yvetot*," he once wrote in this connection, "*donc vaut Constantinople*." Even more interesting is Flaubert's theorizing about the possibility of an almost purely "formal" novel: "What strikes me as beautiful, what I should like to do, is a book about nothing, a book without external attachments, which would hold together by itself through the internal force of its style . . . a book which would have practically no subject, or at least one in which the subject would be almost invisible, if that is possible."[16]

Above, in connection with Shklovsky's views of sentiment and emotion, I had occasion to mention the name of T. S. Eliot. In general, the views of these two critics differ considerably, but a few parallels have been noted. To cite one example, both critics held roughly similar "organicist" opinions concerning the ordering of bodies of literature as wholes. Often quoted are Eliot's words (in "Tradition and the Individual Talent") to the effect that "the whole of the literature of Europe from Homer . . . has a simultaneous existence and composes a simultaneous order" and that this order is modified by the introduction of new works of literature. Shklovsky, whose own holistic views are often neglected in favor of other examples of his "reification of the component part," wrote (again in his *Theory of Prose*) that a work of art is perceived against the background of and in association with other works of art and that a specific form of art is best defined by its relation to forms preceding it.[17] Although the Formalists in general were relativists, many of them citing examples of how radically literary

16. In a letter to Louise Colet, 1852. Quoted in *Documents of Modern Literary Realism*, ed. G. Becker (Princeton: Princeton University Press, 1967), p. 90.

17. See Ewa Thompson, *Russian Formalism and Anglo-American New Criticism* (The Hague: Mouton, 1971), for a study of this and other similarities between specific Formalist critics and critics in the West. Of special interest in this book is the author's search, in both the New Criticism and Formalism, for the "ghostly paradigms" of Kantian influence.

tastes change from age to age, Shklovsky himself went further and wrote that it is not the individual genius or will that creates a work of art but rather that the artist at any given period is simply the point at which external forces are operative. This was one of the few Formalist points of doctrine that could lend itself to Marxist-Leninist adaptation.

The story of Shklovsky's rather hasty retreat, under Party pressures, from his early very radical position to rapprochement and compromise with Marxist-Leninist literary theory is not a pretty one. The real attack was begun by Trotsky in his *Literature and Revolution* (1924). Unlike later less brilliant and much more virulent diatribes against Formalism, Trotsky's criticism is not wholly negative and he has a few good things to say, with wit and sagacity, of both Futurism and Formalism. But he rejects out of hand what he perceives to be idealistic and metaphysical underpinnings of the movement:

> The Formalist school represents an abortive idealism applied to the question of art. The Formalists show a fast ripening religiousness. They are followers of St. John. They believe that "In the beginning was the Word." But we believe that in the beginning was the deed. The word followed, as its phonetic shadow.[18]

Trotsky is critical, too, of Formalism's lack of concern for the sociohistorical environment:

> The architectural scheme of the Cologne cathedral can be established by measuring the base and the height of its arches, by determining the three dimensions of its naves, the dimensions and the placement of the columns, etc. But without knowing what a medieval city was like, what a guild was, or what was the Catholic Church of the Middle Ages, the Cologne cathedral will never be understood. The effort to set art free from life, to declare it a craft self-sufficient unto itself, devitalizes and kills art. The very need of such an operation is an unmistakable symptom of intellectual decline.[19]

Some favorable comments are also found in the writings of Niko-

18. *Literature and Revolution* trans. by Rose Strunsky (Ann Arbor: University of Michigan Press, 1960), p. 183.
19. *Ibid.*, pp. 180–81.

lay Bukharin (executed in 1938), an "old Bolshevik" and called by Lenin "the darling of the Party." But he felt that there was a lack of synthesis in Formalist theory and he put his finger on a patent Formalist weakness when he wrote (in 1925) that "a catalog is simply a catalog; it is, to be sure, a useful thing but please do not call this inventory a science." There was also some strong criticism from Lunacharsky, the first People's Commissar for Education. He rejected the Formalists' slighting of content and their preoccupation with devices, and he asked for a more resolutely ideological art. Lesser figures, such as P. Kogan, were even more outspoken, accusing the Formalists of superficiality and condemning their literary research as "aesthetic gourmandizing."

As the attacks continued, Shklovsky began his search for paths of compromise. His autobiography, *The Third Factory* (1926), shows the growing crisis of his mind: a defiant attempt to hold his ground alongside a somewhat clumsily outlined program for meeting the demands of social engagement. In a study of Tolstoy's *War and Peace*, published in 1928, Shklovsky makes another cleverly formulated but again clumsy attempt to combine his Formalist analysis with Marxist class concepts. He pits literary genre against class in a mechanical fashion (he was later to recognize the crudity of his approach) and manages to arrive at a kind of hybrid conclusion—that the writer's consciousness is determined by the mode of existence of his literary genre. Finally, in 1930, Shklovsky published an article entitled "A Monument to a Scientific Error," in which he makes a public recantation. But in 1963 he wrote in a letter that, despite apparent metamorphoses, he was still the "very same caterpillar."

By 1932, with the establishment of the Union of Soviet Writers, the elimination of all other literary groups, and the imposition of full Party control of the arts, Formalism very quickly became a thing of the past, and the words *formalist* and *formalizm* still remain terms of opprobrium in Russia. Of the Formalists and their followers, some emigrated, some recanted, some turned to literature or journalism, and others turned either to the innocuous editing of texts or to such things as the study of literature and commerce. The versatile Shklovsky kept busy writing scripts and scenarios for films and publishing memoirs. Following the death of Stalin, in the fifties and sixties there was a softening of the attitude toward some aspects of the Formalist method. Certain Formalist studies were partially vindicated and found to be not completely hostile to Marxism-Leninism. Shklovsky himself published several books during this period, including studies of Tolstoy and Dostoevsky. In 1964 Mihajlo Mihajlov, the Yugoslav scholar and writer, visited Viktor Shklovsky—then aged seventy—in his cottage at the Writers' Rest Home outside Moscow. Mihajlov found Shklovsky still active and in very good spirits, and they discussed the renewed interest in Dostoevsky among Soviet scholars, mysticism, and the new French novels. Shklovsky told Mihajlov that he had found two hitherto unknown stories by Tolstoy quite similar to the prose of Natalie Sarraute.[20]

3

Yury Tynyanov (1894–1943) is somewhat better known than Shklovsky for his extra-critical works of prose literature. One of his best short stories, "Second Lieutenant Kizhe" (about a "ghost" lieutenant, the product of a clerical error in military rosters under the eccentric Paul I, who rises through the ranks, is married, becomes a general, dies and is buried with full military honors), was made into a film for which Sergey Prokofiev wrote the well-known musical score. Tynyanov also wrote several very good historical novels (he has been likened to Lytton Strachey), one of which recreates the person and age of the poet and critic Kyukhelbeker (discussed in Chapter II, section 3). But Tynyanov the critic is very little known in the West (except to specialists) and few of his works are readily available in English.[21] This is unfortunate because his major volume of critical essays, *Archaists and Innovators* (1929), is a fascinating and provocative collection of astute observations. It surely must soon be made available in English translation.

Tynyanov, the son of a petty noble, graduated from the University of Petrograd, and by age twenty-nine he was a university professor and well-known literary scholar. He was associated with *Opoyaz* and also knew Gorky and the Serapion Brothers (see Chapter VII, section 10 on Zamyatin). Among the Formalists, Tynyanov is chiefly responsi-

20. Mihajlov's account of his meeting with Shklovsky and other Soviet literary figures may be found in *Moscow Summer* (New York: Farrar, Straus and Giroux, 1965).

21. Three of Tynyanov's essays are included in *Readings in Russian Poetics* (Cambridge: MIT Press, 1971).

ble for two new and significant emphases. The first involves his concept of the dynamic rather than static nature of literary phenomena, i.e., the ever-changing nature of literature, the fluidity of the boundary between literature and life, and a rejection of *a priori* definitions. (It was in fact Tynyanov who caused Shklovsky to pay more attention to the importance of the historical and sociological background in the study of literature.) For Tynyanov, literature is "dynamic verbal structure." Second, taking what we would now call a functional or "systems approach," Tynyanov looked upon literature as a "system of systems" rather than, in Shklovskian terms, a "sum total of literary devices." Here Tynyanov argues for the study of art as dynamic integration, as aesthetic structure, and not as the mere enumeration of coexisting elements, one of the less satisfying aspects of Shklovsky's method. This new Structuralist approach was actually suggested by Tynyanov and Jakobson in an article published in 1928, and the concept was later developed by scholars in Czechoslovakia (the Prague Linguistic Circle and the Czech school of structuralism) and in Poland by critics such as the phenomenologist Roman Ingarden who has "given the most coherent account of a theory which sees that the work of art is a totality but a totality composed of different heterogeneous strata."[22]

It should be remarked here, however, that Tynyanov did not view the components in a system as having equal importance; certain elements predominate and, as he says, sometimes cause the deformation of other elements. It should also be noted that this idea of "dominants" (*dominanta*)—very effectively used by Eykhenbaum, for instance, in his analysis of the poetry of Anna Akhmatova—seems to have been borrowed from the German aesthetician Christiansen.

In his *Dostoevsky and Gogol: On the Theory of Parody* (1921), Tynyanov points out, with a wealth of quotations, the more than accidental echoes of Gogol's notorious *Correspondence with Friends* in the words and character of Foma Opiskin, a "Russian Tartuffe," in Dostoevsky's *The Village of Stepanchikovo* (1859). Though Gogolian influence on Dostoevsky—especially the young Dostoevsky—is very apparent and has been rather exhaustively studied, Tynyanov prefers to use the term "stylization" rather than "influence" in his analysis. He further distinguishes subtle differences between parody and stylization (while admitting the presence of much obvious and characteristic "verbal parody" in Dostoevsky): in stylization we have no clear-cut

22. René Wellek, "Concepts of Form and Structure," in *Concepts of Criticism* (New Haven: Yale University Press, 1963), pp. 67–68.

"displacement" between the two planes (i.e., of a given work and the person or situation being "stylized"). But when stylization is comically motivated, it becomes parody, and this is the opinion of many commentators today. "In *The Village of Stepanchikovo*," writes Mochulsky (who refers to Tynyanov's study), "the writer settles accounts with his 'Gogolian period' and mercilessly avenges himself upon that which was the 'authority of the thoughts' of his youth. Foma Fomich is a caricature of Gogol. He too is a man of letters, a preacher, an instructor of morality."[23]

Tynyanov is intrigued by the subject of "duality of planes" or levels of action in literature. Thus he says that in the poetry of Mayakovsky there has occurred a splitting or separation of two previously merged planes, the lower developing into satirical poems like "The Mayakovsky Gallery" and the higher into the ode ("To the Workers of Kursk"); and with this split the sharpness and "biplanicity" (*dvuplannost'*) of the poet have been lost. Interesting also are Tynyanov's remarks on Pasternak: that we find in his poetry, for instance, a strange kind of visual perspective, much like that of people who are sick and who see very clearly objects that are close to them but for whom objects beyond are, abruptly, infinite space. He also compares the effects of Pasternak's verses on the sensitive reader to what psychologists call paramnesia (the *déja vu* phenomenon). These observations, along with many others on both poetry and prose (including a disappointingly brief look at some relationships between literary texts and their illustrations), are made in the various essays collected in *Archaists and Innovators*. Though his *The Problem of Poetic Language* (1924) is one of the best of many Russian studies, from Bely to the present, on metrics and the language of verse, it is, despite its brilliance, a densely "technical" work in the Formalist manner. Nevertheless, it is still cited with praise by scholars in the field.[24]

Along with the great majority of other Formalists as well as other modern critics with different affiliations, Tynyanov rejects the notion, traditionally very strong in Russian criticism, of literary characters as "beings" who can be discussed and whose "lives" can be subjected to ethical or behavioral criticism. He regards such ontological views as naive; characters in a work of imaginary literature, even if they are

23. Konstantin Mochulsky, *Dostoevsky: His Life and Work*, trans. by Michael Minihan (Princeton: Princeton University Press, 1967), p. 176.

24. E.g., in B. Hrushovski, "On Free Rhythms in Modern Poetry," in *Style in Language*, ed. T. Sebeok (Cambridge: MIT Press, 1960).

portraits or parodies of real-life persons, are merely "verbal products," simply an aspect of the "unfolding of the verbal material." But literary characters precisely as "verbal products," especially when these are so-called charactonyms,[25] were of significant interest to the Formalists and Tomashevsky, among others, has some interesting comments on this subject.

4

A number of other names are of particular note among the Russian Formalists. During his long and active life, Boris Eykhenbaum (1886–1959), already referred to on several occasions, was the author of numerous articles and books and was one of the editors of the Soviet Jubilee Edition of the works of Lev Tolstoy, produced between 1928 and 1958 and filling ninety volumes. Almost all of his major essay, "The Theory of the Formal Method" (1927), is available in English translation,[26] while his name is frequently mentioned in studies of Gogol and Tolstoy in the West. His early (1919) study of Gogol's famous story, "The Overcoat," ostensibly telling us (no one yet has) "how it was made" but actually analyzing the devices Gogol used in his prose, is based upon the concept of "sound gesture." More particularly, Eykhenbaum considers "The Overcoat" to be a system of "mimico-articulatory gestures" and argues that everything in the story, including the name of the principal character, is a matter of the selection and combination of sounds. Under the effect of this "dominant," even the logical structure is deformed, producing the famous Gogolian non sequiturs which Eykenbaum calls "puns" (*kalambury*).

In his study of O. Henry, "O. Henry and the Theory of the Short Story" (1925),[27] Eykhenbaum shows us a highly sophisticated O. Henry using many of the favorite Formalist strategies—defamiliarization, defacilitation, "laying bare the device," etc.—just as if he "had

25. Charactonyms (Aristotle called them *ou ta tuchonta onomata* and Lessing *redende Namen*) are names, the meaning of which fits or supplements the description of the character. See my article on Russian charactonyms in *Canadian Slavic Studies* (Fall 1968), p. 391 ff.

26. See the work cited in note 6, above.

27. There is a translation of this essay in the work cited in note 21, above.

studied the Formalist method in Russia and had frequently spoken with Viktor Shklovsky." But the interpretation, including a comparison between O. Henry and Sterne, seems somewhat forced and tendentious; especially open to criticism is Eykhenbaum's use of O. Henry's first book, *Cabbages and Kings*, as a text for analysis. But the Formalists did not at all limit their studies to "masterworks," and they often remind us of entomologists who, as scientists, study *any* insect and not merely pretty ones. Indeed, one of the aspects of Eykhenbaum's "Theory of the Formal Method" which most Western critics find unacceptable and annoying is the author's insistence that Formalism is strictly scientific (and, in this sense, not incompatible with Marxism).

Eykhenbaum's study of Tolstoy (1928–31) has been called (by Isaiah Berlin) "the best critical work on Tolstoy in any language."[28] This (note the date) is a more traditional literary study of Tolstoy's art against a socio-historical background, although it is replete with the strong and "cosmopolitan" statements so typical of the Formalists, e.g., "To speak bluntly, Tolstoy—in his sources, traditions, and 'school' —is the least Russian of all Russian writers."[29] Eykhenbaum here has moved quite far from his earlier position, but it is often difficult to determine whether he did so out of an eventual and very natural disenchantment with orthodox Formalism or whether the changes occurred as a result of the increasing Party opposition mentioned above.

Boris Tomashevsky (1890–1957) was one of the most scholarly of the Formalists, and it is to him that we owe what is probably the most comprehensive description of Formalist methodology—his *Theory of Literature* (1925). He produced some excellent critical editions of Pushkin's works, including what Mirksy calls a "model edition" of the *Gavriiliada* (an impious parody of the Annunciation), as well as convincing statistical studies of Pushkin's verse rhythms and metrics. Tomashevsky took the view—not at all unique—that the real unit of verse is not the traditional "foot" but rather the verse line as an "intonational segment." He also shows, at least in his early studies, some Formalist iconoclasm when, for instance, he refers ironically to "mes-

28. There is a brief extract in English translation from the first volume of this study in *Leo Tolstoy*, ed. Henry Gifford (Harmondsworth: Penguin Critical Anthologies, 1971), pp. 194–96.

29. An opinion indefensible at the present time in Soviet Russia. Eykhenbaum and many other Soviet writers, critics, and scholars have been criticized at various times for what is called their "bourgeois cosmopolitanism"—finding or drawing parallels between Russian and Western writers. See Solzhenitsyn's sarcastic remarks in *The First Circle*, Chapter 45 ("throwing out the foreigners").

sianism" in Russian Pushkin scholarship, with its tendency (still strong today and in the West) to separate the course of Russian literature into an "Old Testament (before Pushkin) and a New Testament (after Pushkin)."

Of special interest in Tomashevsky's *Theory of Literature* is the section on "thematology" or "thematics."[30] Here the author distinguishes between "bound motifs" (thematic elements which are essential to the narrative) and "free motifs" (motifs which are optional, so to speak, and which are largely determined by literary traditions). His further distinction between "dynamic" and "static" motifs is similar, in criteria, to distinctions made in different terms by contemporary critics and it is often referred to.[31] In a sense, Tomashevsky's *Theory of Literature* is a pioneering venture. It is a brave attempt, even if not quite successful, to describe and classify literature and its elements according to structural features with a minimum of evaluative comment, and it is the prototype of a multitude of similar books published down through the years in Soviet Russia.

Viktor Zhirmunsky (1891–1971) was another distinguished literary scholar who, beginning very early, opposed certain of the more doctrinaire Formalist positions. Thus he was one of the very few who argued against two of Shklovsky's key concepts, those of defamiliarization and defacilitation. In general, he was opposed to the neglect by dogmatic Formalism of the relationships between literature and life, and he advocated a "methodological pluralism" (Erlich). Of lasting importance are a number of Zhirmunsky's studies of poetic language, of rhyme, and of imagery; his close and revealing readings of poems by Pushkin and Blok; and a classic of comparative studies—his analysis of the influence of Byron on Pushkin.

Zhirmunsky was often interested in traditional problems of literary history and criticism, to which he brought, however, some stimulating if not startlingly novel insights. In an essay on "Classic and Romantic Poetry," for example, he distinguished between metonymy and metaphor as tropes characteristic of, respectively, classical and romantic styles. Elsewhere, in a careful analysis of a poem by Pushkin, he shows how the poet shifts his emphasis in a very personal poem from the particular and personal to the general and typical by replac-

30. About half of this is available in English translation in *Russian Formalist Criticism: Four Essays*, cited above, note 6.

31. E.g., by L. Dolezel, "Toward a Structural Theory of Content in Prose Fiction," in *Literary Style*, cited above, note 9.

ing specific words with the "metonymic periphrases" so favored by the neoclassicists. Roman Jakobson carried the distinction between metaphor and metonymy further, theorizing that prose favors the latter, poetry (or verse) the former.

But Zhirmunsky's pluralistic and academic approach in literary studies did not, of course, insulate him against Party criticism (which may be academic at times but is never pluralistic), and in the cultural purges of the late forties his "cosmopolitan" comparative studies came under attack. Though by 1947 he was publishing works such as *The Uzbek Heroic Folk Epic,* he would at least be able to reply, as the Abbé Siéyès did (when he was asked what he had done during the French Revolution): "I lived."

The name of Viktor Vinogradov (1895–1969) is almost always mentioned in discussions of the Russian Formalist movement, but it is correct to point out that his position was peripheral. Although associated in his youth with *Opoyaz,* he very early showed a tendency to deal either eclectically with theoretical problems of broad scope or, in a rather traditional academic fashion, with lexical analysis and "semantic clusters." Thus in his paper "On Developing a Theory of Poetic Language" (1927), he tackled the old problem of genre-divisions, seeing the primary "cut" as that between monolog and dialog. He also contributed to a large body of studies on what in Russian is called *skaz* (i.e., idiolect or "yarn" technique) and wrote interesting lexical analyses of the autobiography of Avvakum (seventeenth century) and of the poems of Anna Akhmatova. In the latter case, his work was criticized by Eykhenbaum for its mechanical procedures and neglect of the aesthetic function of literary devices.

Vinogradov was also a "Pushkinist," the author of books on the language and style of Pushkin, and he participated in the preparation of a useful four-volume *Pushkin Dictionary* (1961). American Slavists are familiar with his study of the history of the Russian literary language which appeared not too long ago in a condensed English version.[32] In 1950 Vinogradov supported Stalin (that "coryphaeus of linguistics," as Solzhenitsyn calls him) in the latter's rejection of the linguistic theories of Nikolay Marr, earlier considered correctly Marxist. Vinogradov was a member of the august Soviet Academy of Sci-

32. *The History of the Russian Literary Language from the Seventeenth Century to the Nineteenth,* a condensed adaptation into English by Lawrence Thomas (Madison: University of Wisconsin Press, 1969).

ences and, before he died, was awarded the Order of Lenin as well as a Stalin Prize.

Roman Jakobson (born 1896) was a member of the Moscow Linguistic Circle (see above, section 1) and was also intimately associated with the Futurists, having been a friend of both Mayakovsky and Khlebnikov (Chapter VII, section 12). After leaving the Soviet Union in 1920, he received his doctorate at Prague (where he was also associated with the Prague Linguistic Circle) and began an impressively long career as scholar, teacher, writer, and lecturer in the United States. He recently retired as Samuel Cross Professor of Slavic Languages, Literature, and General Linguistics at Harvard and Institute Professor at MIT. Jakobson has always been more of a linguist and theoretician of language than a literary scholar or critic, although his extensive bibliography, showing interests ranging from Czech verse and the Palaeosiberian languages to aphasia, contains a considerable number of items dealing with the nature of poetic language.

Jakobson's influence on structural linguistics and derivative studies as well as on other areas of Structuralist thought has been significant. Noam Chomsky's new theories of transformational grammar stem ultimately from ideas elucidated by Jakobson (although these are already being referred to as "old structuralism") and Lévi-Strauss has admitted his indebtedness to Jakobson.[33] But with these contributions, however important they may be, we shall have little further to say here, since they would take us rather far from the subject of literary criticism (as indeed some of the Formalist theorizing already has done).

One of Jakobson's earliest publications, *The Newest Russian Poetry* (Prague, 1921), in addition to containing a discussion of Khlebnikov's poetic devices, is still frequently cited as the source of several Formalist pronouncements. It is perhaps the first Formalist-oriented work in which the necessity is advocated of a more strictly scientific approach to the study of literature. Asserting, as we noted earlier, that the proper subject of literary study (or, more accurately, "literary science") is "literariness" (*literaturnost'*), Jakobson likens traditional literary scholars to policemen anxious to arrest a suspect: in order to make sure they "got their man," they would pick up everyone in the suspect's house as well as passers-by on the street. Thus literary scholars of the past—and of the present—tend to "drag in" everything and

33. See "A Conversation with Claude Lévi-Strauss," *Psychology Today* (May 1972), p. 37 ff.

anything that might possibly help to solve their problems, ransacking in their search for relevancies psychology, history, politics, philosophy, economics—in fact all areas of human knowledge.

But for Jakobson there is one proper object of study—the poem or other literary work as a complex of verbal devices; and it is the literary scientist's job to study and analyze the verbal phenomena and then to formulate the "laws" that govern the relationships and interactions between the various parts and between the parts and the whole, determine the criteria for distinguishing species and genera, etc. It is noteworthy that Jakobson, in addition to pointing out the relevance of modern physics to the new linguistic research, emphasizes as well the significant influence of the pictorial theory and practice of Cubism in helping its contemporaries to see and to understand relationships *within* a work of art. As for critical evaluation, Jakobson considers this a futile pursuit at best, all value judgments (even when based on criteria of defamiliarization and defacilitation) being relative and subjective. To call a student of poetic linguistic phenomena a "literary critic" is as meaningless to Jakobson as calling a linguist a "lexical critic."

Jakobson has continued to make strong claims for the primacy of linguistics in literary study. "Poetics deals with the problems of verbal structure," he wrote some years ago, "just as the analysis of painting is concerned with pictorial structure. Since linguistics is the global science of verbal structure, poetics may be regarded as an integral part of linguistics."[34] But such views are not easy to accept, and there has been much opposition to the Jakobsonian dogma which often appears to be both a classical example of the "fallacy of professional preoccupation" and the results of too close an association with Futurist poetics.[35] Though some of Jakobson's observations are acute and certainly provocative (several have been mentioned earlier in various connections), one never seems satisfied that a lexical, grammatical, or syntactical analysis of a work of literature can yield anything more than a lexicon, a grammar, or a syntax. Indeed, one is often tempted to ask, "So what?" It is as if one were to read a medical textbook on the human body and find here a discussion of pigmentation, here a

34. "Closing Statement: Linguistics and Poetics," *Style in Language,* cited above, note 24, p. 350 ff.

35. See, e.g., Wellek's essay "Stylistics, Poetics, and Criticism," *Discriminations* (New Haven: Yale University Press, 1971), and an article by Leo Bersani, "Is There a Science of Literature?" *Partisan Review* (Fall 1972), p. 535 ff.

list of bones, here a classification of hair types, here statistics on average weight, here a discussion of left-handedness, etc. A medical student might well consult such a reference work in order to pass an examination or a physician in order to make a diagnosis or attempt a cure, but neither he nor anyone else would look there—or in a thousand similar books—for an explanation of the art of a Pavlova. One can describe a chair in great detail, take it apart, weigh the wood and count the nails, show how a chair differs from a table, discuss "chairness" and formulate the "law of four legs"; still, we who are not "scientists" will stubbornly continue to believe that, unless you say something about the chair's function and history, relate it to the human condition and even to the human fundament, and finally—especially if the chair is a Chippendale—seriously consider the subject of beauty, any "objective" or "scientific" analysis is not only incomplete but slightly ridiculous as well.

Despite these strictures, however, we may perhaps agree that from the incisive and analytical approach of linguistically oriented scholars like Jakobson there may yet come, if not any immediate, final, and definitive answers to some of the age-old problems of literature, then at least a continuing flow of brilliant insights helping us to make some sense out of the complexities facing us. We may even hope, when more is known of the human brain and of the nature of language, that some elegant synthesis of what now appear to be disparate *aperçus* may eventually, in fact, bring us closer to more precise knowledge of literary phenomena. We should, I think, remember Ruskin's words: "Between foolish art and foolish science there may indeed be all manner of reciprocal mischievous influence; but between wise art and wise science there is essential relation, for each other's help and dignity." Meanwhile, the seminal influence of Formalist and Structuralist thought continues to be expanded, refined, and evaluated. There has recently appeared an imposing three-volume *Festschrift* in honor of Roman Jakobson on his seventieth birthday, containing essays by various scholars on subjects ranging from anthropology to Slavic history, while many of Jakobson's writings are being made available to American students and critics.

Before we move on to a survey of Russian Marxist literary theory and criticism, one further comment might be made here. It is of particular interest that at the present time in Soviet Russia, although Formalism is still very clearly under a ban, some readable structuralist studies of literature are being written. But Yury Lotman, for example, a number of whose works in Russian are now available in the West (translations should be appearing soon) and whose scholarship is held, it appears, in high repute by American structuralists, still finds it necessary to go out of his way repeatedly to disclaim (in, for instance, his *Lectures on Structural Poetics,* 1964) any connection with Formalism, as if this latter were a concept fathered by Trotsky. He repeats his disclaimer so often, in fact, that one might suspect (if we did not already know) that there *are* significant and indisputable affiliations between Formalism and Structuralism. But scholarship in Soviet Russia—and Lotman's is one of the least notorious examples—has been forced, under the pressure of Communist ideology, to dissemble, to distort, and to lie to a degree hardly equalled in any other area of modern intellectual endeavor.

SUGGESTED READING

Erlich, Victor, *Russian Formalism: History & Doctrine* (The Hague: Mouton, 1969).

Lemon, Lee, and Reis, Marion, trans., *Russian Formalist Criticism: Four Essays* (Lincoln: University of Nebraska Press, 1965).

Matejka, Ladislav, and Pomorska, Krystyna, ed., *Readings in Russian Poetics* (Cambridge: MIT Press, 1971), contains essays by Eykhenbaum, Tomashevsky, Tynyanov, Jakobson, and others.

Field, Andrew, ed., *The Complection of Russian Literature* (New York: Atheneum, 1971), includes excerpts from Eykhenbaum, Shklovsky, and Tynyanov.

Lane, Michael, ed., *Introduction to Structuralism* (New York: Basic Books, 1970), contains two essays by Jakobson, one written in collaboration with Lévi-Strauss.

Thompson, Ewa, *Russian Formalism and Anglo-American New Criticism* (The Hague: Mouton, 1971).

Pomorska, Krystyna, *Russian Formalist Theory and its Poetic Ambiance* (The Hague: Mouton, 1968).

IX MARXIST and SOVIET CRITICISM

1

It is one of the tragic ironies of European history, as Harry Levin notes, that "its most trenchant social critic has become the patron saint of its authoritarian societies." It is not only ironic but shameful that the name of Marx, a man of wide and humanistic learning with an above-average taste in literature, should serve as the aegis under which has been spawned "an artistic school which can be called the most provincial and reactionary in twentieth-century world literature" (Marc Slonim). We will not repeat here the sad story of the unnatural death of one of the great artistic movements of modern times; the suicides and insanities, the murders, corruption, and harassment of an untold number of artists; the forced exile or silencing of countless brilliantly creative minds; the fatuous and futile attempts to produce a "proletarian" literature (an anti-Marxist process and thus deservedly ridiculed by Trotsky); and the pitiful results—the revolting sentiment, the falsities and the affectations, the euphuism and the prettified conventions. Yet this story, sad though it might be, palls before the horrors of the Stalinist regime: the figure, considered modest, of 20,000,000 killed still boggles the mind. It would be a much more pleasant task to discuss the non-Russian Marxist critics: men like the Hungarian Georg Lukács (perhaps the most highly respected Marxist critic) or the German Walter Benjamin (who once remarked that the Nazis turned politics into art and the Communists turn art into politics). But we must at least trace the influence of Marxism on Soviet literary criticism and say something about Soviet literary theory.

A few brief remarks are in order concerning Vladimir Ulyanov (better known as Lenin, 1870–1924); I say "a few remarks," since there is readily available such an abundance of works, ranging from popular surveys to scholarly studies, of his life, activities, opinions, and contributions to Marxist theory that it would really be out of place here to go into any further detail.[1] And, together with Marx, Lenin still occupies such a lofty position in the Communist pantheon that it is somewhat surprising, even for observers in the West, to read of recent daring attacks on his eminence by a very few Soviet dissidents (Vasily Grossman is a prime example). By no means a literary critic, Lenin had a very conservative and quite ordinary taste in literature (we have already referred to his opinion of Mayakovsky in Chapter VII, section 12) and he thought highly of Chernyshevsky. Indeed, he once said (using appropriately rustic metaphor) that his reading of Chernyshevsky had "plowed him over" (*perepakhal*), while his comments on how much he enjoyed, for instance, the music of Beethoven but how he refused to yield to the emotional power of the music lest it distract him from his revolutionary activities remind us of Chernyshevsky's admission quoted above in Chapter IV, section 1.

Of more immediate concern to us, however, than any of these matters is a particular aspect of the Marxist-Leninist theory of knowledge, first propounded by Engels and later elaborated by Lenin. This is the "reflection theory" (or "copy theory"), the fundamental epistemological concept in dialectical materialism and a theory relating matter and knowledge that is also of importance in understanding what is meant, in the special Marxist-Leninist sense, by the reality pictured, say, in literature. According to this theory, not only is matter prior to knowledge, but it is knowable. By means of our sense organs, matter (or the external world in general) is "reflected" in our mind: we have little mirror-images or "copies" of physical objects in our brain. But the process of reflection is not a passive or static one, and it must be regarded as dialectical, involving a "qualitative leap" from perception to thought.[2] Moreover, material reality is variously represented in the minds of men of different social classes but is only perfectly reflected in a fully-developed (i.e., Communist) social consciousness. While one can get a fairly clear idea of the various Marxist-Leninist aesthetic and literary concepts to be mentioned below with-

1. The nineteenth edition (1966) of the *Index Translationum* (published by UNESCO) indicated that the writings of Lenin himself were currently being more widely translated than the Bible.

2. For further details on Marxist theory, see Henry B. Mayo, *Introduction to Marxist Theory* (New York: Oxford University Press, 1960), and Gustav A. Wetter, *Dialectical Materialism* (New York: Praeger University Series, 1963).

out following the intricacies of dialectical reasoning, the "copy theory" should be kept in mind. This is especially true in connection with the doctrine of Socialist Realism.

Georgy Plekhanov (1857–1918) was the first Russian Marxist of any importance. In the 1880s he took part in the formation of what was later to become the Russian Social Democratic (Marxist) Party and was one of Lenin's principal rivals. Plekhanov sought to combine the French and Marxist materialist traditions and believed strongly in the efficacy of the Marxist dialectical method as a tool for analyzing problems of growth and development (it was Plekhanov who introduced the phrase "dialectical materialism"). He once wrote that the primary task of the critic, when dealing with literature, is to translate from the language of art into the language of sociology; this is his concept of the "social equivalent," a notion ultimately derived from Taine. But while he followed Marx's lead in treating art and literature as ideological in nature, he generally avoided the narrow and rigidly doctrinaire (and, it must be noted, essentially un-Marxist) interpretation of later "orthodox" Russian Marxism-Leninism. Though literature is conditioned by the economic milieu and, more specifically, by the class struggle, and though it may reflect this struggle, it is too complex an activity to be solely determined by a single factor. Plekhanov thus advocated a liberal interpretation of Marx on literature, and the influence of his writings was considerable in the Russia of the 1920s (he himself died shortly after the Bolshevik seizure of power). But in the sterner thirties (it was in 1932 that the Party began to gain effective literary control and all writers had to join the Union of Soviet Writers) his views were attacked by orthodox Marxist critics who accused Plekhanov of failing to recognize and emphasize the importance of "Party spirit" (*partijnost'*) in literature.

Plekhanov condemns and rejects such artless works as Gorky's *The Mother* (1907) which Lenin admired and which has always been held up by Soviet criticasters as the prototype of the Socialist Realist novel. He regards it as mere propaganda and points out that propaganda-art has always received the full support of political regimes, whether revolutionary or reactionary. Plekhanov also shows surprisingly little sympathy for utilitarianism in art and literature and criticizes the views of Chernyshevsky and Pisarev. It is interesting, too, that the aesthetic theory of Plekhanov shows in some measure the influence of Tolstoy's *What Is Art?*, though there is more emphasis on art as a social phenomenon than on the communication of feeling.

It is probably appropriate at this time, following the mention of

Gorky and Tolstoy, to say something about "Socialist Realism." Soviet literary historians like to trace the origins of their particular brand of realism back to the iconoclastic and rationalist Tolstoy and the "great tradition" of Russian realism; here Gorky, himself an ardent admirer of Tolstoy and a writer who held himself aloof from the Modernist movement, serves as a convenient connecting link. It was Gorky, speaking at the 1934 All-Union Congress of Soviet Writers, who first outlined the method later dubbed, in a phrase popularized by Stalin, "Socialist Realism":

> To invent means to extract from the totality of real existence its basic idea and to embody this in an image—thus we obtain realism. But if to the idea extracted from the real we add the desirable and the potential and if the image is thereby supplemented, we obtain that romanticism which lies at the basis of myth and which is very useful in that it facilitates the arousing of a revolutionary attitude towards reality.

It is clear, first of all, that what Gorky is describing is a form of *romantic* realism; and, were it not for some particular interpretations given to such terms as "real existence," "the real," "the desirable and the potential," and "a revolutionary attitude towards reality," the passage might well refer to the views of, say, Dostoevsky. But for the Marxist-Leninist it is the "outer" world of material reality (and even a particular aspect of this) which influences or rather determines consciousness, while for Dostoevsky (or Joyce) the situation is much more complex: it is the "inner" world, embodied though it may be in the physical brain, that is the "real" world, and it is this reality, with all its quirks and perversities (its love, for instance, of freedom), its nightmares and buried loves and hates, that is a major determinant. But the Gorkian world is a simple world (especially in *The Mother*) of black and white; in a Socialist (i.e., romantic) Realist novel intervening shades of gray are not only unaesthetic but they are politically suspect, showing lack of "Party spirit." A sophisticated Symbolist technique (and such a technique almost always involves the use of nuances) is, furthermore, positively dangerous, since a clever writer may thus be able to imply or suggest anti-Soviet doctrines.

The "desirable and the potential" refer, of course, to the Socialist order, the "withering away of the state," the future classless society, and all the concomitant blessings of communism. That is, the writer injects into his description of reality either an optimistic view that these things will soon come to pass or he assumes, in the face of quite contradictory evidence, that they have, in part at least, been achieved. It was the Stalinist, Andrey Zhdanov, later a member of the Politburo and notorious for his literary purges, especially the one following World War II (the *Zhdanovshchina*), who introduced obligatory Socialist Realism. Speaking at the same Congress of Soviet Writers in 1934, he said:

> Our Soviet literature is not afraid of being called tendentious, because it *is* tendentious. In the age of the class struggle a nonclass, nontendentious, apolitical literature does not and cannot exist. . . .
>
> In our country the outstanding heroes of literary works are the active builders of a new life. . . . Our literature is permeated with enthusiasm and heroism. It is optimistic, but not from any biological instinct. It is optimistic because it is the literature of the class which is rising, the proletariat, the most advanced and the most prospering class.[3]

This is a good example, by the way, of the Stalinist "*kvass*" style.[4] It is sad that it contaminated Russian literature and criticism, but it is just as sad to read about "Socialist Realism" in science—the fortunately repudiated Lysenkoism in genetics, for example. It is quite obvious that neutrality of any kind is anathema to the Russian Communist. In this connection, I cannot refrain from quoting the sage remarks of a man who was once the head of the Commissariat of Justice of the RSFSR, Nikolay Krylenko:

> We must finish once and for all with the neutrality of chess. We must condemn once and for all the formula "chess for the sake of chess," like the formula "art for art's sake." We must organize shock-brigades of chess-players and begin the immediate realization of a Five-year Plan for chess.[5]

3. Quoted in Edward J. Brown, *Russian Literature Since the Revolution* (New York: Collier Books, 1969), p. 213.

4. *Kvass* is a Russian fermented drink. A Russian equivalent of our "jingoism" is *kvasnoj patriotizm,* a phrase coined by Polevoy.

5. Quoted in Robert Conquest, *The Great Terror* (New York: Macmillan, 1968), p. 270. It appears that Krylenko was later shot.

Similar attacks have been leveled in Soviet Russia against musical instruments: thus in about 1927 resolutions were passed condemning certain instruments (I imagine the saxophone was included) as being of bourgeois provenance and exonerating others because of their "proletarian origin." Humorous as such fulminations may sound, their implications are chilling. Russian music, along with literature and art, has frequently been the object of censorship in Russia, both before and after the Revolution. It is noteworthy that Tolstoy, who so often anticipates Soviet extremes, has his character Pozdnyshev in the *Kreutzer Sonata* say: "In China music is a state matter—that is the way it ought to be." But we must remember that it was Plato (*Republic,* Fourth Book) who first urged that musical innovations should be prohibited as endangering the state; and that Solon, on hearing what he considered to be lies on the stage, once said (according to Plutarch): "If we honor and approve a play like this, we shall find it some day in our business."

2

Lev Trotsky (1879–1940) was born Lev Bronstein in the small village of Yanovka in Kherson province. His parents were Jewish, although his father, who openly denied believing in God, had made himself into a kulak or rich peasant through an unusual set of circumstances. The young Bronstein began his schooling in Odessa but very soon became involved in revolutionary activities which led to his arrest and exile to Siberia. But he escaped and thereafter immortalized the name of a chief jailer in Odessa by assuming his name, Trotsky. The subsequent story of his life—his role in the Revolution, his political career, his eventual fall from grace, and his murder in Mexico by a Stalinist agent —is well known and has been recounted in many books. Here we will be concerned only with Trotsky's comments on literature and, in particular, with his book *Literature and Revolution* (1924). Here, though ending his treatise on a note of almost ecstatic idealism (under communism "the average man will rise to the heights of Aristotle, Goethe, or Marx"), he is essentially a heretic. Nothing makes the fanatically religious nature of Russian communism clearer than the vituperation and execration which have been hurled at Trotsky and his followers ("bandit-cosmopolitan" is but a mild example). As we noted earlier, Trotsky spoke out against the very concept of "proletarian art," arguing that such an idea was quite un-Marxist: the dictatorship of the proletariat is a temporary phase, and the proletariat itself, merging into the Socialist community, will eventually lose its class characteristics and cease to be the proletariat. How therefore can a "culture" be based on it in a classless society? Trotsky also denies that the Party has or can have ready-made solutions for problems of versification or the theater any more than for problems of fertilization or transportation. The actual development of art, he writes, is neither part of the Party's task nor its concern; the domain of art is not one in which the Party should legislate, and it can, at the most, only provide ideological guidance and protection from Russia's enemies. Trotsky compounds his heresy by denying, too, that revolutionary art can be created only by workers.

More interesting, however, are the many passages in *Literature and Revolution* in which Trotsky unleashes with incisive irony his bitter disdain for various individuals and groups. "We cannot say that Merezhkovsky has ceased to be, since he never was." Of Bely and the other religious Symbolists: "Let them chew to the very end the Philistine cat stew with the sauce of Anthroposophy." The writer Boris Pilnyak toys with the typography of his stories and then announces, "Please do not forget—I am a romanticist!" Mayakovsky writes in his poetry about the most intimate of our emotions, love, "as if he were talking about the migrations of peoples." Of some esoteric and "arty" works of the time: ". . . three hundred numbered copies—what hopelessness, what a waste! Better to curse and howl—this at least would resemble life!" Comparing Mayakovsky's famous yellow blouse and Gautier's red vest, he recalls what consternation was caused among the "papas and mammas" by the sartorial and other oddities of the Futurists. But nothing cataclysmic, he remarks, followed these rebellious protests by artists with long hair, yellow blouses, and red vests; indeed, their poetry was very soon canonized by the bourgeois public.

In the previous chapter we saw how Trotsky, while severely criticizing the Formalists, nevertheless recognized some of their contributions. Even more liberal, from the later Stalinist point of view, are the remarks he makes concerning Freud. Castigating Rozanov as a "rascal, coward, sponger, and lick-spittle," he notes that his revelations concerning sex are of immeasurably less significance than the contributions of Adler, Jung, and Freud: even the most paradoxical exaggerations of the latter are richer in insights and more rewarding than the sweeping generalizations in Rozanov. Trotsky's opinion of Dostoevsky is quite low and in no sense either original or perceptive. He sees falseness in Dostoevsky's pious and humble characters, the result of the author's own bad temper and his "perfidious Christianity."

There is nothing subtle or sensitive about Trotsky's comments on art and literature, and his criticism is laid on with a heavy hand. But of course he was not a critic, his interests being primarily political and revolutionary. Yet he is one of the very few figures of consequence in early Russian communism whose names come to mind in reading Zamyatin's remarks on the importance of heretics.[6] Today in Soviet Russia the views of Trotsky, in art as well as in all other areas, are in total disgrace, and his very name is anathema. The fact that this is so is good evidence that he is worth reading.

Anatoly Lunacharsky (1873–1933) was involved in Marxist circles from an early age. He supported Lenin in the early 1900s but later broke with him and joined Gorky and Bogdanov in a Bolshevik faction known as "Forward." Although Lenin severely criticized Lunacharsky for his "revisionism," his interest in Mach and Avenarius, and especially because he viewed Marxism as a natural, anti-metaphysical, and scientific "religion," we remember Lunacharsky chiefly as the first Soviet Commissar of Education in the Russian Socialist Republic (1917–29). He was appointed Soviet ambassador to Spain in 1933 but died in Paris on his way.

It is customary to point out Lunacharsky's pretentiousness in literary matters; but this criticism applies mainly to his own works which, admittedly, are rather poor (e.g., his play *Oliver Cromwell*). As a critic, however, he may justifiably be called "a cultivated and sympathetic literary critic" (John Bayley), especially if we compare him with the great mass of Russian critics who succeeded him. Lunacharsky was sharply opposed, in quite doctrinaire fashion, to both nonobjective art and Formalist literary concepts: for him these approaches reflected the "escapism" of an effete and decadent society. He considered Eykhenbaum's formal analysis of Gogol's "The Overcoat" to be "soulless," and he reminds us in many of his critical comments (as much Russian Marxist criticism does) of Tolstoy's moralistic criteria. To be sure, a good portion of his criticism of contemporary writers is baldly tendentious: thus he finds it illogical that Mitka, the hero of Leonov's novel *The Thief* (1927), should turn out to be apolitical and antisocial, not to mention dishonest, after having served in the Red

6. See Chapter VII, section 10.

Army! On the other hand, Lunacharsky was perceptive enough to note, for instance, the Parnassian nature of Bryusov's "Symbolist" poetry.

In the early twenties, in connection with Lenin's New Economic Policy, Lunacharsky drew up plans for reorganizing not only the educational system of the country but its fine arts as well, since these also fell under his jurisdiction. It is an indication of his comparatively liberal attitude—still possible at this time—that he should have invited Kandinsky (before he joined the *Bauhaus* in Germany) to sit as a member of a board designated to reorganize the art institutes of Moscow. Together with V. Polyansky, Lunacharsky edited *Essays on the History of Russian Criticism* (1929–31) and was also one of the editors of the valuable *Literary Encyclopedia* published in Moscow beginning in 1929 but later discontinued and withdrawn from publication for ideological reasons.

Alexander Bogdanov (pseudonym of Alexander Malinovsky, 1873-1928) served as a military surgeon during the First World War and later became involved in the study of blood transfusions, dying as the result of an experiment on himself. He had joined the Bolsheviks in 1903, and, although a rather important figure in early Soviet philosophy and economics, he will be mentioned here in connection with the influential but brief role he played as a theorist of the movement known as *Proletkult* (an abbreviation of "Proletarian Cultural and Educational Organizations"). Founded by Bogdanov in 1917, this group sought to train proletarian writers in an effort to produce eventually and systematically a new proletarian literature. A large number of training centers were organized throughout Russia where workers were instructed in the art of literature by established writers, including such eminent names as Bryusov, Bely, Zamyatin, and Gumilev. We have noted elsewhere, however, the signal failure of this movement as well as the criticism leveled at it by Trotsky. Because Bogdanov thought that these indoctrinational efforts should be free of governmental and Party control, the *Proletkult* organizations were subordinated to the Commissariat of Education in 1920 and eventually abolished altogether.

Nikolay Bukharin (1888–1938), one of the most brilliant and learned of the Old Bolsheviks, had also opposed Lenin in certain areas. He became a full member of the Politburo after Lenin's death and was considered by the latter as one of his natural successors. Though he supported Stalin against Trotsky, he advocated the continuance of the New Economic Policy and led the "Right Opposition" against Stalin. But Stalin brooked no opposition and Bukharin was eventually arrested, tried at one of the famous "show trials," and executed. Like Trotsky, Bukharin had some good things to say of Formalism. He strongly disparaged the attempts to treat literature as verbal structures apart from the social context; but he urged the usefulness and the necessity of formal literary analysis and he criticized Marxists for ignoring the work of the Formalists. At the Congress of Soviet Writers in 1934, Bukharin also continued to sign his own death warrant by criticizing orthodox poets such as Yefim Pridvorov ("Demyan Bedny") and Alexander Bezymensky, while paying homage to Pasternak as "one of the most remarkable poetic craftsmen of our time." He even dared to criticize the idolization of Mayakovsky, who had committed suicide in 1930 and whom Stalin called the greatest Soviet poet. Bukharin also made some "cosmopolitan" remarks concerning the Belgian poet, Verhaeren, contrasting the richness of his poetry with the bareness of Soviet verse.

Trotsky, Lunacharsky, and Bukharin, primarily political activists and revolutionaries, were important figures in the history of the early Soviet period, and their aesthetic and literary opinions have been mentioned chiefly in this connection. Let us now turn to a scattering of lesser figures of the period whose work was more narrowly limited to literary criticism.

3

Vladimir Friche (1870–1929) was a leading exponent of "sociological poetics" and "economic determinism" in literary studies. We see the Marxist approach in all his works, beginning with his early studies in Western European literature (1908), where he tries in a rather heavy-handed way to establish direct links between modes of production and literary works. For Friche it was the duty of the critic to show how in literature socioeconomic factors are translated into verbal symbols; and, further, how certain styles in prose and poetry correspond directly to certain "economic styles." Thus his "economic equivalent" supplements Plekhanov's "social equivalent." Although some of Friche's comments are at first glance provocative (that, for example, modern free verse echoes the rhythms of the capitalist metropolis), on closer examination they seem quite silly. His approach is now referred to by

Soviet authorities as "vulgar sociology," and Lukács disparages his interpretation of Tolstoy as superficial.[7] Friche believed that, with the coming of socialism and communism, man would become a purely rational creature and that literature would eventually reflect this rationalization of life.

Vladimir Pereverzev (1882–1968) was, like Friche, a radical economic determinist in literary criticism. To really understand a writer, Pereverzev says we may ignore his traditions, his biography, his philosophy, and even his social environment; we must consider solely his position relative to the means of production. It is the economic milieu, the particular class structure in which the writer finds himself, that determines everything—his language as well as his imagery—and it does this without the author's conscious participation. Of special interest is Pereverzev's *The Creative Work of Dostoevsky* (*Tvorchestvo Dostoevskogo*, 1922). Here Pereverzev explains the frequent appearances of and references to "split personalities" in Dostoesvky as projections, so to speak, of the author himself, torn between the exigencies and standards of bourgeois modes of production and his own traditions and pretensions. Western literary scholars occasionally attribute to Pereverzev a few useful insights that may be assimilated, along with certain Civic and Formalist observations, by an eclectic or pluralistic interpretation of Dostoevsky; but his extreme Marxism is, on the whole, repugnant. He did, however, speak in more comprehensible terms when he pointed out, as have many other critics, that "all modern literature is following in Dostoevsky's footsteps . . . to speak of Dostoevsky still means to speak of the deepest and most urgent issues of our present life."

Pereverzev also turned his attention to Gogol. In his *The Creative Work of Gogol* (*Tvorchestvo Gogolja*, 1926), cited by Lunacharsky as an exemplary work of Marxist analysis, all the features of Gogol's literary art are, in effect, made to depend upon the fact that the writer was a petty landowner. But within a few years Pereverzev's studies were condemned and his methods have ever since been denounced in Soviet Russia as examples of "crude sociologism." Whereas Friche's name is mentioned in the *Large Soviet Encyclopedia* (1956), there is no entry for "Pereverzev."

Peter Kogan (1872–1932), a somewhat lesser figure, was a prolific writer of literary studies in the Marxist manner. He has a number of

7. G. Lukács, *Studies in European Realism* (New York: Grosset & Dunlap, 1964), p. 128.

works on ancient and modern literature and is the author of *Belinsky and His Age* (1911). He had some favorable things to say of the "fellow-traveler" writers for the vividness and realism of their descriptions of Russian life, and he praised the "Smithy Poets" (a group of proletarian "forgers of verse") for their faith in the powers of science and labor. But he denounced the Formalists as "naive specialists" (*specy*) who were divorced from the realities of their age. He found nothing at all compatible between Marxism and Formalism, and he regarded the study of form as of no consequence. Although Kogan has not become a "non-person," his name is mentioned with reservations as a critic who failed to produce authentic Marxist criticism and he is routimely accused of "vulgar sociology."

Leopold Averbakh (1903–38) was more of a literary "czar" than a critic. He rose to prominence first as a member of "October," a group of proletarian writers of the 1920s, and later as the leader, from 1927 to 1932, of the Russian Association of Proletarian Writers (RAPP). This was a militant organization, proclaiming the hegemony of the proletariat, whose ostensible mission was the creation of a new revolutionary culture. In his position of leadership, Averbakh exercised a virtual dictatorship over early Soviet Russian literature, directing the active participation of writers in the first Five-Year Plan (1928–32) not only as "observers" but often as laborers. Averbakh was a fanatical Communist and a fierce critic of the "fellow travelers" because of their lack of total allegiance. Though Averbakh (who was Jewish) knew German and had a special interest in Goethe, the RAPP writers were narrowly pro-Russian. But even Averbakh did not believe that specific themes should be dictated to his proletarian writers; despite his own fanaticism, he was uncomfortable with Stalin's much cruder intentions of turning writers into outright propagandists of Party policies. Averbakh assumed that, once writers were "educated" and had acquired an orthodox Marxist outlook based on dialectical materialism, correct literary products would follow. This, however, did not happen, and Trotsky's words remained apt: "If we eliminate Pilnyak, the Serapion Brothers, Mayakovsky, and Yesenin, what will remain of a future proletarian literature except a few unpaid promissory notes?"

In 1932 RAPP, along with all other literary organizations, was dissolved by a decree of the Central Committee of the Communist Party and replaced by the Union of Soviet Writers. This new, officially sanctioned organization, with multi-level branches in all the Union republics, has continued until the present day as the principal means of Party control over literary matters. Averbakh, who had already come under attack, was now blamed for all the failures of RAPP as well as for having used his position to settle personal grudges. For a brief period he was protected by the fact that his brother-in-law was Yagoda, the notorious Security Police chief. But the accusations against Averbakh continued to increase in intensity, and by 1936, when Yagoda was replaced (and subsequently shot), he was in serious trouble. He was "unmasked" as a Trotskyite agent and there were vile denunciations in which even his accent and gestures were caricatured. It appears that he was eventually purged, although the details are not known.

Alexander Voronsky (1884–1943) was also one of the leading Marxist critics of the 1920s. But he was, in the context of the time, a "moderate," favoring a certain amount of tolerance in literature and opposing the concept of a narrowly defined proletarian art. Along with Deborin in philosophy (whose "menshevikizing idealism" was later condemned by the Mechanists), Voronsky supported a "humanistic" interpretation of Marx. More specifically, he wanted the writer to treat reality objectively—to describe, for instance, the vices of the Communist along with his virtues, and the virtues of the class enemy together with his vices. In short, he was more interested in literature than ideology, and this was eventually his undoing. From 1921 to 1927 Voronsky edited *Red Virgin Soil* (*Krasnaja nov'*), a liberal journal which published the works not only of Communists but of non-committed fellow travelers as well. He was also a leading figure amongst a group of writers, formed in 1923, which called itself "*Pereval*" ("The Pass") and which was opposed to enforced proletarianism.

Voronsky was one of the most sensitive of the Russian Marxist critics. Although he never disclaimed his Marxism and liked to cite Belinsky and Plekhanov, he was extremely broad-minded and he was attracted by a great variety of literary topics and ideas from foreign sources. He thought highly of Rabindranath Tagore and read Freud and Bergson. He had necessarily, as a Marxist, to reproach Zamyatin for his hostility, but he praised this writer's verbal skill and his irony and considered the novel *We* an excellent technical achievement.

But with the establishment of RAPP and the regime of Averbakh, Voronsky's moderate position was defeated. He was arrested in 1927, expelled from the Party, and exiled. In 1930 he was permitted to return to Moscow and was even re-admitted to the Party; but he was arrested again in 1937 and disappeared. The date of his death is given officially as 1943, but it is very probable that he died in a prison or a labor camp. He was partially "rehabilitated" in the late fifties, but his views are still considered heterodox and harmful.

Vyacheslav Polonsky (pseudonym of Vyacheslav Gusin, 1886–1932) was also a moderate Marxist. He was the editor of another important periodical, *Press and Revolution,* which had a good section of book reviews, including many books published abroad. Polonsky was outspoken in his rejection of the narrow and dogmatic interpretation of the principle of "social command" (*sotsial'nyj zakaz*) and, like Trotsky, he used Marxist arguments to refute it. He felt that the methods of the proletarian zealots were artificial, failing to recognize or provide an organic link between workers and artists. Polonsky has an especially interesting and still valuable account of the literary movements of the early Soviet period and he has made a number of clever comments regarding some of the early Soviet writers. Of Babel's *Red Cavalry* he wrote: "In *Red Cavalry* the rugged iron of Lenin's skull exists side by side with the faded silken portraits of Maimonides. But they cannot go on living in peace. . . . Maimonides is not compatible with Lenin." He observes the expressionistic nature of Olesha's prose and even uses the Shklovskian-sounding term *ostranenie* (estrangement) to describe Olesha's manner. It goes without saying that Polonsky was very soon accused of counterrevolutionary activities and his voice silenced.

Pavel Sakulin (1868–1930) was one of the more scholarly of the critics of the early Soviet period; of all the figures we have so far mentioned in this chapter, Sakulin's literary studies in nineteenth-century Russian literature are among the most frequently cited by Western scholars. This is due largely to the fact that he was not really a Marxist critic, much less an orthodox one. He was primarily a literary historian who combined the sociological approach with the methods of formal analysis. His works in this area include *Russian Literature and Socialism* (1924), *The Sociological Method in Literary Studies* (1925), and *Russan Literature: A Synthetic Sociological Survey of Literary Styles* (1929). These, although still readable, are not so important as his earlier studies, such as *The New Russian Literature* (1908) and *From the History of Russian Idealism* (1913). Sakulin's name is entered in the *Large Soviet Encyclopedia* (1955) as a critic who attempted a synthesis of formal analysis and Marxist elements; but it is noted that his work is vitiated by the presence of idealistic concepts.

4

The general tenor of literary studies as represented by the preceding group of critics may seem strangely delimited and rather uninteresting to the Western reader. But this early period of Soviet Russian criticism and literary theory was one of rampant liberalism in comparison with the much darker Stalinist period that followed. We have mentioned the establishment of the Union of Soviet Writers in 1932, a date which may conveniently serve to separate the early and the later periods of Soviet literature and criticism. We have also referred to the first Writers' Congress of 1934 and have mentioned some of the literary pronouncements made at this congress. It was both the statutes of the union and the decisions reached during the congress that laid down the law for Russian writers and critics; this new canon was that of Socialist Realism (discussed above, section 1), to be applied not only in literature but in all the other arts as well.

Maksim Gorky (pseudonym of Aleksey Peshkov, 1868–1936) still holds a special place in the Soviet hagiology. A self-taught writer who rose to prominence before the Revolution, he was the author of novels, short stories, plays, and poems, the great majority of which are mediocre and so generally evaluated in the West. The opinion has often been expressed (again in the West) that Gorky's real services to literature lie not in his own fiction but rather in the help and counsel he offered many writers during the period of the Civil War and its aftermath as well as in his valuable reminiscences of Tolstoy. So far as his comments on literature are concerned, these are in no sense original or illuminating; but they are very revealing both of the man and of a certain literary tradition that links the critical realism of the nineteenth century and the later Soviet brand of realism.[8] Certainly Gorky was a good man with a sincere respect for woman and her significance; yet some idea of his general outlook may be had from the remark of one of his characters—"The word 'man'—that sounds magnificent!"—his deification of the people (in his *Confession* of 1908), and his senti-

8. A collection of Gorky's articles, memoirs, and letters dealing with literature is now available in English: *On Literature* (Seattle: University of Washington Press, 1973).

mental "cardiac psychology" (e.g., "It makes me happy to see that you've found the way to the human heart").

Quite understandably, Gorky (who in many of his judgments reminds us of Tolstoy) did not think much of the new literature, either abroad or in Russia. Referring to French literature, he speaks of Proust writing "trivialities in sentences thirty lines long." We earlier quoted (Chapter VII, section 1) Gorky's opinion of the new "decadent" movement, c. 1907–17, as "the most shameful decade in Russian literature." In the early 1900s a publication entitled *Literary Decay* (*Literaturnyj raspad*) was issued, containing articles by Gorky, Friche, Lunacharsky, and others, which was an outspoken condemnation of all Modernist literature. Gorky stood in awe of Chekhov and wept on seeing *Uncle Vanya;* but he was hurt by what he took to be Chekhov's "coldness" and his indifference, "like snow or a blizzard," toward people. He stood, too, in awe of Tolstoy but rejected, as have many Christians and non-Christians (Gorky was an atheist), the doctrine of non-resistance to evil. He also condemned Dostoevsky's irrationalism as well as the doctrines of humility, patience, and salvation through suffering. But Gorky's comments on Tolstoy and Dostoevsky, especially when he says that both writers "lived in a country where the abuse of human beings reached dimensions shocking in their licentious cynicism," apply with even more validity to his own Stalinist period. Still, his opinion of Dostoevsky was, as is so often the case, ambivalent: thus he lists Dostoevsky's novels amongst the greatest ever written.

In the late twenties Soviet critics frequently complained that Russian readers preferred foreign novels to those being produced at home (Jack London, Joseph Conrad, Upton Sinclair, and O. Henry were amongst the favorites). Gorky, in 1925, offered an explanation, claiming that Russians wanted romanticism, more attention paid to plot, and (echoing Shklovsky) unfamiliar descriptions of familiar things. This emphasis on the romantic is found again, as we have seen, in Gorky's 1934 definition of what came to be called "Socialist Realism." At the 1934 Writers' Congress Gorky also indicated quite clearly (and this position has ever since been maintained in Russia) that the older "critical realism" must be sharply distinguished from the new "romantic realism." It was very well for Saltykov-Shchedrin or Tolstoy, living as they did in a corrupt society, to criticize that society; but now under the new regime such a critical view of reality could no longer serve to help mold the personality of the "new man." The new literature had to be optimistic, and the baldest statement of this requirement was made by Zhdanov, to be discussed below.

One of the reasons why the Party decided in 1932 to create a uniform and all-embracing writers' organization was that it had finally realized that such radical tactics as those of Averbakh (and others) had not produced the expected results, although this reason was obscured by Marxist jargon. Other methods had to be introduced that would not only ensure adherence to the Party line but also improve the quality of the new literature. There is little doubt that Gorky, who was one of the first to point out the deterioration in literary output in the late twenties, played a significant role here. "In his campaign for raising the standard of literature," writes Gleb Struve, "he was supported by the most talented among the Communist writers, such as Sholokhov and Fadeev. After the passage of the 1932 resolution Gorky's voice became particularly authoritative in all literary matters and more than ever he came to be looked upon as the *doyen* of Soviet letters."[9]

But the regime of Stalin was especially effective in corrupting or destroying good men. Gorky had been in Russia at the time of the Revolution and was alarmed by the excesses of the Bolsheviks.[10] His criticism of these excesses, his outspokenness in defense of writers, and his humanitarianism created many enemies within the Party, and in 1921 Lenin advised him to leave Russia. He went to Capri and learned there in 1923 that Lenin had ordered the preparation of a list of forbidden books; he wrote angrily that he intended now to renounce his Soviet citizenship. But instead he returned to the Soviet Union in 1928. Torn between the evil he saw and his desire to defend the system in hopes of better things to come, his story thereafter is a sad one. In 1930 at the beginning of the purges he said: "Millions of eyes begin to glow with the same joyous flame!" He wrote "vile articles, merciless and full of sophistry, justifying the worst trials on grounds of Soviet humanism"—these are the words of Victor Serge who saw Gorky in the early thirties riding alone in the rear of a big Lincoln, shrunken and with the hollow eye-sockets of a skeleton. Although all the details are not known, it now appears likely that Gorky was murdered in 1936 on orders from Stalin.

Andrey Zhdanov (1896–1948) is without a doubt the most notorious figure in the entire history of Russian politico-literary relation-

9. *Russian Literature Under Lenin and Stalin, 1917–1953* (Norman: University of Oklahoma Press, 1971), p. 254.

10. See an article in *Encounter* (March 1972), pp. 92–94, for some excerpts from Gorky's denunciations of Lenin.

ships. An ideologue of incredible fanaticism, his name and his activities—"Zhdanovism" (*Zhdanovshchina*)—have become synonymous with what is very possibly the ultimate in the politicization of literature and the arts. Zhdanov joined the Bolsheviks in 1915 and from 1924 to 1934 headed the Party organization in Nizhny Novgorod (later Gorky). After the assassination of Sergey Kirov (very likely on orders from Stalin), Zhdanov took over the Party organization in Leningrad which he headed until 1944. He became a full member of the Politburo in 1939. During World War II Zhdanov played an important role in the defense of besieged Leningrad; after the War he and Malenkov established the Cominform (Communist Information Bureau).[11] Zhdanov is also given credit for having re-established in the Soviet educational system, which had deteriorated severely during the twenties, much of the rigor and discipline of prerevolutionary Russian schools.

Zhdanov's name is especially associated, so far as literature is concerned, with two periods: that of the Writers' Congress of 1934 and that of the purge of literature and the arts which began in 1946. At the 1934 Congress in Moscow, Zhdanov was proud to quote Stalin who referred to Soviet writers as "engineers of human minds." In addition to lauding the optimism, enthusiasm, and tendentiousness of Soviet literature, Zhdanov officially defined Socialist Realism. What does it mean, he asked, to be a Soviet writer? It means to depict life truthfully, not as "objective reality," however, but as life in its "revolutionary development." To combine this unusual brand of realism with the ideological re-education of the masses—this was to be the new approach in fiction and criticism, the method to be known as Socialist Realism. While accepting the need for romanticism, he was careful to distinguish between the old romanticism, "which depicted non-existent life and non-existent characters," and the new revolutionary romanticism, glorifying real-life heroes and their military and labor feats (*podvigi*).[12] This disparagement of the creative imagination and emphasis on a "literature of fact," a concept which owed much to some of the later Futurists and even to Shklovsky, can be seen in a good deal of Soviet literature, especially in many of the so-called five-year-plan novels. One of the leading exponents of "factography" was N.

11. The Cominform "coordinated" the activities of the Communist parties within the USSR, the satellite countries, and France and Italy. It was dissolved in 1956.

12. This term occurs with great frequency in Soviet literature and journalism. The word *podvig* earlier had strong religious connotations. See Billington's note (52) in *The Icon and the Axe* (New York: Vintage Books, 1970), p. 651.

Chuzhak (pseudonym of N. Nasimovich) who edited a collection of articles called *The Literature of Fact,* published in 1929. Chuzhak, who regarded fiction as "opium for the people," wanted to "concretize," "technicize," and "rationalize" literature.[13] But this factual literature was not exactly what the Party wanted either, and the tendency in this direction was more than balanced by "revolutionary romanticism" which soon developed into a sentimentalism that is often worse than maudlin.

If Chuzhak's contentions seem absurd, they were rather mild in comparison with the concepts and formulations of a number of minor critics in the thirties and forties. Though these matters may be of significance in a specialized study of Soviet Russian Marxist-Leninist aesthetic theory, it would be of little interest or benefit to treat them, even cursorily, here. There was, for example, M. Gelfand, whose virulent and savage attacks against Formalism and other areas of "ideological sabotage" are minor classis of senseless vituperation. He once wrote, for example, "Formalist philosophy . . . is utterly false, because it is completely reactionary, and it is reactionary because it is utterly false."[14] Or there was M. Serebryansky's neat aesthetic formulation (1938): "Artistic truth means being able to tell everything that needs to be told but to tell it correctly—that is, from a definite Bolshevik point of view." Of the theoretical problems which were discussed during this period and afterwards, there is one that perhaps deserves mention. This concerns the theory of the "single stream" (*edinyj potok*). It was natural right after the Revolution, when there were fanatic attempts in many quarters to break completely with all vestiges of the tsarist past, for a number of critics to theorize that, with the establishment of a Socialist (not to mention communist) state, a radically new culture and, with it, a radically new literature would arise. This was essentially the argument of the proletarian zealots. But as time went on, many features of the former regime returned (this was especially true of the Stalinist period during and after World War II); and many critics argued in this connection that the new Soviet literature was but a continuation of the great Russian realist tradition—that, in effect, here was a "single stream" of Russian literature, from past to present. It was a knotty problem, and many clever arguments have been propounded, pro and con. At times the "single stream" theory has been regarded as a heresy, since theoreti-

13. Chuzhak seems to have been purged in the thirties.

14. Quoted in Erlich, *Russian Formalism,* p. 138.

cally it militates against the cherished concept of the uniqueness (*svoeobrazie*) of Soviet literature viewed as something qualitatively different from prerevolutionary literature. The general position now, however, is an ambivalent one: Soviet Russian literature *is* original and unique, yet at the same time it *is* a continuation of an older tradition.

One other important matter must be touched upon here before we turn to the purge of 1946. Also appearing at the 1934 Congress was no less a figure than the former prince, Dmitry Mirsky, the author of *A History of Russian Literature* so frequently cited in earlier chapters of this book. At the Congress it was, surprisingly, he who launched the campaign against James Joyce and the pernicious influence (from the orthodox point of view) of his radical experiments in prose. Thus Mirsky, who had yet to know the real nature of the rabble and hacks he had joined, found himself on the side of such characters as Karl Radek, for whom Joyce's works represented a "heap of dung." Since Mirsky is an important Russian critic, the whole story must be told.

Prince Dmitry Svyatopolk-Mirsky (1890–1939?), usually referred to as D. S. Mirsky, was born of an old aristocratic family and educated at the University of St. Petersburg. During the Civil War he served as an officer in the White Army; after their defeat he emigrated first to Greece and then to England where he became a lecturer at the London School of Slavonic and East European Studies. During the 1920s he wrote numerous reviews and articles for both English and French periodicals on a wide variety of literary topics and in 1926 he published his renowned *History of Russian Literature*. This, of course, he wrote in English, and it is certainly one of the most readable literary histories ever written. Though many readers and scholars may disagree radically with many of Mirsky's judgments (the book is by no means "scientific" or even "objective"), most readers of taste have been unanimous in praising the book's sparkling prose style and elegant wit. It is a literary history eminently in the English manner, and Sir Isaiah Berlin, a greater scholar than Mirsky but a sympathetic critic, has written the best general appraisal of it:

> Mirsky wrote with confidence, spontaneity, and a combination of fastidious taste and intellectual gaiety which communicated to his books the brilliance and freedom of the best and most illuminating kinds of conversations about literature. His judgments were recklessly personal, and his facts and dates sometimes inaccurate. He lavished magnificent encomia upon authors,

> who, for reasons not altogether clear, delighted or excited him, and launched violent personal attacks on writers both great and small, men of genius and forgotten hacks, who happened to bore or annoy him. His use of English was very vivid and very original, his judgments were first hand and derived from direct contemplation of the object. In everything he wrote there was a play of ideas which sprang from a wide if undisciplined knowledge of all the great European civilizations, assimilated without residue into the loose but rich texture of his own mental life, and expressed with that astonishing mixture of elegance, high spirits, and directness of vision which is the specific property of the best Russian liberal intelligentsia; of this unique society he was perhaps the most accomplished representative among the émigrés of the twentieth century. He was not a systematic critic, and there are large and capricious omissions in his work; but his confidence in his own literary insight was unbounded and, armed with it, he succeeded in rescuing various authors from undeserved oblivion, and by introducing figures hitherto little known outside Russia in a manner which arrested the attention of western readers to their great and abiding profit.[15]

"Encomia" there surely are in Mirsky: exaggerated praise is one of the noticeable features of the book, and occasionally it is inconsistent. Thus of Vladimir Soloviev he writes: "Next to Pushkin (who has no rivals), Soloviev is no doubt the best of the Russian letter writers, with Chekhov as a good third"; but elsewhere: "Griboyedov stands next to Pushkin as a letter writer." Few critics would agree with Mirsky when he claims that Pushkin's poem *The Gypsies* is "the most temptingly universal work in the Russian language," although his opinion concerning *Tsar Saltan* ("The longer one lives, the more one is inclined to regard *King Saltan* as the masterpiece of Russian poetry") is clearly a personal predilection, but one not too far from the truth. Mirsky's opinion of Shestov's prose, albeit hyperbolic, is one that most Russian readers of discrimination who know Shestov might well share: "His prose . . . is the tidiest, the most elegant, the most concentrated—in short, the most classical prose—in the whole of modern Russian literature."

Mirsky does not seem to have cared much for the theater in general, and his opinion of Chekhov's plays shows little understanding:

15. *Partisan Review* (July–August 1950), p. 617.

"There is no subject matter in Chekhov's plays, no plot, no action. They consist of nothing but 'superficial detail.' They are, in fact, the most undramatic plays in the world." And Mirsky concludes his discussion by stating that Chekhov "is a classic who has been temporarily shelved"! Few scholars or Russians who know Chekhov well would agree that "he had no feeling for words" and that his language is colorless and lacking in individuality. Mirsky's view of Dostoevsky is a traditionally dark one: "The real Dostoevsky is food that is easily assimilated only by a profoundly diseased spiritual organism." Whereas Tolstoy was "a Euclid of moral quantities," Dostoevsky "deals in the elusive calculus of fluid values." Tolstoy, he claims, is a puritan, Dostoevsky a Symbolist; and he dwells on the "purity" of Tolstoy versus the "impurity" of Dostoevsky. He speaks highly of the idiolect skill of both Tolstoy and Dostoevsky and acknowledges the great impact of the latter as a "phenomenon" but not as a writer.

His opinion of Tolstoy is very high. Of the *Confession,* he writes that "it is the greatest piece of oratory in Russian literature" and, in some ways, Tolstoy's "greatest artistic work." He notes, as others have, the epic or Homeric qualities of *War and Peace* and *Anna Karenina* but criticizes (again as others have) the figure of the peasant Karataev and the "theoretical chapters on history" in the former novel. "It is an essential of Tolstoy's art," he writes, "to be not only art but knowledge." Mirsky uses Shklovskian terminology ("making it strange") in discussing examples of Tolstoy's characteristic manner of debunking cherished romantic illusions, and he explains the peculiar individuality of Tolstoy's prose style as a combination of a very pure colloquial vocabulary and a rather involved gallicizing syntax. Of the other major Russian novelists, the pages devoted to Gogol have won the approval of Vladimir Nabokov. While agreeing that *Oblomov* is a great novel, Mirsky rejects the "professor-of-literature" view of Goncharov as a great stylist: his prose "has all the flatness of mediocrity." The comments on Turgenev, e.g., that his style was weak and ineffective when it was divorced from concrete and familiar objects, are quite conventional.

Mirsky is at his best with poetry. He wrote some poetry himself, but early came to the logical and wise conclusion that his true gifts lay in criticism rather than in lyricism. True, his criticism very often is, as Berlin points out, impressionistic and idiosyncratic, but references to Mirsky's judgments and pithy comments on the Russian poets in Western studies of the subject are overwhelmingly favorable. Of special interest is his separate study of Pushkin, published in 1926. "Despite the fact," writes George Siegel, "that Pushkin is a notoriously dim and difficult figure to apprehend for the foreigner, Mirsky does succeed in giving the non-Russian reader a sense of Pushkin's style."[16] Finally, there are, to be sure, odd passages and quaint observations in the *History*, but they make the book all the more interesting and refreshingly different from similar works by "professionals." In his account of Artsybashev's "decadent" novel *Sanin*, for example, Mirsky writes that "the author of *Sanin* cannot be exculpated from having contributed to the moral deterioration of Russian society, especially of provincial schoolgirls." This is a passage that only Trotsky might have done justice to.

In 1931 Mirsky joined the British Communist Party, setting forth his reasons for doing so in a French periodical, and in the following year the "Comrade Prince" returned to Russia. Unlike Count Aleksey Tolstoy (a distant relative of Lev Tolstoy) who returned to the Soviet Union in 1923 to become a popular Soviet author and a Stalin Prize laureate, Mirsky very soon ran into trouble. In 1934 he wrote an article criticizing one of the novels of Alexander Fadeev from an almost ultra-Marxist point of view. But the journal in which Mirsky's article had appeared was later obliged to recant, and the critics pounced on Mirsky for having dared, as a recent convert, to attack a Communist writer. Although Gorky came to his defense, Mirsky was arrested in 1935. He was soon released but thereupon spoke up in favor of Boris Pasternak, who was also under attack by Communist critics and wrote an article on Pushkin that was denounced. He was arrested again in 1937, exiled, and apparently perished in a concentration camp.[17]

5

As soon as the Great Patriotic War was over in 1945, the Party turned its attention promptly and resolutely to the tightening of ideological controls in all areas, including the arts and literature. Those naive observers in the West were sadly mistaken who had believed that, following the many contacts established at various levels between the Soviet Union and the Western democracies during the war, extensive changes

16. Introduction, D. S. Mirsky, *Pushkin* (New York: Dutton, 1963), p. ix.

17. See Edmund Wilson's memoir, "Comrade Prince," *Encounter* (July 1955), for further details.

for the better would occur in Russia. There had been, necessarily, some relaxation in limited areas during the war years, but it was never at all significant. Indeed, rigorous censorship continued in the arts during this period and many writers, including Erenburg, Fedin, and Zoshchenko, were censured for sundry ideological shortcomings. The Stalinist cult of the state and of a quite idolatrous patriotism, an especially repugnant aspect of Soviet Russia, was given added impetus by the War. This statism which, like so much else in modern Russia, stands in blatant contradiction to the teachings of Marx, Engels, and Lenin, was peremptorily pronounced as official doctrine by Stalin in 1950. By this time, too, official histories had removed earlier statements acknowledging the contributions of the Allies in defeating Hitler.

On August 14, 1946, the Central Committee of the Communist Party passed a resolution which severely criticized the editorial policies of two Leningrad periodicals: they were accused of publishing the works of Zoshchenko, the "scum of literature," and the poet, Anna Akhmatova, whom Zhdanov described as "a cross between a nun and a whore." These remarks give a rough idea of the tone of the period that was to follow. Both Akhmatova and Zoshchenko were expelled from the Union of Soviet Writers, one of the magazines that had published their works was closed down, and the other was placed under the editorship of a Party official. There were immediate and far-reaching repercussions at all levels. Chairmen and members of various branches of the union were replaced or severely censured, and lax Party control was criticized; the editors of other periodicals were summarily removed, while alert staff members of still others attacked their own editorial boards; grave warnings were issued to all concerned, writer after writer was attacked, and an especially virulent anti-Western campaign was begun.

Short shrift was given now to certain deviationist views—e.g., the poet Selvinsky's theory of "social symbolism" as a substitute for Socialist Realism or the bold assertion of a minor Ukrainian writer that authors should be allowed to err. The gist of Zhdanov's onslaught, however, was that writers had forgotten not only Lenin's 1905 admonition that Socialist literature must be "Party-spirited" but that they had also forgotten the basic principles of Socialist Realism. The Soviet writer must always remember that literature is an instrument of Socialist education, that it must be accessible to the masses and not merely serve, as in the West, as a private enterprise catering to special tastes, and that Russian literature must oppose "blow for blow" the slanderous attacks from the decadent West. Of the Russian literary heritage, only the materialist, realist tradition must be drawn upon.

In previous chapters we have referred occasionally to the traditional Russian suspicion and mistrust of the West as the source of corrupting and dangerous influences—political, cultural, and religious; and during the early Soviet period the Western states, both monarchies and democracies, continued to be condemned and vilified by Soviet spokesmen. But now, beginning in 1946, this tradition was intensified, and there began an almost incredible campaign against not only the contemporary bourgeois cultures of the West—especially America—but also against Russian writers, artists, scholars, and critics who had, in one way or another, shown a deference to or interest in foreign ideas or who had fallen under the influence of bourgeois modes of thought or principles of art. This attack was by no means limited to literature and the arts but was also directed at music and even science. Thus the leading composers Shostakovich, Prokofiev, and Khachaturian were accused of "Western Modernism," "Formalist perversions," and "anti-democratic tendencies," while the view was promulgated that there could be no such thing as a "world science," since science in the Soviet Union, based upon Marxist principles, was necessarily the only true science, qualitatively different from and superior to bourgeois science.

A study by a prominent Soviet scholar and critic, I. Nusinov, *Pushkin and World Literature* (1941), in which the author had quite legitimately discussed Pushkin's works in relation to European literature and had called Pushkin a "European writer," was now severely criticized by the novelist Fadeev. He accused Nusinov of having neglected Marxism and of writing about Pushkin as if the Russian writer were a universal figure and a "pan-European." But the matter did not end here, since the real culprit behind this and other examples of "kowtowing (*nizkopoklonstvo*) to the West" was now exposed: he was Alexander Veselovsky (see above, Chapter VI, section 5), the literary scholar, historian, and comparativist who died in 1906. There was almost immediately a deluge of articles condemning "Veselovskyism" (*Veselovshchina*) and Veselovsky was called the "grandfather of deference to the West"; he was posthumously blamed for having fathered a whole school of literary scholars, such as Nusinov, who discussed the classics of Russian literature as derivative, secondary, and imitative works or who dared to believe in the "interdependence of all literatures." The attack was taken up by the critic Valery Kirpotin (himself later to be denounced) who summed up the charges against the dead Veselovsky in numerous articles. Although some voices were raised in Veselovsky's defense (including Skhlovsky and Zhirmunsky), Zhdanovism and the Party triumphed in the end: whereas in the 1928 edition of the Soviet Encyclopedia Veselovsky is described as one of the "great architects" of Soviet literary science, the 1951 edition explains that Soviet literary scholarship has revealed the "complete worthlessness of his liberal-positivistic methods."

The disciples of Veselovsky (of whom there were many in Russian universities), as well as others who had "kowtowed to the West," were dubbed "cosmopolites," the noun frequently being preceded by such adjectives as *rootless, kinless,* or *bourgeois.* Coming under particular attack in this connection were Jewish writers, critics, and artists (Nusinov was Jewish), and the term "cosmopolite" (*kosmopolit*) has come to have marked anti-Semitic overtones in Soviet usage. But America was also singled out as a source of "cosmopolitanism" and of the heretical concept of the "interpenetration of cultures." The poison of American cosmopolitanism, a weapon of imperialism and a cloak for great-power chauvinism, was among the themes used in a multitude of anti-American novels, short stories, and plays which now appeared in rapid succession. In the course of the campaign, many names were resurrected for ritual execration. Anatoly Tarasenkov, a critic who took part in the attack on Veselovsky's legacy, included the "Jesuit Bukharin" as well as the "cosmopolitan" Trotsky amongst those who gave an impetus to contempt for Russia and its culture. A few years later (in 1949) this same Tarasenkov further clarified the meaning of Socialist Realism. He wrote that if a Soviet writer notices contradictions in life (i.e., between correct Socialist principles and vestiges of the past), he must not describe these objectively, but must, knowing that under conditions of "Soviet reality the new is bound to win," take sides and see indeed that "the new" wins. Unless he does so, he shows himself to be "hostile to realism."

As the campaign went on, official histories of various literatures were scrutinized, and serious errors were found. The authors of a Soviet history of French literature were criticized for referring too often to the influences exerted by various French writers on Russian literature of the eighteenth century; the same faults were found in a history of English literature. A course of study prepared for use by Soviet theatrical institutes was accused of suggesting that the nineteenth-century Russian dramatist, Alexander Ostrovsky, had borrowed from Western playwrights the age-old device of "recognition," ultimately of

Greek origin (*anagnorisis*). The authors of an official Russian history were criticized for having devoted too much attention to the influence of such figures as Leibniz, Helvétius, and Rousseau on the eighteenth-century writer, Alexander Radishchev. The scholar Boris Eykhenbaum (Chapter VIII, section 4) was accused of exaggerating the influence of Schopenhauer's philosophy on the thought of Tolstoy. A scholarly specialist in eighteenth-century Russian literature, Grigory Gukovsky, a student of Veselovsky, was the author of a study of Pushkin and a contributor to a Soviet history of eighteenth-century literature. Because he did not respond sympathetically to the denunciation of Veselovsky and the attack on "comparativism," his books were withdrawn from publication and he himself soon disappeared. Following his "rehabilitation" after the death of Stalin, it was revealed, euphemistically, that he had been "illegally repressed" in 1950.[18] A specialist in the morphological analysis of folk and fairy tales, Vladimir Propp, had published in 1928 a book that is still a classic in its field, *The Morphology of the Folk-tale* (*Morfologija skazki*).[19] In 1946 the University of Leningrad published another of his books, and this was now severely criticized for the frequent references to foreign authorities in the fields of folklore and anthropology.

It would be of little avail to continue listing similar cases of the execration and denunciation of literary scholars, both living and dead, by fanatic and hack Marxist critics. But enough has been said to illustrate the nature of this utterly fatuous and revolting period, a period that would be absurd and ridiculous were it not for the fact that many good writers, scholars, and critics either had their serious and honest research radically interrupted, had their reputations ruined, or were themselves destroyed during its course. This, certainly, was the period that Gorky, were he still alive, might well have called the most shameful era in Russian literature. Along with this anti-Western campaign there also developed an ultra-nationalistic tendency in many quarters to ascribe to Russian inventors many of the inventions traditionally and quite correctly attributed to Westerners: thus it was claimed that printing was known in Russia prior to Gutenberg. But most ignominious of all were the obsequious and unctuous homages paid in the following years to the omniscience of Stalin by men in all fields of study

18. I am indebted for much of the information in this section to Chapter 28 in Gleb Struve's *Russian Literature Under Lenin and Stalin, 1917–1953.*

19. Available in an English translation by Laurence Scott, ed. by L. A. Wagner (Austin: University of Texas Press, 1968).

as well as by critics. The critic V. Yermilov, for example, commenting on Stalin's description of the writer as "an engineer of the human mind," exclaims how deep a respect for the writer is revealed in this definition by Stalin, "for whom there is nothing more precious on earth than man."

6

Of particular interest is the Dostoevsky criticism of the early Soviet period, the reaction against such criticism which began in the thirties and continued during and after the *Zhdanovshchina,* and the subsequent relaxation in this area in connection with the "thaw" following the death of Stalin in 1953. We have already commented on the marked preoccupation of many of the critics during the Modernist period, prior to the Revolution, with the works and thought of Dostoevsky (Chapter VII) and have referred to several of the ambivalent views of this novelist expressed by early Marxist or Marxist-oriented critics (e.g., Pereverzev and Gorky): while decrying his "reactionary" opinions in many domains, they had necessarily to admit his contemporary significance. It is also a commonplace to point out the noticeable Dostoevskian influence on such early Soviet writers as Leonov, Zamyatin, and Pilnyak. Although the antipathy toward Dostoevsky and his works that we find in the criticism of Belinsky, Dobrolyubov, Pisarev, and Mikhaylovsky never abated after the Revolution, and although Lenin as well as many other Russian Marxists expressed a stern—and quite understandable—dislike of both his works and his influence, during the first two decades after 1917 Dostoevsky's writings were published in what are still the best Russian editions of his works, and many critical studies of the novelist were written. In the thirties, however, there was a radical change, and for almost twenty-five years, until 1956 in fact, the publication of Dostoevsky's novels and other writings was severely limited, while practically all serious Dostoevsky research was halted.

One of the most important of the critics writing on Dostoevsky in the early Soviet period was Leonid Grossman (1888–1967). Grossman, who was closely associated with Formalist trends, began writing studies of Dostoevsky before the Revolution (e.g., "Balzac and Dostoevsky," 1914;[20] "Dostoevsky and Europe," 1915; and "Problems of Realism in Dostoevsky," 1917), and he has provided us with a valuable account of Dostoevsky's reading in *Dostoevsky's Library* (1919). In *The Creative Art of Dostoevsky* (*Tvorchestvo Dostoevskogo,* 1921) he traces the influence of Schiller on Dostoevsky, and in *The Poetics of Dostoevsky* (*Poètika Dostoevskogo,* 1925) he has a number of essays dealing with various facets of the novelist's art, including the influence of gothic novels on Dostoevsky's fiction. In an article entitled "Dostoevsky and the Theatricalization of the Novel" (1927) he takes up the dramatic aspects of Dostoevsky's prose, a subject that has attracted numerous critics. Grossman also produced some interesting biographical studies of Dostoevsky, such as *The Way of Dostoevsky* (*Put' Dostoevskogo,* 1924). He continued his scholarly output in the thirties with articles and introductions—e.g., "The City and the People of *Crime and Punishment*" (1935). In an introduction to Dostoevsky's *The Manor of Stepanchikovo* written in the same year he suggests that Foma Fomich is a caricature of Belinsky, but his arguments are weak. Grossman also wrote an historical novel based upon Dostoevsky's notorious gambling sprees in Germany (*Roulettenburg,* 1932). But Grossman had written on other Russian writers, including Gogol and Tyutchev, and during the Zhdanov purge he was taken to task for finding biblical and oriental motifs in the poetry of Lermontov. By 1948 Grossman was still doing comparative literature, but now in an inoffensive way—e.g., by writing on the influence of Mayakovsky on Aragon.

Vladimir Yermilov, whose Stalinist effusion was quoted earlier, was a notorious and rather repugnant figure in Soviet criticism. He had shown his obtuseness in the late twenties by waxing enthusiastic over the figure of Andrey Babichev in Olesha's *Envy,* a grotesquely ironic caricature which he took to be the portrayal of a good Communist, and he had been attacked as a bureaucratic hanger-on in some verses of Mayakovsky. Despite his *faux pas,* he was able to survive by denouncing others and by cannily attacking writers and critics at the appropriate times in accordance with the prevailing Party line. In 1947 the official view of Dostoevsky was represented in an article by another critic of the same caliber as Yermilov, D. Zaslavsky, entitled "Against the Idealization of the Reactionary Views of Dostoevsky." This was followed by Yermilov's article in 1948: "Against Reactionary

20. Now available in English translation by Lena Karpov (Ann Arbor: Ardis, 1973).

Ideas in the Works of F. M. Dostoevsky." But after the death of Stalin and the Twentieth Party Congress in 1956 there was again a marked change. The year 1956 was also the seventy-fifth anniversary of Dostoevsky's death, and a ten-volume edition of the novelist's *Collected Works* was published (1956–58). This in turn was followed by a veritable spate of books and articles on the life and times as well as the literary works of Dostoevsky.[21] Yermilov was again on hand, this time with a book on Dostoevsky which was made available in English translation by the Foreign Languages Publishing House. But it is a book, as Donald Fanger notes, that is "unlikely to be consulted for insight into the problems of Dostoevsky's art." Writing some years later (in 1959), another Soviet critic claimed that Dostoevsky had never really been under a ban in Soviet Russia, although he admitted that the absence of new research concerning the writer had been a "serious shortcoming."

In the more relaxed atmosphere of the fifties, Grossman returned to his Dostoevsky studies with, for example, his article "Dostoevsky as Artist" (1959), in which the recurrent images and situations in Dostoevsky are likened to Balzac's technique of *"le retour des personnages."*[22] In addition, his valuable *Life and Works of F. M. Dostoevsky: A Biography in Dates and Documents,* first published in 1935, was reissued in summary form, and he continued publishing into the sixties (*Dostoevskij,* 1962).

Another important Dostoevsky scholar was Arkady Dolinin (pseudonym of Alexander Iskoz, born 1883). In the early Soviet period he published numerous studies of Dostoevsky, such as his essay "Stavrogin's Confession" (1922), and he edited a two-volume collection of articles and material on Dostoevsky (1922) as well as an excellent collection of Dostoevsky's letters (four volumes, beginning in 1928). In 1935 he published more important archival material on Dostoevsky. But after the publication in 1947 of his *In Dostoevsky's Creative Laboratory* (a study of Dostoevsky's notebooks showing the genesis of the novel, *A Raw Youth*), Dolinin was accused of having shown too lax an attitude toward the novelist's reactionary views. Given the

21. For further details on Soviet Dostoevsky criticism see Vladimir Seduro, *Dostoyevski in Russian Literary Criticism, 1846–1856* (New York: Octagon Books, 1969).

22. These phenomena in Dostoevsky have also been referred to as "situation rhyme." See J. Meijer, *Situation Rhyme in a Novel of Dostoevskij* (The Hague: Mouton, 1958).

maleficent nature of the time, however, we can be lenient in understanding why Dolinin, together with a number of other scholars, "mounted the rostrum in turn," as Gleb Struve writes, "and abjured their comparativist sins." But after 1956 Dolinin returned to his former studies, and in 1964 his collection, *F. M. Dostoevsky in the Memoirs of Contemporaries,* was published in two volumes.

Mikhail Bakhtin (born 1895) was another outstanding Dostoevsky scholar with Formalist affiliations, one of whose theories is perhaps better known in the West than those of any of his contemporaries. I refer to his *Problems of Dostoevsky's Creative Art* (*Problemy tvorchestva Dostoevskogo*, 1929) in which he theorized that, unlike Tolstoy's "homophonic" novels (one can always clearly make out, in the exposition of various arguments, the voice of the author), Dostoevsky's novels, with their predominance of dialogue, are "polyphonic": we hear many voices but it is difficult—rather, quite impossible—to distinguish amongst them the voice of Dostoevsky.[23] As N. S. Trubetskoy expresses it in his book, *Dostoevsky as Artist,*[24] in this writer "*alle Weltanschauungen der handelnden Personen* [*sind*] *gleichberechtigt.*" Though we can certainly see a marked difference in this respect between Tolstoy and Dostoevsky (and in this sense Bakhtin's differentiation is as valid as most generalizations), one must agree with René Wellek when he concludes that Bakhtin is patently false in claiming that "there is no final word in the world of Dostoevsky." One has only to read the *Notes from Underground,* not to mention *The Possessed* and passage after passage in the other novels, to see that Dostoevsky does indeed make final statements and that we can indeed very often hear the voice of Dostoevsky quite as clearly as we hear the voice of Tolstoy. Bakhtin, who liked to add Marxist sauce to his work from time to time, goes on to argue that the development of the "polyphonic" novel became possible only wih the rise of capitalism; and, further, that the peculiar development of capitalism in Russia favored an exemplary type of "many-voiced" novel, reflecting a great variety of distinctly different and often contradictory opinions.

Although Bakhtin's works were for a time suppressed and he himself forced into academic exile at the University of Saransk (Mordovian Autonomous Republic), in 1963 his 1929 opus, revised and en-

23. Bakhtin's work, *Problems of Dostoevsky's Poetics,* is now available in English (Ann Arbor: Ardis, 1973).

24. *Dostoevskij als Künstler* (The Hague: Mouton, 1964), p. 14.

larged, was republished with a slightly altered title (*The Problems of Dostoevsky's Poetics*). Following the "rehabilitation" of Bakhtin in the late fifties, another grimly orthodox Soviet critic, A. Dymshits, ventured to attack him again; but now a large contingent of Dymshits' colleagues among the so-called eminent Russian critics (including Yermilov) defended Bakhtin. The work of Bakhtin, Dolinin, and Grossman was complemented by the studies of many other Dostoevsky scholars, including M. Davidovich, A. Tseytlin, and P. Bitsilli. In 1959 a volume of over 500 pages, *The Creative Work of Dostoevsky,* was published by the Academy of Sciences. This contains a selection of monographs written by various scholars in connection with the anniversary of Dostoevsky's death.

7

The year 1956, with its Twentieth Party Congress and the Dostoevsky jubilee, was a significant date in several other respects as well. It was, for instance, the year of Alexander Fadeev's suicide, which caused a considerable stir in Soviet literary circles. Fadeev, the Soviet novelist mentioned earlier in connection with the Zhdanov era, was himself denounced during the Twentieth Congress, most notably by another famous novelist, Mikhail Sholokhov (author of *And Quiet Flows the Don*). Sholokhov criticized Fadeev in scathing terms not only as a novelist but also as the secretary general of the Union of Soviet Writers. He was a secretary general, Sholokhov said, who had turned the Writers' Union into a sort of military organization or penal colony and had, in effect, forced writers to stand at attention before him. Fadeev had revised—and thereby mutilated—his own novel, *The Young Guard,* in accordance with Party demands, had slavishly followed Stalin in regimenting writers, and had also (it was rumored) been instrumental in denouncing Babel (who was arrested in 1939 and died later in a labor camp) as well as other writers.

Also in 1956 a scholar by the name of P. Berkov published an article in which he was happy to claim that the period of "bibliography phobia" (*bibliografiobojazn'*) seemed to be over. This "fear of bibliography," which "hampered the development of Soviet science in general and literary scholarship in particular," was a noticeable feature of the Stalinist era. It was dangerous, whether you were writing a book on Pushkin or a book on the growing of turnips, to include a bibliography: one never knew whether any of the authorities in your list, living or dead, had already been, or were about to be, denounced. And if your bibliography was found to contain one or more names of "enemies of the people," this was evidence of your own guilt.

Ever since the doctrine of Socialist Realism was first enunciated and attempts made to define it, there have been innumerable discussions and polemics in the Soviet Union concerning its true nature. Some of these matters have already been commented on, and, it is clear that the doctrine advocates a literary realism that is so strongly tendentious, militantly partisan, highly selective, melioristic, and oriented toward the future (i.e., teleological), it no longer appears to be a form of realism at all, despite the wide range of meanings we give this word in the West. These discussions concerning Socialist Realism continued through 1946 and after 1956, with some critics taking a hard and narrow line, others attempting from time to time to inject a modicum of common sense. It has been said that only Zhdanov really knew what Socialist Realism is and that he took the secret with him to the grave. But in 1959 there was printed in a French monthly the French translation of an article by a Russian writer, "Abram Tertz." This soon appeared in English translation as "On Socialist Realism," and it was subsequently learned that "Abram Tertz" was the pseudonym of the writer and critic, Andrey Sinyavsky.[25] The bulk of the original essay was written in 1956, although the final pages outlining the author's concept of "fantastic realism" were added in 1958. This is an extremely enlightening essay, replete with wit and irony, by a critic of considerable learning and taste, and without a doubt one of the best things ever written on Socialist Realism. It must be read in full to be duly appreciated, but here several of the highpoints will be mentioned.

Perhaps the first thing one notices in the essay, aside from the general tone of irony, is the use of theological terminology. Thus the author emphasizes that Soviet art, like the whole of Soviet culture, is thoroughly teleological, the final end or Purpose being of course communism. Further, the splendor of the Purpose is so ineffable that one can only use the negative definitions of apophatic theology to describe it at all. There are numerous—and not always gentle—references to the West and Christianity and many comparisons are drawn between

25. *The Trial Begins and On Socialist Realism* (New York: Vintage Books, 1965). The translation of "On Socialist Realism" is by George Dennis.

these and Marxism. Like any true faith or orthodoxy, communism is not tolerant of heterodox opinions and heresies. Stalin is quoted but in a refreshingly new manner: not, as he had been for decades, to substantiate some pompous foolishness, but to illustrate the utter inanity of his language and thought. Occasionally Sinyavsky is effectively rhetorical when recalling the events of the recent past, as in this passage summing up what was done in the name of the Purpose:

> So that prisons should vanish forever, we built new prisons. So that all frontiers should fall, we surrounded ourselves with a Chinese Wall. So that work should become a rest and a pleasure, we introduced forced labor. So that not one drop of blood be shed any more, we killed and killed and killed.
>
> In the name of the Purpose we turned to the means that our enemies used: we glorified Imperial Russia, we wrote lies in *Pravda* [*Truth*], we set a new Tsar on the now empty throne, we introduced officers' epaulettes and tortures. . . . Sometimes we felt that only one final sacrifice was needed for the triumph of Communism—the renunciation of Communism.[26]

There is an interesting (but obviously selective) list of literary works early in Part Two of the essay, some of them by Western authors, the others Soviet. The Western titles (such as *Death in the Afternoon*) all suggest darkness, death, or pessimism, whereas the Soviet titles (such as that of Pavlenko's novel, *Happiness*) suggest optimism and meliorism. Sinyavsky then speaks of that Soviet shibboleth, the "positive hero," which he calls the "Holy of Holies" of Socialist Realism. He reviews briefly the nature of literary heroes in nineteenth-century Russian literature who, with all their defects, are so different from—and so much more interesting than—the Soviet versions. In Part Three he advances the proposition that Soviet literature, as typified especially by the doctrine of Socialist Realism, far from being either something qualitatively new or a continuation of the great nineteenth-century realist tradition, is actually more akin to the eighteenth century. Quoting some verses from odes by the eighteenth-century writer Derzhavin, Sinyavsky likens them, in language and content, to the spirit of Soviet literature. Furthermore, this Soviet literature, with its tendency to be serious and severe, reflects the coming of a new faith

26. *Ibid.*, p. 162.

in the infinite perfectibility of man and the consequent disappearance of irony, "the faithful companion of unbelief and doubt."

As the classical literature of the eighteenth century was fond of the ode, with its lofty language, fixed epithets, and nice circumlocutions, so "official" Soviet literature of the twentieth century, whether poetry or prose, observes the same proprieties and sense of decorum. "We became classicists," Sinyavsky writes, "We represent life as we would like it to be and as it is bound to become, when it bows to the logic of Marxism. This is why socialist realism should really be called 'socialist classicism.' "[27] And as classical literary formulas tend to become frozen into the only acceptable canons of usage, so the "new" Soviet literature, rather than displaying romantic rebellion, experimentation, and the rejection of formal niceties, is given to ponderous didacticism and pompous simplicities. "The river of art was covered with the ice of classicism. As art became more precise, rational, and teleological, it squeezed out romanticism."[28] Sinyavsky quotes the art critic, N. Punin, who noted as early as 1918 a marked classical tendency in some of Mayakovsky's poetry, and goes on to quote examples of the new "classical" style from Soviet prose and poetry.

Toward the close of his essay, Sinyavsky has more ironic comments on Stalinism and the eclectic nature of Soviet art; but he ends by advocating

> . . . a phantasmagoric art, with hypotheses instead of a Purpose, an art in which the grotesque will replace realistic descriptions of ordinary life. Such an art would correspond best to the spirit of our time. May the fantastic imagery of Hoffmann and Dostoevski, of Goya, Chagall, and Mayakovski (the most socialist realist of all), and of many other realists and non-realists teach us how to be truthful with the aid of the absurd and the fantastic.
>
> Having lost our faith, we have not lost our enthusiasm about the metamorphoses of God that take place before our very eyes, the miraculous transformations of His entrails and His cerebral convolutions. We don't know where to go; but, realizing that there is nothing to be done about it, we start to think, to set riddles, to make assumptions. May we thus invent something marvelous? Perhaps; but it will no longer be socialist realism.[29]

27. *Ibid.*, pp. 200–201.

28. *Ibid.*, p. 206.

29. *Ibid.*, pp. 218–19. Sinyavsky himself has written fiction illustrative of these

After reading Sinyavsky's essay with its irony, sharpness of language, and forthright criticism, one can easily understand why, even following the so-called Thaw, he got into serious trouble and was eventually arrested, tried, convicted, and sentenced to seven years of forced labor in 1965. In reading his essay, too, we can see rather clearly the influences of Modernism and Formalism and hear many echoes of earlier "heretics," writers and critics in the Gogolian-Dostoevskian tradition such as Zamyatin. More will be said about Sinyavsky's literary criticism in the following chapter.

8

Many of the literary events of the Thaw are now familiar to readers in the West—from the appearance of Erenburg's novel, *The Thaw* (1954), looked upon by optimists both within and outside Russia as the harbinger of better things to come, to the publication in 1962, with Khrushchev's approval, of Solzhenitsyn's novella, *One Day in the Life of Ivan Denisovich.* But we all know now the reaction in the Party hierarchy to Khrushchev's dalliance with liberalism as well as the eventual results. Erenburg was, before he died in 1967, criticized on numerous counts, while the subsequent harassment of Solzhenitsyn by Soviet authorities is perhaps one of the aspects of contemporary Russian culture most familiar in the West. It is interesting that the conservative critic Dymshits (referred to earlier in connection with Bakhtin) surprised many of his colleagues in 1962 with a favorable review of Solzhenitsyn's story; but his opinion was not shared by others, and one of the first critics to speak out against Solzhenitsyn, thus heralding the much stronger measures that were to follow, was Lidiya Fomenko. She pointed out (also in 1962) that Solzhenitsyn's work, despite its formal virtues and its truthful revelations, was essentially in error, since it did not disclose the "entire dialectic of the time": that is, it did not balance the bad of Stalinism with the good (as if this had ever been a practice in Socialist Realism). How much in error, too, was the poet Robert Rozhdestvensky when he proclaimed, in No-

---

concepts. A collection of his stories is available in English translation: *Fantastic Stories* (New York: Grosset & Dunlap, 1967).

vember of 1962, that Russian writers need no longer fear that others were doing the thinking for them!

In the sixties, although again many polemics concerning various issues took place which we shall here ignore, there was a noticeable alignment of Soviet writers and critics into two principal camps, an alignment which is still apparent today in Soviet Russia. These two categories may be called, following Ronald Hingley and others, the "hards" and the "softs." The former are the hard-line, conservative apologists of orthodox Party doctrine, intolerant of dissident opinions, whether political or literary; the latter are the more liberally inclined (but by no means anti-Communist) writers, critics, and artists whose views of the proper relationsship between creative thought and Party principles are reminiscent of those of Trotsky, for example, and therefore potentially dangerous. But this opposition is nothing new, being essentially a modern instance, as noted earlier in this book,[30] of older divisions separating thinkers or writers in Russia along certain clearly defined lines. In the sixties, two good examples of "hards" were Aleksey Surkov and Vsevolod Kochetov. Surkov, of peasant origin and outlook, was primarily a versifier and Stalinist bard. In the thirties he had criticized the poet Pasternak for his idealism and for seeming to take seriously a number of readers who considered him a modern classic (as we do in the West). Surkov, in addition to criticizing poets and writers, also defended the liquidation of the kulaks as enemies of the people. At the 1956 Party Congress Sholokhov had disparaged his importance for younger writers, but Surkov continued to see in "humanistic phrases" and such terms as "sincerity" and "directness of expression" potentially dangerous ideas. In 1959, at the Twenty-First Party Congress, Surkov (who had replaced Fadeev) was himself replaced by the novelist Konstantin Fedin as general secretary of the Writers' Union.

In 1967 the Secretariat of the Board of the Soviet Writers' Union met under the chairmanship of Fedin to take up the matter of Solzhenitsyn, his fiction (notably that published abroad), and his charges against the Union set forth in two strongly worded letters. Fedin, who was now seventy-five, had written a good, technically sophisticated novel in the early Soviet period (*Cities and Years,* 1924) but had been criticized during the Zhdanov purge for his Formalist leanings and for having belonged to the Serapion Brotherhood. In 1948 he published another novel, *No Ordinary Summer,* in which (carrying fiction

30. See above, Chapter III, section 1 (*ad fin.*).

to a new extreme) he attributed to the tactical genius of Stalin the defeat of General Denikin's White forces. Fedin is quite unimpressive in his exchanges with Solzhenitsyn, and Surkov, although he has little to say in accordance with his reduced importance, is still on the alert for heresy. He makes the point that Solzhenitsyn is more dangerous than Pasternak: Pasternak, a dreamer and a poet, was clearly divorced from life, while Solzhenitsyn has an "ideological temperament" and is a man of principles. But Surkov fails to understand an allusion in Solzhenitsyn's novel, *The Cancer Ward,* to some Baconian terminology and suspects that the reference to "idols of the marketplace" is an ironic comment on an as yet unerected monument to Marx in a Moscow square.

Vsevolod Kochetov (died 1973) was a novelist of very limited ability, a sort of "primitive" among Socialist Realists, a political conservative and Party dogmatist. His novel, *The Yershov Brothers* (1958), beyond its hackneyed plot, is a tendentious attack on the liberals who wanted freedom of expression in literature and who chafed under Party controls. Even *Pravda* had to acknowledge the novel's crudeness. Earlier, Kochetov had criticized a better novel by Vera Panova for what he called its "naturalism," i.e., its objectivity and lack of "Party spirit" and Socialist Realist commitment; he also expressed shock, in 1959, at an article by the novelist Paustovsky complaining of the harassment of writers when they touch upon "unpleasant truths" in their fiction. When Erenburg's memoirs began to be serialized in 1960, Kochetov made some pointed remarks about writers "burrowing in the rubbish heaps of their crackpot memories" to drag out once more "decayed literary bodies" and to pass them off as still living things. Tertz/Sinyavsky, in his novel *The Makepiece Experiment* (written in 1962 but not published abroad until 1965), was bold enough to refer to Kochetov by name as an agent and informer. Later, in 1969, Kochetov wrote another novel, *What Do You Want?,* in which he continued his artless attack on dissident intellectuals. But Kochetov's novel is belletristic in comparison with another that was published in 1970—*In the Name of the Father and the Son* by Ivan Shevtsov. This novel is not only an attack on Western culture and Israel (Stalin is here said to have rescued Russia from Trotsky and Zionism) but also on Modernism and liberalism in general as well as on several prominent but unorthodox Russian writers. Picasso is called a pornographer; the poets Andrey Voznesensky and Bella Akhmadulina are parodied in the characters of, respectively, "Vozdvizhensky" and "Novella Kaparulina"; and the United States is referred to as a country that needs a beating it will remember for a hundred years. Thus the "hards" are not merely political and cultural conservatives; they are most often fierce and bellicose jingoists and anti-cosmopolitans who quite obviously long for a return to Stalinist law and order.

Amongst the "softs" the name of Alexander Tvardovsky (1910–72) is an important one. Of peasant origin, Tvardovsky was primarily a poet. He became a journalist in his late teens, continued to write poetry, joined the Party in 1938, won a Stalin Prize in 1941, served in the Red Army, and eventually became editor of the literary journal, *New World* (*Novyj Mir*). Although he had earlier published some tributes in verse to Stalin and although his poetry is not of a very high order, he did distinguish himself on several occasions as an advocate of increased sincerity in literature and as a defender of persecuted writers. Tvardovsky was among the initiators of the post-Stalin Thaw in literature, and in his poem, "Far Distances," he makes clear his opinion that a great mass of Russian readers have only contempt for the obvious insincerity of Soviet writers as well as for their contrived and unreal plots. But in 1954 he was replaced as editor of *New World* for having allowed the publication of an article, "On Sincerity in Literature," by the young and rather brash critic, Vladimir Pomerantsev. In a style that was itself more impressionistic than didactic, Pomerantsev criticized the artificial psychology in Soviet fiction, the avoidance of actual human problems, and the periphrastic and politicized jargon of Soviet literary characters. Greater subjectivity, too, was needed in Russian literature: the great writers of the past had written confessions as well as sermons. He pressed for more sincerity in prose fiction and urged that this, rather than "Party spirit," be the principal criterion. The primary task of Soviet criticism, he felt, is to inspire both this sincerity and a greater breadth in fictional themes. Russan readers should be able once more to get something unique out of literature, not simply quaint fictionalizations of pieces out of *Pravda* and *Izvestia.*

However, Tvardovsky was reinstated as editor of *New World* in 1958. Whereas Dudintsev's *Not by Bread Alone* was published in this journal in 1956 but Pasternak's *Doctor Zhivago* was rejected in the same year, under Tvardovsky, beginning in the sixties, Erenburg's memoirs were serialized and Solzhenitsyn's *One Day in the Life of Ivan Denisovich, Matryona's Home,* and *An Incident at Krechetovka Station* were accepted and published. Tertz/Sinyavsky also had a number of his critical articles accepted and printed in *New World,* which now gained the reputation of being a liberal and "soft" organ as opposed to the "hard" journal, *October,* edited by Kochetov. At the

Twenty-Second Party Congress in 1961, Tvardovsky, one of the very few non-members of the Writers' Union, criticized the excessive and unseemly boasting that still characterized much Soviet writing and criticism as well as the exaggerations and glorification of "positive heroes" in Soviet fiction, figures who are certainly virtuous but with whom it would be very tedious to have to associate in real life. Tvardovsky was also bold enough to parody the beginning—we should rather call it the exordium—of a typical Soviet story in a style much beloved of the "hards":

> The bright rays of the setting sun were still gilding the tops of the silver birches in the yard of the "Road to Communism" Collective Farm, when Grunya the milkmaid, after evaluating her capabilities, decided to milk so many liters in excess of the obligations which she had assumed.

In 1963 Tvardovsky's own poem, "Tyorkin in the Other World," was published in *New World.* This had previously been read to Khrushchev (Sartre, Simone de Beauvoir, and Robbe-Grillet were also present) at the Premier's summer residence, and it had appeared in *Izvestia.* It is a humorous anti-Stalinist satire in which Tyorkin (the hero of an earlier poem by the same author) descends to the nether world and there encounters an inferno with the same censorship, secret police, and heavy-handed bureaucracy that he had known so well on earth under Stalin. In 1964 V. I. Lakshin, one of the liberal editors of *New World,* published his article "Ivan Denisovich—His Friends and His Enemies" in this periodical. Lakshin here staunchly defended Solzhenitsyn against his many critics but was himself attacked in turn by almost the entire Soviet press. In 1972 Alexander Solzhenitsyn surprised many people by appearing at Tvardovsky's funeral and sprinkling a handful of earth on the coffin, thus paying public homage to one of the few figures who had befriended him and other dissidents.

9

In 1964 Mihajlo Mihajlov, a Yugoslav author, critic, and lecturer in Slavic literatures, visited the Soviet Union. His report on this visit, "Moscow Summer, 1964," was written for a Belgrade literary journal.

As a result of Soviet protests, Mihajlov soon found himself under attack in his native country and was subsequently arrested, tried, convicted, and sentenced to a term in prison. An English version of his report appeared in issues of the American magazine, *The New Leader*, in 1965.[31] Mihajlov seemed to feel that there was a clearly discernible aura of liberalism in Russia at the time, a view which has, unfortunately, been darkened by later developments. He noted an interest in the works of Kafka and mentions studies of him by the critic D. Zatonsky which not only ridicule the traditional Soviet evaluations of Kafka but which also provide a "cosmopolitan" bibliography (including works by Max Brod and Robbe-Grillet). Though some of Rimbaud's verse was published in 1963, Mihajlov was pessimistic about the possibility of Russian translations of a number of other modernists, such as Beckett, Virginia Woolf, and Ionesco, although he found that some Russian scientists and inquisitive students were reading the works of Erich Fromm, Jaspers, Lucien Goldmann, and Heidegger in the original. He saw a copy of Joyce's *Ulysses* on sale for about eleven dollars.

Mihajlov was surprised by the popularity of Solzhenitsyn, and he was told that during the preceding year four graduate theses on Solzhenitsyn had been submitted to the Philosophy Department of Moscow University. Although the works of Zamyatin were still officially unavailable, Pilnyak was being rehabilitated and one of his hitherto unknown stories was being published. The Acmeist poet, Gumilev (executed in 1921), was becoming popular, especially among the young. One of the most interesting aspects of Mihajlov's account is what he says of the continued and growing interest in the writings of Dostoevsky. The revised and enlarged edition of Bakhtin's famous study of Dostoevsky had been published the year before Mihajlov's visit, and during his stay in Moscow another large volume on Dostoevsky by G. Fridlender appeared.[32] Before coming to the Soviet Union, Mihajlov had heard of another Dostoevsky scholar, Yakov Golosovker. In 1963 the Academy of Sciences had published his study, *Dostoevsky and Kant*, which follows up certain interesting parallels (noted earlier by Shestov) between Kant's *Critique of Pure Reason* and the fiction of Dostoevsky, most notably in *The Brothers Karamazov*. But Mihajlov was never able either to see Golosovker (who was seventy-four in

31. See especially the issue of 29 March 1965. Mihajlov's report is also available in book form: *Moscow Summer* (New York: Farrar, Straus and Giroux, 1965).

32. The impact of Dostoevsky on modern Russian literature is emphasized in several of the chapters of Mihajlo Mihajlov's book, *Russian Themes* (New York: Farrar, Straus and Giroux, 1968).

1964) or even find out exactly where he was, although it seemed clear to him that the old scholar was very ill and in some kind of a hospital.

Mihajlov also noted, in speaking with various Soviet intellectuals, that writers like Sholokhov were regarded, especially by the young, as "monuments of the past." It was his impression that many young Russian writers, besides indicating an interest in Dostoevsky and some of the hitherto "blacklisted" authors (both Russian and non-Russian), were also showing a remarkable interest in several less familiar but highly romantic writers. One such writer was Alexander Grin (Grinevich), a sort of "Russian Tolkien" and something of an anomaly in Soviet literature. Grin, who died in 1932, wrote a series of strange but entertaining novels and stories, some of them set in a never-never land of fantasy called "Grinland," which must surely have supplied for many Soviet readers a refreshing if not very sophisticated change from the monotonous literary fare. Yet not everything that Mihajlov encountered was promising. Though many of the people he spoke with associated Socialist Realism with Stalin and Zhdanov or disparaged this concept in one way or another, the "hard" critic V. Chalmaev wrote an article in 1964, "The Hero and the Heroic in Soviet Literature," which upheld the orthodox and dogmatic viewpoint with only slightly less militancy than did Zhdanov.

Mihajlov talked with a number of critics, scholars, novelists, and poets. In a conversation with the novelist Leonid Leonov, who was still in the process of rewriting some of his earlier fiction that had been reworked for ideological reasons under Stalin, Mihajlov was surprised to hear the novelist claim that he had never read Remizov. At the home of the poetess, Bella Akhmadulina, he learned that she possessed a set of the rare 1929 four-volume Russian translation of Proust's *À la Recherche du temps perdu* with a Preface by Lunacharsky. Mihajlov also visited the flamboyant Ilya Erenburg in his Moscow apartment with its unusual collection of masterpieces of nonobjective and abstract art. Erenburg, as he drank Turkish coffee and smoked a Cuban cigar, made fun of Khrushchev's primitive tastes and described his earlier meetings with such figures as Shestov and Bely. Mihajlov was pleased to learn that Erenburg was acquainted with developments in Yugoslav painting but was vexed and finally angered by Erenburg's talk of "liberated humanity." In the classless society of the future, given unlimited freedom through the achievements of science and technology, people would spend their time reading, listening to fine music, and engaging in intelligent conversation. There would be no more wars, no more boredom. But Mihajlov disagreed and cited in refutation a passage from Tolstoy (he might have found much better material in Dostoevsky). The meeting ended somewhat unpleasantly with Erenburg calling Mihajlov a "fanatic" and "dogmatist," and the latter very disappointed with Erenburg's myth of the "orderly ant-hill where all troubles will have been eliminated by science."

10

Erenburg, as mentioned previously, died in 1967 shortly after the Fourth Writers' Congress held in May of the same year. His absence in Italy at the time of the Congress was noted ironically by Sholokhov. This Congress, unlike preceding ones, was remarkable for its general tone not so much of moderation as of apathy. There was no doubt a good deal of disillusionment with many of the topics usually discussed at such gatherings as well as with the possibility of things ever really changing for the better; but the simple fact that on this occasion only a little over 12 percent of those attending were under forty must have been a factor.[33] Although the critic Novichenko mildly chided *New World* for its distrust of "lofty and heroic" themes, he also criticized *October* for "oversimplifications." It was in fact Sholokhov (now in his early sixties) who made the strongest statements. In 1966 he had castigated Sinyavsky and Daniel, condemning them as outright traitors and asserting that their punishments were too mild. Now he was disturbed by the absence of a number of writers and by their apparent indifference toward clear signs of continued intellectual rebellion. This was especially true, he said, among the young writers where bad examples of the recent past, coupled with irresolute Party action, had become sources of spreading infection. There was a spirit of defiance in the air: many of these young writers were not observing "accepted canons of behavior" and seemed to have "other things" on their minds as well. Sholokhov, who considers himself a Communist first and a writer second, was especially incensed by the fact that some writers were even asking for such things as "freedom of the press" in response to certain voices in the West demanding freedom of artistic expression for Soviet writers. But these were the voices, according to

33. At the First Congress in 1934, 71 percent of the delegates were under forty.

Sholokhov, of the CIA, White Guardists, U.S. senators, and vicious defectors like Stalin's daughter.

Since the middle sixties and in the early seventies we have learned of numerous brave acts by individuals and groups in Soviet Russia protesting in one way or another what they consider to be either undue repression of individual freedom of thought and action, especially in the creative arts, or—in a wider sense—a betrayal of the Revolution by Stalin and his successors. Such acts have had, it appears, little effect upon a regime which has seen what ensues when even a modicum of that heady draught we call freedom is permitted, and there seems to be little hope that any radical changes will occur in the near future. The Party is resolutely committed to opposing in every way any reconciliation with "bourgeois ideologies." In 1970 an editorial in *Pravda*, entitled "Irreconcilability to Bourgeois Ideology," asserted this claim quite clearly: the struggle against the influences of Western ideologies (including such concepts as free speech, free elections, and the idea that artists should be able to do what they want) is a struggle, it said, for the "spiritual purity and strength of Soviet man." There was little doubt, from the tone of the editorial, that the Party has no intentions of even listening to suggestions that present policies be modified. In 1972 a play was produced in Moscow dealing with the relations between Pushkin and Tsar Nicholas I. Pushkin, one of the most cosmopolitan of all Russian writers, was never able to leave Russia: he never saw London, Paris, Berlin, or Rome. But the official critic, Yury Zubkov, complained that the author of the play (V. Kostylev) failed to make clear (and hence had intimated modern instances) that the Tsar was wrong in his treatment of Pushkin *because* he was the Tsar and not simply because he had considered the interests of the state to take precedence over the poet's art. Zubkov had little to criticize, however, in Yevtushenko's play, *Under the Skin of the Statue of Liberty*, in which actors reenact the assassinations of John and Robert Kennedy and Martin Luther King and in which there is a strong vein of anti-Americanism. Another voice of the establishment, M. Yenkovsky, manager of the Comedy Theater in Leningrad, provides us with a typically profound Soviet observation when he explains the blandness of the Soviet stage when it comes to social criticism: "You in the West have sharper contradictions in your society, so you have sharper plays."

Recently the Soviet Union has joined the International Copyright Convention, ostensibly to demonstrate cooperation with the community of free nations. But acute observers in the West as well as certain persistent critics of the repression of civil rights within the Soviet

Union, notably Andrey Sakharov, the physicist, have correctly pointed out that the Party has agreed to adhere to the convention in order to control not only what is published in Russia but to secure control over the publication of works by dissident writers abroad. Other naive onlookers in the United States thought they observed a promising shift in Soviet views regarding Modernism in the arts when some of the "forbidden" works of *avant-garde* Russian painters were to be exhibited in this country. But these works are in fact being used, as Hilton Kramer has noted, as "counters in a game of international finance," and there is not the slightest evidence to suggest that the Party has changed its position with respect to abstract art.

Despite the dark outlook for anything resembling the free development of art and literature in Soviet Russia, literary studies are still being written. Much of this is of the conventionally Marxist and Party-line variety and much is purely academic, the authors managing at least to carry on their research even in the face of strict censorship and what must be disturbingly severe restrictions for intellectually curious scholars and critics. But one hopes the heretics will continue to appear from time to time in Russia, as they have in the past, to question accepted values. Though we might have gone on from this point to discuss some of the more interesting work in literary studies and criticism in Russia at the present time (the writings of Y. Lotman, for instance, in structural poetics seem particularly noteworthy), the whole subject of contemporary trends and developments in Soviet criticism really deserves, because of the special complexities involved, separate treatment. In the following chapter, however, we shall conclude by looking at some of the literary opinions and criticism of several non-Marxist Russian writers.

SUGGESTED READING

Trotsky, Leon, *Literature and Revolution* (Ann Arbor: University of Michigan Press, 1960).

Gorky, Maxim, *On Literature* (Seattle: University of Washington Press, 1973).

Grossman, Leonid, *Balzac and Dostoevsky* (Ann Arbor: Ardis, 1973).

Bakhtin, Mikhail, *Problems of Dostoevsky's Poetics* (Ann Arbor: Ardis, 1973).

Field, Andrew, ed., *The Complection of Russian Literature* (New York: Atheneum, 1971), contains brief excerpts from Gorky, Grossman, and Erenburg.

Gifford, Henry, ed., *Leo Tolstoy* (Harmondsworth: Penguin Critical Anthologies, 1971), contains excerpts from Lenin, Plekhanov, and Gorky.

Edie, James, and others, eds., *Russian Philosophy* (Chicago: Quadrangle Books, 1965). Volume III contains excerpts from Lenin, Plekhanov, and Bogdanov.

Tertz, Abram (Sinyavsky, Andrey), *The Trial Begins and On Socialist Realism* (New York: Vintage Books, 1965).

Ehrenburg, Ilya, *Memoirs: 1921–1941* (New York: Grosset & Dunlap, 1966).

Seduro, Vladimir, *Dostoyevski in Russian Literary Criticism, 1846–1956* (New York: Octagon Books, 1969), Part II on Soviet Literary Criticism.

Hayward, Max, and Crowley, Edward, eds., *Soviet Literature in the Sixties* (New York: Praeger Paperbacks, 1964).

Simmons, Ernest, ed., *Through the Glass of Soviet Literature* (New York: Columbia University Press, 1961).

Struve, Gleb, *Russian Literature Under Lenin and Stalin* (Norman: University of Oklahoma Press, 1971).

Hall, Vernon, *A Short History of Literary Criticism* (New York: New York University Press, 1963), Chapter 27, "Marxism and Literature."

X REACTION

1

In this concluding chapter we shall look briefly at some of the critical comments and writings of five Russian authors. One of these, Boris Pasternak, is dead, while the others now live and write outside the Soviet Union. Although these five represent a rather heterogeneous group, they have at least two things in common: they are in various ways and to various degrees opposed to Soviet Russian literary theory and practice; and they all show a predilection for quite divergent, personal opinions regarding literature. Following some brief remarks on Pasternak and Solzhenitsyn, the criticism of Andrey Sinyavsky will be examined, and in the third and fourth sections some of the criticism of Wladimir Weidlé and Vladimir Nabokov will be discussed.

Boris Pasternak (1890–1960) was preeminently a poet, at his best either writing poetry or talking about poetry. In his remarks on prose writers (e.g., Tolstoy), he shows a sensitive taste but really says nothing new or striking. One is strongly tempted, too, to agree with Nabokov, who, in his gentle manner, once called *Doctor Zhivago* a "sentimental and vulgar novel." As in the case of Blok, Pasternak's comments on poetry, as well as on life in general, are very often apt to be highly subjective, almost lyrical statements of implicit rather than explicit significance. Thus in reading a small volume of Akhmatova's verse in the late afternoon of an autumn day, he wrote: "There were two kinds of evening in the book. One lay across it with a light rosy hue. The other was made up of the contents and the soul of the poems published in it."[1] Speaking of two of his own poems, "Venice" and "The Railway Station," Pasternak tells us that his hopes in writing these

1. *I Remember: Sketch for an Autobiography,* trans. by David Magarshack (New York: Meridian Books, 1960), p. 82.

were modest: all he wanted was that the former contain the city of Venice and that the latter contain a certain railway station. But occasionally his meaning is quite clear. Discussing the poetry of Bely and Khlebnikov, he refers to these innovators as "rummaging about" in such thing as vowels and consonants, whereas the true poet, when he is authentically inspired, expresses his "new word" in the old and traditional poetic language and does not worry about formal novelties. Although he seems to admit the importance—to students at least—of Bely's statistical studies of Russian verse, he always believed that the music of poetry is not at all a purely acoustical phenomenon but that it depends rather upon a subtle relationship between the meaning and the sound of words.

A key concept in Pasternak's remarks on poetry is quite naturally that of metaphor. "Metaphorical language," he writes, "is the result of the disproportion between man's short life and the immense and long-term tasks he sets himself. Because of this, he needs to look at things as sharply as an eagle and to convey his vision in flashes which can be immediately apprehended. This is just what poetry is. Outsize personalities use metaphor as a shorthand of the spirit."[2] His views of sex in literature are conventional, almost puritanical. Sex is "repugnant" and it is useful to Nature by virtue of this repugnancy; but sex in literature has, in his opinion, something unbearably trivial about it. These are hardly ideas that the great majority of writers and poets in the West would share, nor would most dissident writers in Russia agree. Speaking through the character of Zhivago, Pasternak writes that "only the familiar transformed by genius is really great" and cites the works of Pushkin and Chekhov as classical examples. This, again, is a conventional opinion, shared by many critics (e.g., Blackmur) in the West. Pasternak shows here and elsewhere little recognition of or sympathy with the work of the Formalists and their preoccupation with such matters as defamiliarization.

There runs throughout Pasternak's poetry, his memoirs, and his novel a clear vein of Schellingian or Stoic holism, and he frequently seems to have put all caution aside in commenting, with little obliquity, on Soviet anthropomorphism:

> The unity with the whole was the breath of life to them. And the elevation of man above the rest of nature, the modern coddling and worshipping of man, never appealed to them. A social

2. *Ibid.*, p. 126.

> system based on such a false premise, as well as its political application, struck them as pathetically amateurish and made no sense to them.[3]

Even more outspoken is the following:

> . . . But revolutions are made by fanatical men of action with one-track minds, geniuses in their ability to confine themselves to a limited field. They overturn the old order in a few hours or days, the whole upheaval takes a few weeks or at most years, but the fanatical spirit that inspired the upheavals is worshipped for decades thereafter, for centuries.[4]

Critics have frequently noted parallels between the allusive, elliptical nature of much modern painting and similar devices in Pasternak's poetry (or vice versa). Pasternak, the son of a well-known but not great Russian painter, was always interested in modern art; he was close to the cubist-oriented Futurists and had lavish praise for Mayakovsky, although he himself followed another path in poetry. In his novel he also makes an unusual reference to art:

> These scenes and incidents had the strangeness of the transcendental, as if they were snatches torn from lives on other planets that had somehow drifted to the earth. Only nature had remained true to history and appeared in the guise it assumed in modern art.[5]

Alexander Solzhenitsyn (born 1918) is in many ways much more conventional than Pasternak. Indeed, the chief criticism leveled against him in the West is that he seems quite aloof from or to have quite simply rejected all the resources and effects provided by Modernist innovations in prose fiction as well as all the formal devices made available as the result not only of foreign but of Russian experiments with such things as Symbolism and Neorealism. He has chosen rather to deal with those particular aspects of reality which interest him in a very traditional novelistic manner. In some cases, the criticism goes further and accuses him of writing journalism rather than literature.

3. *Doctor Zhivago*, translated by Max Hayward and Manya Harari (New York: Pantheon Books, 1958), pp. 501–502.

4. *Ibid.*, p. 454.

5. *Ibid.*, pp. 378–79.

This criticism of Soltzhenitsyn, however, has a familiar ring and reminds us of much earlier criticism of, in particular, the Russian novel of the nineteenth century. Solzhenitsyn is clearly, in fact, in a Russian tradition which has been described by many scholars, and I here quote at length Mirsky's very relevant comments:

> Another obligation generally recognized by the realists was the duty of choosing their subjects exclusively from contemporary or almost contemporary Russian life. This was owing not only to their honest desire to speak of nothing but what they actually knew, but also the social position of fiction in mid- and late-nineteenth-century Russia. The novelists were expected to react, sensitively and significantly, to the current life of the nation. Partly owing to the severity of the censorship for other branches of literature, fiction, from the forties onward, became an important and widely listened-to mouthpiece of social thinking, and the critics demanded that every time a novelist gave his work to the world, it should contain things worth meditating on and worth analyzing from the point of view of the social issues of the day. As a rule, the novelists took the obligation very seriously and never ignored it, at least in their more ambitious work. This "social" (*obshchestvenny*) or "civic" (*grazhdansky*) coloring is a general characteristic of the European novel of the mid-nineteenth century, but it is nowhere more apparent than in Russia. It gives it an almost journalistic character and makes it tempting as an actual source of information on Russian social history.[6]

There is nothing "arty" about the novels of Solzhenitsyn nor any suggestion that he feels, as many of his contemporaries do, that literature must remain detached from and unsullied by the problems—especially the moral problems—of life. As we read his novels, it becomes quite clear that the author recognizes a close and almost natural connection between literature and morality. There is a "human smell" about his fiction so noticeably lacking in a multitude of modern novels which seem, "everything having turned into words, every set of words into musical jugglery" (Kazantzakis), well on their way to becoming "pure literature." But Solzhenitsyn has a deep respect for language,

6. *A History of Russian Literature,* p. 172. Cf. the similar remarks by Gerald Brenan concerning the Spanish writer in *The Literature of the Spanish People* (New York: Meridian Books, 1957), p. 116.

and, as critics have noted, he shows a marked concern for the debasement, during recent decades, of the Russian literary language.[7] Some of the "primitive," unsophisticated, and traditional quality of his prose appears to be the result of an effort to cleanse and reestablish the language in a manner that reminds one of Günter Eich's attempt to "begin all over again" after the Nazi desecration of the German language:

> Dies ist meine Mütze,
> dies ist mein Mantel,
> hier mein Rasierzeug
> im Beutel aus Leinen.

Throughout Solzhenitsyn's novels there are many passages of outspoken criticism of the Soviet regime. Even if we limit ourselves to the author's comments on literature, it is difficult to separate neatly the political from the literary. Thus in *Cancer Ward* a character who is a willing and simple-minded mouthpiece of the Party line explains the mysteries of Socialist Realism: "You must understand this. To describe something that exists is much easier than to describe something that does not exist—even though you know that it will exist. What we see today with the unaided eye is not necessarily the truth. The truth is what we must become, what will happen tomorrow. This wonderful tomorrow of ours is what writers should be describing today." Asked what writers will describe when tomorrow comes, this character replies that they will then write about the day after tomorrow. In *The First Circle* Solzhenitsyn expresses his opinion of official Soviet literature in considerable detail. The "zeks" or prisoners who staff the "Mavrino Institute" have little to read, and what they do have is, aside from a few cherished copies of works such as *The Count of Monte Cristo,* proper but drab Soviet pablum. There is, for example, a copy of the *Selected Works* of the "famous writer Galakhov."[8] But this seems, writes Solzhenitsyn, material for simpletons who know nothing of life and who "in their feeble-mindedness are thankful for any kind of childish amusement [*pobrjakushka*]." Amidst the pile of books available to the inmates there is a collection of *American Tales* by leading "pro-

7. In *Count Julian,* by the Spanish *émigré* novelist Juan Goytisolo (New York: Viking Press, 1974), the author is also much concerned with what he very obviously takes to be the debasement, over the centuries, of the Spanish language.

8. The character of Galakhov may be a composite of two Soviet writers, Nikolay Gribachev and Vsevolod Kochetov.

gressive writers." In every story there is "obligatory" venom directed at America and such nightmarish descriptions of American life that one is "surprised Americans have not fled their country or have not hanged themselves." In none of the books is there anything that stirs the heart; even in novels about the war the injection of "Party spirit" and Socialist Realism has turned otherwise comprehensible stories of suffering and sacrifice into specious and melodramatic fantasies. But volumes of certain Soviet "classics" serve a useful function: windows are held open "by [the thickness of] one volume of Erenburg" or "by one Mayakovsky."

The daughter of a Party official, reviewing her experiences with the study of literature in Soviet schools, remembers how correct but tedious Gorky was, how "progressive" but boring were Saltykov-Shchedrin's works, and how a teacher had once advised his students not to read the long novels of Tolstoy, since this would upset the interpretations set forth precisely in critical essays. All her literature courses had stressed the social issues involved, and she wondered why she had to read the writers representing "brother peoples" of the Soviet Union whose works were so unintelligent and unimportant. Gleb Nerzhin recalls the period following the death of Kirov—the suicides, the mass arrests, and the ritual public confessions—and realizes that it must have been Stalin who had Kirov murdered. But it was all so crude, so blatantly false, and so overdone. And what did Russian writers do? "Russian writers who made bold to trace their genealogy back to Pushkin and Tolstoy praised the tyrant with sickly-sweet words, while Russian composers, trained in the Herzen Street Conservatory, jostled one another as they thrust their obsequious hymns at the foot of his statue." Volodin, a principal character in the novel, speaks directly on one occasion to Galakhov: "A great writer is, so to say, a second government. Therefore no regime has ever loved its great writers, only its minor ones." But Galakhov replies that this is true only of bourgeois regimes. Later, Galakhov, who is quite aware of his own incompetence, asks himself why he should seek immortality. Even if one cannot write the truth, it is after all the present that really matters: the official publication, promotion, and mass distribution of his books, the acclaim, the awards, and the comforts of life.

In his *Nobel Lecture*[9] Solzhenitsyn has also revealed many of his views on the nature and function of literature. "The artist," he writes, "has simply been given the ability to sense more poignantly than oth-

9. Trans. by F. D. Reeve (New York: Farrar, Straus and Giroux, 1972).

ers the harmony of the world as well as the beauty and ugliness of man's contributions, and to communicate all this poignantly to people." Here and elsewhere in Solzhenitsyn's thought we can see lingering vestiges of the "organic" philosophy (mentioned earlier in connection with A. Grigoriev and Dostoevsky); certainly when he writes, "By means of art we are sometimes sent, dimly and briefly, such revelations as rational thought could never yield," we think not only of Ivanov (*a realibus ad realiora*) but of Dostoevsky as well. Not surprisingly, Solzhenitsyn quotes one of Dostoevsky's most idealistic utterances (spoken by Myshkin in *The Idiot*): "Beauty will save the world." He claims now to understand the meaning of these words as prophetic; perhaps the "old trinity of Truth, Goodness, and Beauty" is not as ridiculous as many (including Dostoevsky himself in *Notes from Underground*) would have us believe. Solzhenitsyn returns later in the Lecture to Dostoevsky's *The Possessed:* what appeared to many as a "provincial, nightmarish fantasy of the preceding century" is again prophetic of our present age.

In the winter of 1973–74, a startling book by Solzhenitsyn was published in Paris by the YMCA Press in a Russian edition. This is his *The Gulag Archipelago, 1918–1956,* a chilling account of the Soviet system of prison camps and secret police. A six hundred-page documentation of Soviet police terror, this work is especially explosive because it shows quite convincingly that the "excesses" now ascribed to Stalin alone had their beginnings under Lenin. The attacks on Solzhenitsyn intensified and he was accused, for telling the truth, of "malicious slander against the Soviet state." Faced with the apparent dilemma of either allowing this writer to go unpunished (and thereby encouraging other brave Russians to emulate him) or of silencing him at once, despite the fact that his name and his tribulations are now known around the world, the Soviet regime decided to expel Solzhenitsyn against his will. The regime has thereby both punished the writer and removed from its midst a focus of dangerous infection.

2

Andrey Donatovich Sinyavsky (born 1925), some of whose works were mentioned in the preceding chapter, is an important figure in both modern Russian fiction and literary criticism, and he deserves special attention. After brief military service, Sinyavsky entered Moscow University in 1945 and concentrated in Russian literature. He wrote a rather orthodox dissertation on Gorky's unfinished novel *Klim Samgin* (accepted in 1952) and later used some of the material in this for a monograph that appeared in the first volume of the official *History of Soviet Russian Literature,* published under the auspices of the Academy of Sciences. After passing the state examinations, Sinyavsky received a teaching appointment at Moscow State University. He also became affiliated with the Gorky Institute of World Literature, where he did research in the area of early Soviet literature.

In the forties and fifties Sinyavsky seems to have developed some serious misgivings about the nature and course of Soviet literature in general and of the doctrine of Socialist Realism in particular. As related in the preceding chapter, he wrote his now famous essay "On Socialist Realism" in the late fifties, and this appeared abroad in 1959. He had also begun writing fiction in the fifties, and his collection, *Fantastic Stories,* appeared abroad in 1961. Also in 1961 a long monograph of his, "The Literature of the Period of the Great Patriotic War" (i.e., World War II), was published in the third volume of the *History of Soviet Russian Literature.* But in the same year there appeared in *New World* two articles by Sinyavsky of clearly liberal orientation which attracted the attention of Party watchdogs. The consequences of his defiantly liberal attitude have also been described briefly in the previous chapter, and we shall turn now to some of his critical articles, a number of which are available in English translation.[10]

One of the best of these is his essay on the poetry of Yevgeny Yevtushenko, written prior to the author's arrest and trial, the Russian text of which first appeared abroad in 1967. Although this article is specifically a harsh indictment of Yevtushenko's poem, "The Bratsk Hydroelectric Station," in a more general sense it is an indictment of Yevtushenko the poet and provides a refreshing and incisive counterweight to much of the adulation of this versifier both here and in the Soviet Union. In his poem, Yevtushenko contrasts, quite unconvincingly, the image of the Egyptian pyramid as a symbol of "unbelief" with the Bratsk Hydroelectric Station, which represents the concrete results of sincere faith. The basic concept of the poem is effectively demolished by Sinyavsky:

10. *For Freedom of Imagination* (New York: Holt, Rinehart and Winston, 1971) contains nine articles trans. by L. Tikos and M. Peppard.

. . . To be sure every poet has the right to understand in his own way images of the past, but the treatment of the pyramid jarred us: one of the great architectural wonders, based on a faith remote from our life, mysterious, but strong and deep, with an extraordinarily firm and integral conception of the world, one that down to our times serves as a symbol of immortality, creative power, monumental grandeur, for the most varied cultures—such a thing is assigned the most nihilistic program. No, whoever else might have suffered from skepticism, the pyramids did not, and they had their own thoughts evidenced in the unity of style, the harmony of detail in idea and composition, all of which creates a grandiose whole. Properly speaking we maintain in defense of their honor that Yevtushenko lacks precisely what made the fame of the pyramids, and that what is needed for any Cyclopean work in the art of yesterday and today is a firm monolithic foundation, profound thought, and artistic unity.[11]

Much more interesting and to the point is Sinyavsky's criticism of the poetical style of Yevtushenko, who (he writes) "is easy for the reader and hard for the critic": easy for the reader, because he knows how to ingratiate himself and evoke sympathy, hard for the critic, because Yevtushenko has criticized himself so often that it is awkward for anyone to take up this criticism again. Nevertheless, Sinyavsky does not find the task too difficult and he directs his criticism precisely at Yevtushenko's principal weakness (the principal weakness of all poor poets): his fondness for the "ambiguous pairing of words," in oxymora and paradoxical statement, which creates the illusion of dialectical contradictions and profundity of thought through a sort of poetical "begging of the question." "Such tropes and sophistries," writes Sinyavsky, "may succeed in certain contexts, but they have long since become a Yevtushenko trade-mark. Most often they are hardly pleasing, since in a very primitive way they produce only the illusion of significance." Another example of *postiche* noted by Sinyavsky is the "name-dropping" in Yevtushenko's poem: "Wishing to point out the lofty intellectual level of the men who built the power station, Yevtushenko introduces, in addition to popular names, some rarer and more unusual ones"—the names of Scriabine, Fellini, Saint-Exupéry, Gauguin, Cézanne, and Degas, for instance. The most absurd example in the poem

11. *Ibid.*, p. 18. There is another translation of this article by Henry Gifford in *Encounter* (April 1967).

is the appearance of Rodin's *The Thinker* sitting on the edge of the dam. But the names of Tolstoy and Dostoevsky are also invoked, as well as the image of Gorky carrying a baby in his arms.

In his essay on Pasternak, Sinyavsky has the opportunity to reflect on the work of a poet of somewhat greater vision.[12] It is exactly this peculiar Pasternakian vision which all good critics have noted and commented on in one way or another. It will be remembered that the Formalist, Yury Tynyanov, felt obliged to resort to clinical terminology, likening Pasternak's poetic vision to the abnormal visual perspective some of us may recall having experienced during an illness, when objects lying nearby on the bed-table, for example, loom large and in unusually vivid detail. Sinyavsky's comment in this connection is similar—that Pasternak's poetry is the "poetry of the concrete and the nearby." But he comes close to speaking in Hegelian terms of the "concrete universal" in enlarging upon the poet's ability to combine in his imagery the particular and the abstract, the temporal and the eternal; and close to Ivanov's concept of *a realibus ad realiora* in his references to Pasternak's "expanded meanings" and the constant shift from details to a "higher and general level." But the philosophical implications are not fully interpreted, since this article, we should remember, was prepared for an official Soviet publication. There are even some formal references to the Revolution at the beginning of the article, while toward the end Sinyavsky's remarks on the "higher aims" of art are left purposefully ambiguous.

A considerable portion of the essay deals with Pasternak's metaphor which is more often than not actually either metonymy or synecdoche. "Pasternak will frequently tell the reader about the weather at a given historical moment rather than explain the full chronology and sequence of events"; or in poems about cities he writes about the suburbs, and in poems about the first of May he tells us about the end of April. "Pasternak likes," says Sinyavsky, "to define a thing by referring to the borderline that divides it from other things." Indeed, much of the difficulty in Pasternak stems from his frequent use of what may more precisely be called metalepsis, i.e., the substitution of one metaphor for another. Sinyavsky quotes the almost pathetic words of Gorky who found it particularly hard to follow the far-reaching associations that Pasternak's metalepses entail.

12. This essay was originally written as an introduction to a Soviet edition of some of Pasternak's poetry published in 1965. It is included in *For Freedom of Imagination,* while an abbreviated version appeared in *Encounter* (April 1966).

The extensive use of metonymy that we find not only in poets such as Pasternak but also in novelists like Tolstoy has often suggested to critics the term "Impressionism." Sinyavsky, however, objects to the use of this word in connection with Pasternak's poetry. Impressionism, he claims, deals only with the emotionally perceivable surfaces of things and not with essential qualities; it is not concerned with "eternal values" but only with the flow of impressions emanating from objects in this world. Immersed in a sea of sense impressions, the impressionist carefully avoids (Sinyavsky would have us believe) *a priori* knowledge and ideas that might disturb the "purity of his perception." But this is only true to a limited extent: the "purity" of the Impressionists is very often mere illusion, their technique involving quite as many *a priori* notions as other forms of nineteenth-century realism. In any case, Sinyavsky prefers the phrase "Impressionism of the eternal" as most applicable to Pasternak's manner, a phrase which Pasternak once used of his own inclinations and which seems to encompass both the concrete and the abstract. Though one might wonder what exactly this means, it is a signal indication of how far some contemporary Russian critics have gone in returning to various romantic concepts of the nineteenth century in their search for "fresh" critical principles. Sinyavsky, for instance, seems often to be a twentieth-century disciple of Apollon Grigoriev and "organic criticism" and to have little sympathy with either the idiotic demands of Socialist Realism, the frigid tenets of Formalism, or the excesses of "democratic" criticism. One may well imagine the caustic remarks that such a phrase as "the Impressionism of the eternal" would elicit from either Roman Jakobson, for example, or from a Soviet Marxist critic.

In his essay on science fiction, Sinyavsky notes how many features of the literary treatment of space travel have long since become commonplaces and how often descriptions of such phenomena as weightlessness go hand in hand with traditional matter derived from the works of Jules Verne; or how often space travelers very conveniently encounter forms of life resembling those of earlier—especially prehistoric—periods on Earth. In Soviet science fiction the devices of the spy thriller and detective story are very often introduced to enliven the plot, with saboteurs and foreign agents intent on upsetting well-laid plans. Particularly good are Sinyavsky's comments on the language of science fiction—its clichés and "cheap elegance."

Sinyavsky also finds in the poetry and prose of Olga Berggolts the author's tendency to raise concrete phenomena to a higher, abstract level. (Olga Berggolts is a Soviet Russian poet whose verse is often reminiscent of Akhmatova, especially in its close association with the city of Leningrad.) But Sinyavsky seems to exaggerate this tendency when he refers to the poet's ability to raise such phenomena to the "level of universal philosophical categories," thus attaining "the highest symbolic meaning and universal significance." She "transforms," "spiritualizes," "sublimates," and "illumines" reality. What I suppose Sinyavsky means is that Berggolts very frequently uses abstract phrases like "true existence" where one can indeed find, if not "philosophical categories" in any technical sense, an admittedly very broad range of connotations.

In a short essay on the poetry of Robert Frost, written for a volume of Frost's poems published on the occasion of the American poet's visit to the Soviet Union in 1963, Sinyavsky again discovers an integral view of man and nature and of the "unity of universal reality." But Frost's technique does not depend upon the frequent use of "loaded" abstract nouns; rather there is in his poems something like, as Sinyavsky puts it, a "stereoscopic effect" which allows the reader to perceive philosophical depth behind the poet's scrupulous attention to concrete details. With all his references to the "universal" qualities in Frost, Sinyavsky realizes that some Russian readers might find it strange that Frost's "all-embracing poetic world" does not include the city. One might expect here a comparison with a poet like Pasternak whose "organic" philosophy also pretty much excludes urban elements; but Sinyavsky, perhaps intentionally, does not refer to the Russian poet and simply writes that Frost is in a great American tradition of rural regionalism, the pioneer spirit, and the struggle for independence.

In the preceding chapter the name of the Soviet novelist, Ivan Shevtsov, was mentioned in passing. Sinyavsky has an essay on this person and another of his classic novels, this one entitled *Plant-Louse* (*Tlja*), in which the forces of goodness and truth are pitted against the forces of evil and corruption. The former are "progressive" artists, exponents of orthodox Socialist Realism, while the latter are the promoters of "pure art"—aesthetes, Formalists, Modernists, and cosmopolites. In short, the novel is a blatantly tendentious attack on dissident Soviet artists who, because of their refusal and failure to follow the Party line in the arts, are considered as clever criminals, saboteurs, and incendiaries. But the novel is incredibly bad, and Sinyavsky must have enjoyed writing this article which appeared in the liberal *New World* in 1964. One of the representatives of "decadent," "pure art" in the novel, Boris Iulin, has in his room colored reproductions of several famous paintings of nude women, including Giorgione's *Venus* and a Renoir. Shevtsov explains that the presence of these pictures inspired Iulin to seduce innocent young girls.

It must be granted—and Sinyavsky notes this fact—that a great many reviewers in a number of periodicals condemned Shevtsov's novel. At the end of his article, wondering whether Shevtsov now sees himself, a devoted "realist," being persecuted by the critics just as the "progressive" artist-heroes of his novel were dogged by Modernists and distorters of reality, Sinyavsky again goes back to the eighteenth century (which he does, it will be remembered, in his "On Socialist Realism") for a quotation that might serve as an afterword to Shevtsov's novel. He cites a long passage from an obscure book published in St. Petersburg in 1789 about the fall of large hailstones which the author quaintly likens to abuse and calumny: hailstones frighten us and cause damage but they disappear very quickly without a trace.

In the summer of 1973, it was learned that Sinyavsky had been released from confinement and had managed to emigrate to France where he is living at the present time. It was rumored, while he was still imprisoned, that Sinyavsky was working on a study of Jonathan Swift. While it is difficult to imagine any commentary on Swift that would not, in the Soviet Union, leave an ironic critic like Sinyavsky open eventually to even more severe attack, now that he is free we look forward without uneasiness and with greater expectation to such a study from the pen of a Russian critic. We may expect, too, more tales of fantasy and more organic criticism.

3

Though Wladimir Weidlé (born 1895) is a Russian *émigré* critic of an older generation, quite unsympathetic with much that we consider modern, he is not altogether different from a younger Russian critic like Sinyavsky. He is a bitter opponent of the Soviet regime and, as we shall see, an eloquent spokesman of the view that Russia is essentially a Western nation: that ever since 1917 she has been receding from the West and that it is time she returned to the West. Born in St. Petersburg, Weidlé was educated at the University of St. Petersburg and later became a lecturer there. Shortly after the Revolution he left Russia, settled in Paris, and eventually became a French citizen. He was appointed Professor of Christian Art at the Russian Theological

Academy in Paris, and many of his subsequent writings have been concerned with art and art history.

Many of Weidlé's articles dealing with literature are either in French, German, or Russian, but quite a few works are available in English translation. Perhaps his best-known book (translated from the French) is *Russia: Absent and Present.*[13] This book, however, is more philosophical than critical (suggesting, for instance, that Russians are prone to steal because of their profoundly communal nature!), while most of the remarks concerning Russian writers are quite conventional—e.g., "Tolstoy is an epic poet transplanted, by a strange freak, into the era of the naturalistic novel." Weidlé is also prone, because of his special interest in painting, to draw frequent analogies between art and literature or between art and culture: thus he finds a peculiar affinity between Jordaens' *Family Portrait* (in the Hermitage) and what he considers to be the very strong Russian feeling for the "family nest" or the *rod* (clan). But it is in this book that Weidlé argues very effectively for a better understanding of Russia and Russian culture (and he includes Russian music, painting, and philosophy) as essentially Western in tradition and orientation. "In the last fifty years of European literature," he writes, "there have been no names more thoroughly European than those of Dostoevski and Tolstoy; and the spirit in which writers like Turgenev or Chekhov have been read by Englishmen or Frenchmen is far from being that of mere infatuation for exotic forms of art, like Japanese prints or Negro sculpture. If Europe came to understand the great creations of Russian culture and to love them, it was no escapism but a rediscovery of its own true image."[14] It is noteworthy that Weidlé singles out Vladimir Nabokov as the most Western of all Russian writers, an opinion with which Russian Marxist critics would also be inclined to agree.

Another book by Weidlé that is familiar to critics, especially European critics, is his *The Bees of Aristaeus* (*Les Abeilles d'Aristée,* 1954). The gist of this study is that the whole of modern culture, including its literature, music, art, and architecture, is in a state of degeneracy and decay, but that out of the corruption a new art will emerge as the bees of Aristaeus emerged, in the Greek legend, from the decayed carcases of animals. Poems and paintings have been reduced, according to Weidlé, to machines designed to produce aesthetic satisfaction, and his condemnation of modern literature is almost total. Mod-

13. New York: Vintage Books, 1961.

14. *Ibid.*, pp. 61–62.

ern decadence is attributed to the loss of communal spirit and the absence of authentic modes of communion. There is no remedy for this situation other than a return to some form of religious or mystical communion; for Weidlé this involves more specifically a "new union of art and religion, of the creative imagination and the Christian faith." Despite the wide range of knowledge at Weidlé's command and the elegance of his style, his arguments are neither new nor convincing, reminding us, however, of much contemporary talk in the West about the need to return to irrational "fundamentals." Some years ago the French critic Claude Mauriac wrote a book which appeared in English translation as *The New Literature*[15] and which contains a chapter devoted to Weidlé's *The Bees of Aristaeus.* Mauriac subjects this work—and especially the view that a return to faith will result in an aesthetic renaissance—to rather harsh criticism. He points out, for example, that Weidlé seems reluctant to acknowledge the fact that it is exactly in Soviet Russia that a "common religious faith" is being reborn. But surely, despite the many comparisons that have been made between Christianity and communism, this is not what Weidlé means; nor has the religion of communism yet produced, or shown any signs of producing, anything of striking artistic merit. Despite Weidlé's severe strictures on Modernism, he admires individual writers. Commenting on Proust's remark that, when he dined in town, he failed really to see his fellow guests because he always tended to "X-ray" them, Weidlé writes: "Fortunately for his art, it was precisely the opposite that happened: however much he desired to be a technician, he could not help remaining a poet."

It goes without saying that one will hardly find any references to Weidlé's literary studies in collections of Formalist or Structuralist criticism. Nevertheless, in spite of his rather old-fashioned approach, all his writings are not concerned with historical, philosophical, and metaphysical speculation, although he has remained a staunch advocate of criticism as judgment and evaluation. Thus in a recently published collection of scholarly articles entitled *Problems of Literary Evaluation*[16] one of Weidlé's essays is included, along with studies by Roman Ingarden, Luc Benoist, David Daiches, and others. Weidlé's article, "The Appreciation and Understanding of a Work of Art," describes the results of what the author calls the "aesthetic fallacy." Since about 1750

15. New York: George Braziller, 1959.

16. *Yearbook of Comparative Criticism,* Vol. II (University Park: Pennsylvania State University Press, 1969).

and the "birth of aesthetics" (Weidlé is referring to the introduction of the term by Baumgarten) there has been an ever-widening gap between the understanding of a work of art and the appreciation of it. Prior to 1750 there was universal acceptance of the view that "art speaks, that the work of art has something to say," and that appreciation and understanding are inseparable. But from 1750 to the present, under the deleterious influence of aesthetic theory, works of art have come more and more to be judged solely on the basis of effect. And since now, in particular, art is judged only by its effect, it has ended by producing only effects. There is nothing, Weidlé feels, which requires understanding in non-objective art, and a painting without an "image" is silent. "Nor is there anything that calls for understanding in functional architecture which remains mute about the human meaning of its function, in atonal music which can just as well be played in reverse as not, in so-called concrete poetry which may intrigue or amuse me but is completely incapable of telling me anything at all."[17]

Although we can agree with some points in this well-argued essay (notably the comments on literary and other works of art produced, it seems quite clear, only for effect), Weidlé's criticism strikes us on the whole as extreme. Certainly his views are not at all unique, especially in the context of Russian criticism: critics from very early times have both expounded and denounced so-called affective theories, while Weidlé has many modern critics on his side. But many others would not at all concur with his frequent statements to the effect that non-objective art is "silent." Regardless of the theories of individual artists, there are many works of non-objective art (literary, musical, and graphic) which "speak to us" and tell us, in fact, much more than a great mass of nineteenth-century art which, though communicating explicitly, communicates inanities. Weidlé is clearly in a European tradition but more particularly in a Russian tradition which requires, as we have noted earlier on several occasions, that artists communicate relevantly and explicitly. It must be said, too, that Soviet Marxist critics of non-objective art would take a stand very similar to Weidlé's, although the language might be different. It is ironic in a way that Weidlé should hold the opinions he does while other Russian artists and critics in Soviet Russia are today struggling, often at the cost of personal freedom, for the prerogative to do what he condemns.

It is interesting that in this essay Weidlé uses technical terms such as "semantemes" and tries to distinguish differences and formulate his

17. *Ibid.*, p. 156.

ideas more neatly by using letter-symbols (P, L, PL, L_1, L_2, L_3, etc.), all of which gives his article a kind of pseudo-scientific appearance but which really does little to supplement the author's excellent prose style. He also refers in his notes to two studies of his written in German, the titles of which indicate his interest in language: *"Das Kunstwerk: Sprache und Gestalt"* and *"Die zwei Sprachen der Sprachkunst."*

4

Vladimir Nabokov (born 1899) stands apart from just about every other modern Russian critic so far mentioned. Despite the differences between, say, Sinyavsky and Weidlé, both seem monolithically identical as critics when both are contrasted with Nabokov. Of course, Nabokov is not a critic in any conventional sense, having achieved a sort of notoriety as a writer of fiction; but he has, from time to time, voiced his opinions on his own art and the writings of others, and these, if not unique, are at least representative. Several books have been written on the subject of Nabokov, his life, and his fiction; numerous articles have been devoted to various aspects of his writings; and he himself has left us an autobiographical memoir, *Speak, Memory.* Nabokov, who was born in Russia and educated at Cambridge University in England, became an American citizen in 1945. In 1962, during a BBC television interview, he stated that he had found not only his "best readers" in America but minds closest to his and an "intellectual home" as well. He now lives in Montreux, Switzerland.

Nabokov's favorite Russian poem (if we can accept what he says in the BBC interview) is one he wrote himself for a character in his novel, *The Gift,* which was originally written in Russian. He also tells us here that he "thinks in images" and has the gift (granted, he claims, to one in a thousand) of *"audition colorée." Lolita* he calls a special favorite of his and his most difficult work, since the theme was so remote from his own emotional life. He says that he has "no general ideas to exploit" but likes to compose riddles and then enjoys finding elegant solutions to his own riddles."[18] But a more readable introduction to Nabokov as critic may be found in his small book on Gogol.[19]

18. *The Listener* (22 November 1962), pp. 856–58.

19. *Nikolai Gogol* (New York: New Directions, 1961).

This is a brief but refreshingly different commentary on Gogol's life and major works, especially the novel *Dead Souls* and the famous short story, "The Overcoat." Nabokov's eccentric English style is here quite appropriate to his subject matter, some of the most eccentric fiction in Russian literature. Happily, the text of Nabokov's essay is not excessively larded with obsolete, obsolescent, or rare English words, although the author cannot refrain from referring to leeches as "chaetopod worms," punning on "stratagem" ("a treasure in a cave"), and using words like *insolite.*[20] Indeed, Gogol's eccentricity and his linguistic idiosyncrasies seem to be of particular interest to Nabokov as criteria for his giving a very high evaluation to the Russian writer, "the greatest artist that Russia has yet produced." Even Pushkin's prose, writes Nabokov, is "three-dimensional" as compared with the "four-dimensional" prose of Gogol. As Zamyatin utilized the concept of entropy in his criticism, Nabokov here refers to concepts of non-Euclidian geometry:

> . . . Gogol's world is somewhat related to such conceptions of modern physics as the "Concertina Universe" or the "Explosion Universe"; it is far removed from the comfortably revolving clockwork worlds of the last century. There is a curvature in literary style as there is curvature in space—but few are the Russian readers who do care to plunge into Gogol's magic chaos head first, with no restraint or regret. The Russian who thinks Turgenev was a great writer, and bases his notion of Pushkin upon Chaikovsky's vile libretti, will merely paddle into the gentlest wavelets of Gogol's mysterious sea and limit his reaction to an enjoyment of what he takes to be whimsical humor and colorful quips. But the diver, the seeker for black pearls, the man who prefers the monsters of the deep to the sunshades on the beach, will find in *The Overcoat* shadows linking our state of existence to those other states and modes which we dimly apprehend in our rare moments of irrational perception.[21]

"Gogol was a strange creature," Nabokov writes, "but genius is always strange; it is only your healthy second-rater who seems to the

20. The word *insolite* (*unaccustomed, strange*) is entered in *Webster's New International Dictionary of the English Language* (Second Edition, 1960) "below the bar" and is noted as "obsolete." Thus the word is what it means.

21. *Nikolai Gogol,* pp. 144–45.

grateful reader to be a wise old friend, nicely developing the reader's own notions of life. Great literature skirts the irrational."[22] But Nabokov, despite his emphasis on strangeness and the irrational, is a stickler for accuracy in *realia,* as many a critic and reviewer have found out. His ideas thus remind one of such assertions, similar to that of C. E. Montague's, that the best of imaginative literature has its leaves in the light and its roots in the darkness. One also thinks of various remarks by the German romantic critics concerning the aesthetic value of "strangeness." Even more interesting, from a comparative point of view, are Nabokov's remarks elsewhere on inspiration ("afflation"), some of which are quite Longinian in tone, e.g., "The bolt of inspiration strikes invariably: you observe the flash in this or that piece of great writing, be it a stretch of fine verse, or a passage in Joyce or Tolstoy, or a phrase in a short story, or a spurt of genius in the paper of a naturalist, of a scholar, or even in a book reviewer's article."[23]

It is obvious, from Nabokov's phraseology at the beginning of the preceding paragraph, that he does not think much either of naive readers or of authors as "wise old friends." His contempt for books that "make one think" and for readers who yearn for "facts," "true romance," and "human interest" is always made very clear. Even more obvious is his disdain for mediocrity of any kind, and mediocrity for Nabokov covers a very large terrain. But special objects of his scorn seem to be linguistics and Freudian psychology. One of the best parts of his book on Gogol is the excursus on the significance of the Russian word *poshlost'* (as exemplified by Chichikov in *Dead Souls*), a word which means essentially *vulgarity.* He cites several examples of *poshlust* (as he transliterates the word), including Goethe's *Faust.* Explaining how the word is to be pronounced, he goes out of his way to use descriptive terms that would shock a "professional linguist":

> . . . Various aspects of the idea which Russians concisely express by the term *poshlost* (the stress-accent is on the puff-ball of the first syllable, and the final "t" has a moist softness that is hardly equaled by the French "t" in such words as "restiez" or "émous-

22. *Ibid.,* p. 140.

23. "Inspiration," *Saturday Review of the Arts* (January 1973), p. 32. This is one of Nabokov's best short pieces on literature. He quotes inspired passages ("divine vibrations") from works by Cheever, Updike, Salinger, Gold, Barth, and Schwartz.

> tillant") are split among several English words and thus do not form a definite whole. On second thought, I find it preferable to transcribe that fat brute of a word thus: *poshlust*—which renders in a somewhat more adequate manner the dull sound of the second, neutral "o." Inversely, the first "o" is as big as the plop of an elephant falling into a muddy pond and as round as the bosom of a bathing beauty on a German picture postcard.[24]

Elsewhere and frequently he leaves no doubt as to what he thinks of Freud and "Freudian drivel" in language that sometimes, however, is revealingly peevish ("the garbage cans of a Viennese tenement").

Nabokov, presumably having in mind the much-renowned Celtic imagination as well as some interesting parallels between the Ukrainians and the Irish, says that "none but an Irishman should ever try tackling Gogol" (i.e., to translate him). More to the point than either this remark or the geometrical metaphor is his comment on the "curiously physical side of Gogol's genius": that, for instance, the "belly is the belle of his stories, the nose is their beau." But this "physical" aspect of Gogol's fiction has been pointed out by numerous critics (often in conjunction with Gogol's hypochondria), though in language less quaint. Typical of Gogol is the sudden emergence from time to time in his fiction of odd characters who may, before they disappear, be described in considerable but Sternean detail (e.g., the "Lieutenant from Ryazan" at the end of Chapter VII in *Dead Souls*). It seems natural now to use Nabokov's terminology and refer to these as "peripheral characters," the products of a kind of "spontaneous generation."

Though there are many literary observations, both explicit and implicit, in Nabokov's stories and novels (notably in *Pale Fire* and *Ada*), one of his novels has the distinction of having been called a "work of literary criticism" (S. Karlinsky). This is *The Gift* (*Dar*), written in Russian in the thirties and now available in a new English translation done by Michael Scammell in collaboration with the author. Nabokov has himself spoken highly of this novel of his in particular ("the last novel I wrote, or ever shall write, in Russian") and tells us in the Foreword to the English version that the heroine of the work is, in fact, Russian literature. The novel is a complex one, replete with literary and other allusions and rich in verbal sleight-of-hand. But it is a splendid evocation of a world that is gone. "Gone," writes the

24. *Nikolai Gogol*, p. 63.

author, "are Bunin, Aldanov, Remizov. Gone is Vladislav Khodasevich, the greatest Russian poet the twentieth century has yet produced. The old intellectuals are now dying out and have not found successors in the so-called Displaced Persons of the last two decades who have carried abroad the provincialism and Philistinism of their Soviet homeland."[25] At the end of Chapter I in the novel there are some witty and epigrammatic comments on a number of nineteenth-century Russian writers set forth in an imaginary conversation between two of the characters. The opinions of one, Godunov-Cherdyntsev, seem to be those of Nabokov himself. Goncharov's character Oblomov is called the "joy of social critics," while in the same writer's *The Precipice* the language used (e.g., "rosy moisture shimmering between his lips") reminds Godunov-Cherdyntsev of certain stylistic peculiarities in Pisemsky. The Anglicisms in Leskov are noted with some distaste and the novel *Cathedral Folk* (*Soborjane*) might "easily be condensed to two newspaper *feuilletons*." Criticism of Pushkin is rejected, since he is the "gold reserve" of Russian literature, and "Chekhov's hamper . . . contains enough food for years to come." Dostoevsky is punningly reduced to "Bedlam turned back into Bethlehem." The "maudlin endings" of Turgenev's chapters are mentioned and unspecific references made to all sorts of howlers in his (and Tolstoy's) hunting scenes, but his "graceful sentences" with their "outstretched hind legs" are commended. In Chapter II there are numerous references to Pushkin (for whom Nabokov has a very high regard)—e.g., the accuracy of his language and the "absolute purity" of his conjunctions. To read Pushkin often is to breathe a revivifying air and to have the capacity of one's lungs enlarged.

In Chapter III there are some interesting remarks on poets and poetry, much of the latter rather fastidiously technical in a Pickwickian sense. The amphibrachic foot, which Nabokov feels is used excessively in Russian poetry, is seen in the "shape of a sofa with three cushions—the middle one dented." Godunov-Cherdyntsev (i.e., Nabokov) was especially attracted to Bely's studies of the distribution of "half-stresses" (*poluudarenija*) or—to use Nabokov's own term—"scuds." Associations and juxtapositions being of great importance to Nabokov, he tells us, in discussing rhymes, that *glaza* (eyes) appear blue when rhymed with *biryuza* (turquoise), while the rhyming words *svechi* (tapers), *plechi* (shoulders), *vstrechi* (meetings), and *rechi* (speeches) "created the old-world atmosphere of a ball at the Congress of Vi-

25. Author's Foreword, *The Gift* (New York: Capricorn Books, 1970), p. 10.

enna." The associations here are similar to (but do not go so far as) those made by Khlebnikov in connection with his theory of the "internal declension" of words.

Discussing his self-imposed training as a poet, Godunov-Cherdyntsev comments on his own tendencies to use, as well as his efforts to avoid, hackneyed poetic words and phrases, and he touches at one point on something that reminds us of Eliot's "dissociation of sensibility":

> . . . I clutched at the first hackneyed words available, at their ready-made linkages, so that as soon as I had embarked upon what I thought to be creation, on what should have been the expression, the living connection between my divine excitement and my human world, everything expired in a fatal gust of words, whereas I continued to rotate epithets and adjust rhymes without noticing the split, the debasement and the betrayal.[26]

The fourth chapter in *The Gift* is a biography of the Civic critic, Nikolay Chernyshevsky, discussed in Chapter IV of this book. But this is a chapter in a novel, and, although one is impressed by the cleverness, the scholarship, and the attention to significant details, it is a peculiarly one-sided treatment. Chernyshevsky's life and works are subjected to satirical and very often harsh criticism. Indeed, the criticism of Chernyshevky, a figure much admired by Marx, Lenin, and the Russian Communists as well as by liberal *émigré* intellectuals and former members of the Social Revolutionary Party, is so severe, that when the novel first appeared serialized in a Paris Russian-language journal, this fourth chapter was omitted. There are, of course, some amusing remarks about Chernyshevsky's preoccupation with his "perpetual motion" machine and about his novel, *What Is to Be Done?* ("Today, it seems, only Marxists are still capable of being interested by the ghostly ethics contained in this dead little book"). Of Chernyshevsky's notions of "communal love" set forth in the novel, Nabokov writes: "For of course the inevitable happened: the eminently pure Chernyshevski (who had never been to a brothel), in his artless aspiration to equip communal love with especially beautiful trappings, involuntarily and unconsciously, out of the simplicity of his imagination, had worked his way through to those very ideals that had been evolved by tradition and routine in houses of ill repute."

26. *Ibid.*, p. 165.

On some naive philosophical remarks by Chernyshevsky concerning the "objective existence" of trees, Nabokov makes a valid point: "the 'materialists' ' constant appeal to trees is especially amusing because they are all so badly acquainted with nature, particularly with trees." Chernyshevsky, Nabokov goes on to say, had no technical knowledge of such down-to-earth things as plows, confused beer with Madeira, and was completely unfamiliar with all wild flowers except the "wild rose," making up for his deficiencies in these and other areas by "generalizing." A major fault in Chernyshevsky as thinker and critic is summed up thus: "Chernyshevski had . . . a dangerously wide range, a kind of reckless and self-confident 'anything-will-do' attitude which casts a doubtful shadow over his own specialized work." Nabokov also enjoys referring to Chernyshevsky's silly dismissal of Lobachevsky, the great Russian mathematician, as a fool and of the poet, Fet, as an idiot. It goes without saying that Nabokov is also justifiably caustic on both Chernyshevsky's horrible style and his solecisms as well as the critic's pathetic comments on the "senseless combinations of words" in Pushkin and on poetic language in general (his utter inability, for instance, to understand *audition colorée*). Like all revolutionaries, Nabokov claims, Chernyshevsky "was a complete bourgeois in his artistic and scientific tastes." Chernyshevsky, he notes, also equated genius and "common sense." If Pushkin had really been a genius, Chernyshevsky reasoned, his words should have flowed effortlessly from his pen, since common sense always knows exactly what it wants to say; yet Pushkin's drafts show a multitude of corrections, from which it follows that Pushkin seems merely to have bungled his way through poetry.

If one seeks enlightenment of any kind from Nabokov's criticism, one will not find it in his general statements (such as "Great literature skirts the irrational"), which are unoriginal and of little value in themselves. What we can learn from him, however, is precisely the dangers inherent in fanciful generalizations and in any fatuous allegiance to one or another "school" of literary interpretation. We also learn from him the importance of exact knowledge and scrupulous attention to detail. One is struck, in all of Nabokov's fiction and his critical comments, by the fastidious judgment and the precise weighing, not of gross structural elements, but rather of minor—one might even say minute—particulars: the nice placement of an adjective, the appositely relevant etymological connotations of a word, or the precisely chosen and allusive phrase. The work of Nabokov is thus wholly illustrative of Harry Levin's assertion, to the effect that technicalities may often help us more than generalities. One would be hard put to call Nabokov's critical theory either romantic or classical. Thus such things as his attention to particulars and his emphasis on the irrational may be traditionally romantic; but his sense of decorum and propriety as well as his strong feeling for tradition and his respect for exact usage and clarity of expression are eminently classical qualities. Though Nabokov is himself a scientist (a lepidopterist), it is gratifying that he makes no claim for the scientific validity of either his own literary opinions or for any all-embracing "theory of literature." It is also gratifying (and in this he differs from both the great mass of Soviet Russian critics and many of his fellow *émigrés*) that he shows a keen and perceptive interest in much modern literature, including the works of Proust, Joyce, Kafka, and many others.[27]

5

The statement made at the beginning of Chapter I of this book, that Russian criticism (i.e., official criticism within the confines of Russia) begins and ends badly, is still, I think, a valid one. It is a sad but true commentary on the state of contemporary Russian literary criticism that the best of this should come either from dissident writers who have recently left Soviet Russia (Sinyavsky, Solzhenitsyn) or from Russian-born writers and scholars now residing abroad (Jakobson, Weidlé, Nabokov). In 1917 V. Rossikov observed (in an article on Russian criticism at the beginning of the twentieth century) that the history of Russian literary criticism was essentially a history of the development of "social awareness" in Russia. But the value of this "social awareness" in the mainstream of Russian criticism from Belinsky to present-day Marxist criticism in Soviet Russia seems minimal, judging by the end results, while the very term "social awareness" in the context of Russian communism seems to us (with all our faults) to border on the ridiculous.

There is, however, another and lesser current in Russian criticism, represented, since the beginning of the twentieth century, by such figures as Zamyatin and a small number of successors down to the pres-

27. There has recently been published a collection of Nabokov's interviews, letters to editors, and articles in *Strong Opinions* (New York: McGraw-Hill, 1973).

ent day who, if not wholly free of the tendency to systematize, are skeptical, radical, and cosmopolitan. Not only, unfortunately, are they a small contingent, but many of them are dead or dying, either internal exiles cut off from the intellectual variety and stimuli of pluralistic societies, or expatriates cut off from the living nourishment of their mother tongue. Both those who have come to the West and those who have never been able to leave Russia or who have chosen to stay (but whose works we know of) have enriched, directly and indirectly, our knowledge of literature and our critical thought; but neither will have any appreciable effect on the course of Soviet Russian criticism which is dominated by a quasi-religious orthodoxy which tolerates neither skepticism, radicalism, nor cosmopolitanism.

SUGGESTED READING

Pasternak, Boris, *I Remember: Sketch for an Autobiography,* trans. by David Magarshack (New York: Meridian Books, 1960). Also included is Pasternak's essay "Translating Shakespeare."

Solzhenitsyn, Alexander, *Nobel Lecture* (New York: Farrar, Straus and Giroux, 1972), is a bilingual edition.

Tertz, Abram (Sinyavsky, Andrey), *The Trial Begins and On Socialist Realism* (New York: Vintage Books, 1965).

Sinyavsky, Andrei, *For Freedom of Imagination* (New York: Holt, Rinehart and Winston, 1971).

Mauriac, Claude, *The New Literature* (New York: George Braziller, 1959), contains a chapter on Weidlé.

Strelka, Joseph, ed., *Problems of Literary Evaluation* (University Park: Pennsylvania State University Press, 1969), contains a contribution by Weidlé.

Nabokov, Vladimir, *Nikolai Gogol* (New York: New Directions, 1959).

Nabokov, Vladimir, *Strong Opinions* (New York: McGraw-Hill, 1973).

Field, Andrew, ed., *The Complection of Russian Literature* (New York: Atheneum, 1971), contains a brief excerpt from Weidlé on Nabokov and two excerpts from Sinyavsky.

INDEX

UNIVERSITY LIBRARY
NOTTINGHAM

Russian Literary Criticism

by R. H. Stacy

was composed in ten-point Caledonia, leaded two points; and printed on 55-pound Perkins and Squier Special Book; case bound in Joanna's Devon. It was composed in Linotype and printed letterpress by York Composition Co., Inc., York, Pennsylvania; bound by Vail-Ballou Press, Binghamton, New York; and published by

SYRACUSE UNIVERSITY PRESS
Syracuse, New York

NOTES

NOTES

NOTES

NOTES